BLAZING
THE WAY WEST

From a contemporaneous sketch in Hennepin's "A New Discovery of a Vast Country in America."

Iroquois Warriors Torturing Captives by Fire

BLAZING
THE WAY WEST

by

BLISS ISELY

CHARLES SCRIBNER'S SONS · NEW YORK
CHARLES SCRIBNER'S SONS · LTD · LONDON
1939

ACKNOWLEDGMENTS

THIS BOOK is made possible through the generous assistance of a great many librarians of the United States and Canada who have been unfailingly helpful. Particularly do I wish to mention Miss M. Alice Isely, reference librarian at the University of Wichita; Mrs. Hortense Balderston Campbell, now Mrs. John Gibson, former reference librarian at the Wichita City Library; her successor, Miss Genevieve Newel, and Miss Winifred Schott, Wichita children's librarian.

Acknowledgments are also due to Miss Beatrice Paddock, of the Wichita City Library staff, who translated documents, letters and books from the original French; and Miss Jacquetta Downing, professor of French at the University of Wichita, who aided with the vocabulary, which is designed to help non-French-speaking Americans and is not intended for French students.

BEAVER TRACKS

It was the mode for furs in Paris that drove intrepid adventurers to explore the unmapped wilderness of North America. Men crossed beyond familiar horizons because fashion decreed that every well-dressed woman should adorn herself with the warm fur of the beaver, and that her lordly escort should wear a hat of the same material.

Although North America was then a dark and savage continent, her small streams, from southern swamp to Arctic timberline, were obstructed by the dams of sixty million beaver, whose web-like footprints in the mud spelled incredible riches to those who could read their sign. Perhaps no other era has produced so rich a fabric for the weaving of historical romance. There was as much adventure ahead of the daring little bands of Frenchmen as ever awaited the men who quested for the gold of Ophir.

This book, however, deals not in fiction but in truth concerning the deeds of men, some greedy, some noble, some hating, some loving; who endured scurvy, loneliness, homesickness, intrigue, and Indian warfare in order to gain for their king the right to rule over a large portion of North America. For themselves they gained the death of heroes if they fell, and wealth and influence if they lived to bring back to France a shipload of precious beaver peltry.

Champlain and Frontenac, Duluth and Jolliet, Cadillac and La Salle, Bienville and Tonty and a band of other paladins, answering the call of fortune, were the first white men to mark the course of the St. Lawrence, first to hear the thunder of Niagara, first to sail the Great Lakes, first to float down the Mississippi's flood, and first to trail across the sun-bright plains to clamber up the Rockies. They built fur-trading capitals at Quebec and Mackinac, Mobile and New Orleans, Detroit and Vincennes, St. Louis and Laramie. But the entire winnings of their valor and devotion were staked on the gamble of war by their king, who played for European domination. He cast and lost.

Silent are the French rondeaus that once resounded from river and prairie and forest. Yet if we will but close our ears against the drone of airplanes, the honk of motor cars, and the clang of progress, we still may catch the lilt of the voyageur's notes; for our maps are studded with French names of mountains, streams and cities, among them the capitals of one territory and six states. Then, too, our mightiest rivers and all but two of the states of our Middle

West hear the picturesque Indian names remembered and kept alive for us by our French predecessors.

How we wish we might roll back the years to don buck-skins and moccasins and a bright red sash and explore America with them; to crouch in a canoe and, paddle in hand, give voice to a chanson as our bark splits the foam; to see America with deer drinking at the springs and beaver splashing in the streams; to smell and hear America with her tang of balsam and her bleat of fawns!

CONTENTS

ILLUSTRATIONS

MAPS

BLAZING
THE WAY WEST

CHAPTER I

THE LADY OF BELLE ISLE

COD fishermen were the first to bring back beaver from America. Arriving from France on the heels of John Cabot, who discovered Newfoundland in 1497, they tried their luck at fishing. Luck was so good that they thereafter crossed the Atlantic summer after summer to catch cod for the Friday fish market. The fishermen did not make their permanent home in America, but the land-locked harbor of St. John on the southeast coast of New-foundland provided them a safe haven, to which they might fly in times of summer storm. From that harbor they explored the coast both south and north.

To the north in the straits between Newfoundland and Labrador, they came to a grim, desolate rock, three miles wide and nine miles long, whose forbidding heights rise 700 feet above the surges of the Atlantic. We call this rock Belle Isle, a very appropriate name when we reflect that here, as far as we can learn, was born the first white child in America north of the Spanish settlements in Cuba. The fishermen, however, named it the Isle of Demons, because of confused and inarticulate voices that are heard there.

Should we visit the island, we could learn from the

clear-eyed lighthouse keeper that voices are as clamorous today as they were four centuries ago. Sometimes at night, when the gales are especially savage, noises like blood-curdling shrieks rise from several quarters at once. In explaining the source of the shrieks the lighthouse keeper tells us that Belle Isle stands in the flood of the cold Labrador current, which streams south from Greenland, carrying ice floes and icebergs that grind against each other or shatter their lofty pinnacles headlong against the isle's granite ramparts. He tells us that the crashing of ice and not the howling of demons causes the clamor.

The fishermen, however, gave the island wide clearance as they crossed the Straits of Belle Isle to Labrador. On the shores of Labrador they met Indians wearing beaver skins, much larger and finer than the furs bought by the Paris hat makers from the trappers of Sweden and Germany; for the pelt of the American beaver weighs from a pound and a quarter to two pounds. Although the skins were extra fine, the Indian was glad to accept a fish hook in exchange for a fur, which a cod fisherman could sell to a Paris hat maker for a piece of silver.

The fact that beaver skins could be bought for a fish hook came to the attention of the king of France, who sent Jacques Cartier, his ablest mariner, on a voyage of exploration. Sailing around Newfoundland to the westward, Cartier surveyed the Gulf of St. Lawrence in 1534 and in 1535 voyaged up the broad St. Lawrence River into the heart of the continent for five hundred miles to the Lachine Rapids just west of the present Montreal. He came home with enchanting tales of the beauties of the forest and of the plentitude of beaver, and he asked the king to name him governor of those lands and rivers.

The foolish king, however, named Jean of Roberval as governor, he being a favorite court politician. Cartier had to be content with the appointment of captain general under Roberval. For six years the governor laid plans for the founding of a colony on the St. Lawrence. As a beginning he directed Cartier to go in advance with a crew of men to select a site and build a fort. In obedience to the command, Cartier entered the St. Lawrence in the autumn of 1541 and built a fort at Cap Rouge, eight miles from the present Quebec. All went well until winter. Then scurvy appeared and destroyed one half the garrison. In the spring Cartier and the other survivors fled from the scene of death. As they came to the southeast corner of Newfoundland, they put in at the Harbor of St. John to fill their water casks before the long voyage home across the Atlantic. There a surprise awaited them.

While Cartier was spending the winter at Cap Rouge, Roberval had made ready a fleet of four ships. Early in the spring he sailed with a colony, which included a few women, one being his niece Marguerite, and another her old Norman nurse. The fleet crossed the ocean and stopped at the Harbor of St. John for drinking water. On the evening before Roberval was ready to continue his voyage, Cartier and his emaciated survivors sailed through the narrow, rocky gateway into the harbor.

Upon seeing Cartier, Roberval became violently angry. He summoned the captain general to come aboard the flagship where he denounced him as a coward for deserting his post. In vain did Cartier plead that half of his men were dead and the remainder little more than living skeletons. Roberval commanded him to have his men fill their water casks that very evening so that all might sail back to Cap Rouge the following morning in company.

Cartier returned to his own ship, directed his men to

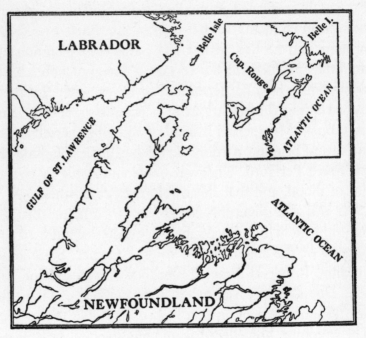

Belle Isle and Surroundings

fill all water casks and make the ship ready to sail at once. That night he had his men weigh anchor so that the ship might glide silently from the harbor with the ebbing tide. Once outside, they spread sails to a westerly breeze, which carried them eastward far out of sight upon the broad Atlantic before break of day.

We can imagine Roberval's fury the next morning when he awoke. He was still grinding his teeth in baffled anger when an officer approached to report that one of the seamen had seen Marguerite walk on the deck in the evening with a young, handsome, penniless colonist from Perigord. Since Roberval was from one of the noblest families of France, he regarded it as a great offense for his niece to be seen in company with a man of low birth. She was an orphan, and he had reared her as his own daughter. He doubtless planned for her to marry a man of noble blood. Summoning her, he demanded to know what she meant by accepting the attentions of a penniless youth of ordinary birth. Marguerite, instead of throwing herself on her knees and begging pardon, defied her uncle. She said that she loved Perigord, who was brave and noble of heart if not of blood, and that she would marry no other.

At this the governor determined to inflict a dreadful punishment, which no doubt was made yet more terrible because of the anger he felt toward Cartier. Summoning his pilot, Roberval directed him to set his course for Belle Isle. The pilot was frightened at the command, for he had heard about the demons that lurked upon that lonely rock. The governor, however, directed him to obey without further words. And so under a cold, sullen sky the fleet drew alongside the southern shore of the isle. Here Roberval had the crew put off a boat, which carried Marguerite and the old Norman nurse to the rock, where the men cast the two women ashore with no other supplies than four arquebuses, a supply of powder and lead and one ax. Having performed this heartless task, the crew rowed back to the ship as fast as men can row when in mortal fear of demons.

As this was being accomplished, Perigord ran to the ship's armory where he slung two arquebuses on his back, tied several lead bars to his waist and tucked a waterproof bag of gunpowder under an arm. Before Roberval suspected his purpose, Perigord leaped over the rail and into the icy waves.

Even without the weight of the lead bars and the arquebuses a very good swimmer could hardly hope to live in that cold, surging water. Yet to the amazement of every one and to the chagrin of Roberval, Perigord outswam the sea. He swam through the bellowing breakers, and when the sea found it could not swallow him, a writhing billow flung him through the white of the foaming surf against the jagged rocks. He grasped a granite boulder and, clambering to safety, ran to the arms of Marguerite. Perhaps he waved a mocking farewell to the discomfited Roberval, who turned his back as his fleet sailed westward through the Straits of Belle Isle until lost to sight beyond the horizon.

The story of Roberval and his colony is quickly told. His fleet passed westward across the Gulf of St. Lawrence and up the St. Lawrence River to Cap Rouge. That winter the scurvy came. Men died by scores. The living suffered from the scourge until they had not strength to bury the dead. They had scarcely enough strength to cast them into the snow drifts for the wolves. The colony failed, and eventually the survivors fled in their ships to France, where, as long as they lived, they told all who would listen of the horrors of life in America.

As for Marguerite and Perigord, we wish they had kept a journal so that we might have an account of their remarkable adventures on the Isle of Demons. The accounts we do have are contradictory and incomplete, but

BELLE ISLE

Above is the lighthouse. Below is Black Jake Cove. The two scenes show the rocky character of the island where was born the first white child in North America north of the Spanish settlements in Cuba and Mexico.

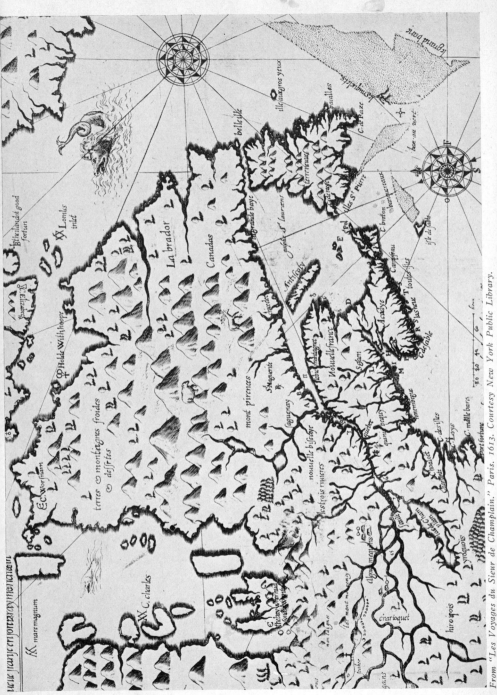

From "Les Voyages du Sieur de Champlain." Paris. 1613. Courtesy New York Public Library.

we will relate what we have reason to believe is the truth.

Soon after landing they determined to be married; and since no clergyman was there to perform the ceremony, they said their vows to each other and to God with the old Norman nurse as their only witness. They probably built a hut of rocks and driftwood and prepared for winter. We will have to guess what they had to eat, but we know that they had six arquebuses; and we also know that Belle Isle abounded in bears, foxes and caribou, which could supply both meat and clothing. Probably the castaways found berries, for berries grow there today in an interior valley. No doubt they found mushrooms. Today mushrooms can be gathered there in summer and dried for storage. In winter they need only be soaked in water to freshen them, and those who eat them never have scurvy.

The shores of the island were strewn with driftwood brought down the St. Lawrence and through the Straits of Belle Isle. We believe that Perigord not only cut up wood for winter, but that he also dragged a pile of wood together so that it might be lighted as a signal fire in case a sail should be sighted. Winter arrived and the three inhabitants of the rock remained in good health. The next summer a baby was born, and for the first time the cry of a white child was heard in that part of the North American continent.

Happiness, however, did not endure. Early the second winter the baby grew ill and died. Next Perigord followed the baby to the grave. Finally the nurse died, leaving Marguerite to face the terror of the demons alone. In the night, when their shrieks and howls sounded above the moan of the gale, she fired an arquebus; but that did not quiet the clamor. The winter passed. Then hungry bears came from the caves to steal her food. Many times they rushed to attack her. Always she kept the six arquebuses loaded and ready for defense. She killed many bears—three of them, so it is related, with coats as white as an egg.

Two years and five months passed when one afternoon Marguerite saw several fishing boats cruising to the south along the coast of Newfoundland, keeping as far as possible from Belle Isle. Long had she watched and waited for such an opportunity. Hastily she carried a firebrand from her hut to light the signal fire. The wood was dry and a column of white smoke rose upward to beckon the fishermen.

At the sight some of the fishermen made the sign of the cross and turned their boats to row away as fast as they could. They feared that the fire had been lighted by demons as a device to lure them to destruction.

It chanced, however, that the crew in one of the boats was made up of stout-hearted men. They steered toward the isle, and when they did so, the others, ashamed, followed at a distance. The stout-hearted fishermen, fearless of demons, drove their boat through the surf to the landing. As they drew near they saw a strange creature clad in the skins of beasts. Her figure was like that of a woman, but as she came near they saw that her hands were rough and calloused. Yet her face was as lovely as that of any woman they had ever seen and they knew she could be none other than the niece of the heartless Roberval. Gladly did these hardy fishermen take her into their boat. They conveyed her to the Harbor of St. John, and that autumn, as they sailed home with their catch of cod and their bales of beaver, they took her back to France. There she made her home in the land of Perigord and was loved and honored by all the people.

CHAPTER II

WESTWARD BY CANOE

Harrowing tales of suffering brought back from the St. Lawrence by Roberval ended for more than sixty years attempts at building a New France. Not until long after the death of Marguerite did a new leader arise whose fortitude, whose love of adventure and whose interest in geography impelled him to dare the hazards of the American wilderness. This new leader was Samuel of Champlain, born in 1567 at a seacoast village of western France. We know that he loved adventure, for he left home while yet a boy to follow the sea; we know that he was fascinated by geography, for he early learned the art of map making and was always eager to visit foreign places; we know that he had fortitude, for he served King Henry IV of France in fifteen years of wars fought against overwhelming odds. His cheerful disposition in defeat as well is in victory won the affection of the king, who, when the wars were ended, chose Champlain as his constant companion, offering him a pension for life so that he might live at ease at the royal court.

Champlain, however, had no desire to fritter away his time in Paris. He rejected the pension and, sailing as captain of a Spanish merchant ship, saw the West Indies, Mexico and Central America and crossed the Isthmus of

Panama to gaze spellbound upon the Pacific. As the waves of that ocean rolled eastward from China to break on the shore at his feet, he asked himself:

"What is to hinder me from sailing westward up the St. Lawrence River right through America to China?"

That seems like a strange thought to us, but in Champlain's day no one dreamed that North America was 3000 miles broad at the latitude of the St. Lawrence and that the vast Central Plain and the Rocky Mountain region barred the way.

After two years in Spanish service, Champlain came home to Paris in 1603, just in time to sail as the map maker of an expedition to found the French colony of Acadia on the North American seacoast south of Newfoundland. Champlain drew maps of Acadia, of Newfoundland and of the New England shore line. Then he sailed up the St. Lawrence as far as Tadoussac, where he traded with the Algonquin Indians. Here, he saw an opportunity to found a French fur-trading colony, which would give to France the leadership of the world in the manufacture of fur coats and beaver hats and, at the same time, would provide a base for an explorer to voyage westward to seek a route through the continent to China.

Back to France sailed the geographer and obtained from King Henry permission to found the colony. In 1608 he again arrived on the St. Lawrence with twenty-eight adventurers—all men—and founded Quebec on the north bank of the river where lofty hills abut the stream and provide a natural fortress. Champlain's men erected a stout trading fort, to which he invited the Algonquins to come and trade furs for articles of French manufacture, such as iron knives, axes and kettles, colored cloth, paint, beads and mirrors. This the Indians were glad to do, for prior to the coming of Champlain, they had no knives and axes but those of stone, no cloth but the tanned skins of wild animals, no beads but the quills of the porcupine, no paint other than what they brewed from vegetables and no mirrors other than the surface of a quiet pool or spring.

The summer and autumn of 1608 passed; the last goose honked southward; and the Algonquins withdrew for shelter to their villages. Solid ice bridged the St. Lawrence; the temperature fell to zero and below zero. Never before had Champlain and his men felt such bitter cold. They shut doors tight, rolled logs into the fireplace and made themselves cozy before the blaze.

All went well until mid-winter. Then a man complained of gnawing pains in his body. The next day another said he ached all over. Soon every man felt illness. Their faces turned to an ashen color. Their flesh sagged between their ribs. Their teeth rattled in their heads and became so loose that one man went so far as to pick teeth from his mouth.

"Scurvy," he moaned.

At the word his companions shivered with dread and recalled what old men back home had told of Roberval's ill-fated colony, which had been driven from New France by scurvy. As weeks passed, the illness grew worse. One man died. The twenty-seven frightened survivors scooped away the snow, chopped a grave into the frozen earth and laid the body in an ice-ribbed grave. A few days later a second died. Funeral followed funeral. Only the resolution of Champlain kept up the courage of the dwindling survivors. When spring finally came back, only eight hollow-eyed men remained to totter out of the fortress gates to bury the twentieth victim of that ghastly winter. Fortunately spring brought leaf buds and the shoots of wild vegetation. Such food contains the vitamins so necessary to health; and when the men ate the buds and leaves, their strength returned. The spring also brought back the Indians laden with packs of beaver furs. By the time the ship arrived from France in the early summer, the eight surviving adventurers had a large cargo of beaver skins for shipment to Paris. The arrival of the ship brought its temptations, too, for it offered escape from that plague spot to the homeland.

But Champlain was too busy with plans for a journey into Iroquois-land to think of retreat to France. The Iroquois were a murderous confederation of Indians, who made a practice of coming to the St. Lawrence every summer to rob and kill the Algonquins. When the Algonquin warriors came to Champlain with a request that he help them fight the Iroquois and defend their villages, he offered a better plan. Instead of sitting at Quebec to await the Iroquois, who would have all the advantage of a surprise attack, Champlain proposed that the Algonquins make a raid into the Iroquois country. If they would go on such a raid, he offered to lead them.

What a man to stir the savage imagination! By this one decision Champlain forged a brotherhood to bind the Algonquins and the French forever. With only two other Frenchmen and sixty Algonquin warriors, the governor of New France boldly set out to attack the most ferocious and domineering confederation of warriors in North America. Riding in twenty-four canoes, the warriors ascended the St. Lawrence to the mouth of the Richelieu River, which flows into the St. Lawrence from the south, and paddled against the current of the stream toward a beautiful lake, which the Indians reported was the mother of the Richelieu River. Each night the canoes were drawn up on the shore while the war party feasted on fresh venison and slept on the ground.

Champlain was in his element, visiting lands which no white man had ever seen before and extending the world's knowledge of geography. One day the river broadened into a lake. It is a lovely body of water 15 miles wide and 121 miles long and is called Lake Champlain in honor of the explorer. As Champlain looked to the west and saw the rugged Adirondacks in the present state of New York and looked eastward to other mountains mantled in their green forests, he exclaimed:

"*Voila les Verts Monts!*" (Behold the green mountains.)

It is from this exclamation that the Green Mountain State takes its name of Vermont.

The warriors coasted southward along the western shore of Lake Champlain until they came to a cape between two bays where later was to rise Fort Carillon—called Fort Ticonderoga by the English—which was to make history through three wars. It was ten o'clock of the evening of July 29 when they arrived at the cape. Here the lookout in the first canoe spied in the fading light a fleet of approaching Iroquois. At the same instant the Iroquois spied the Algonquins and quickly put ashore to hew trees with their stone axes and to throw up an *abatis* for defense. The Algonquins also put ashore. Thereupon the Iroquois sent a messenger to ask if they had come to fight.

In taunting tones the Algonquins answered that they had come a long way for no purpose other than to fight. Now indeed were the Iroquois dumfounded, for the Algonquins had never before dared to seek battle. The surprise was all the greater because the Iroquois numbered 200 men while the Algonquins had but sixty-three; but of course the Iroquois had no means of knowing that three of the invaders were white men from across the ocean. Indeed, it is not likely that the Iroquois had ever heard of white men and their terrible guns, which could shoot thunder and lightning.

Through the night the two opposing bands of warriors remained awake and shouted insults at each other. At sunrise Champlain deployed his men for an attack. He directed his two French followers, each armed with a gun, to take to the woods on either flank, while he remained in the center with the main body of the Algonquins. We will let Champlain tell what followed in his own words as translated from the French:

"I saw the enemy go out of their barricade, nearly 200 in number, stout and robust in appearance. They came at a slow pace towards us with dignity and assurance which greatly impressed me, having three chiefs at their head. Our men also advanced in the same order, telling me that those who had three plumes were the chiefs and that they had only these three, and that I should do what I could to kill them. I told them I should do all in my power. Our men began to call me with loud cries, and in order to give me a passageway, they opened in two parts, and put me at their head where I marched some twenty paces in advance of the rest until I was within about thirty paces of the enemy, who at once noticed me and, halting, gazed at me as I did also at them.

"When I saw them making a move to fire at us, I rested my musket against my cheek and aimed directly at one of the three chiefs. With the same shot two fell to the ground, and one of their men was so wounded that he died some time after. I had loaded my musket with four balls. When our side saw this shot so favorable to them, they began to raise such loud cries that one could not have heard it thunder. Meanwhile the arrows flew on both sides. The Iroquois were greatly astonished that two men had been killed so quickly, although they wore armor woven from cotton thread with wood, which was proof against arrows. This caused great alarm.

"As I was reloading, one of my companions fired from the woods, which astonished them anew to such a degree that, seeing their chiefs dead, they lost courage, took flight and, abandoning the fort and camp, fled into the woods, whither I pursued them, killing still more. Our savages also killed several of them and took ten or twelve prisoners. Fifteen or sixteen were wounded on our side with arrow shots, but they were soon healed.

"After gaining the victory, our men amused themselves by taking a great quantity of Indian corn and meal and also their armor, which they had left behind that they might run the better. After feasting sumptuously, dancing and singing, we returned three hours later with the prisoners."*

Although the Iroquois were defeated by these white men who seemed to handle thunder and lightning, another

*From *The Voyages of Samuel de Champlain*, C. P. Otis, translator, reprinted by permission of the Prince Society, Boston.

From a statue in Quebec. Courtesy of the Library of the Quebec Legislature.

SAMUEL DE CHAMPLAIN

He was the father of New France, founder of Quebec, discoverer of Lake
Champlain, of Lake Huron and of Lake Ontario.

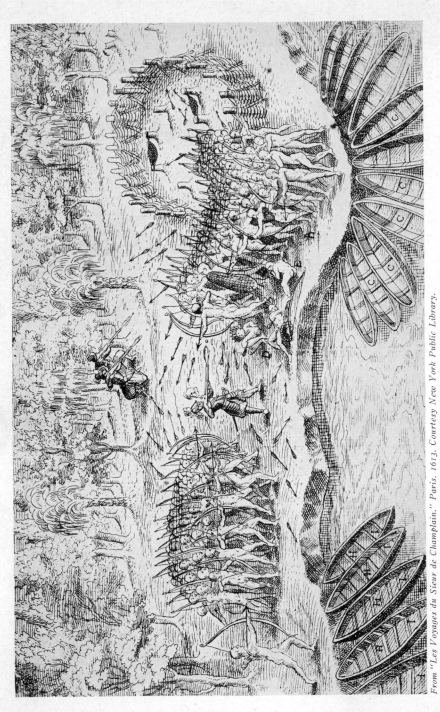

From "Les Voyages du Sieur de Champlain." Paris. 1613. Courtesy New York Public Library.

Defeat of the Iroquois at Lake Champlain

day would come. The Iroquois believed that the soul of a
slain warrior could not rest until his blood had been
avenged. Consequently wars of vengeance and counter-
vengeance would come between the Iroquois and the
Frenchmen until grand-daughters of unborn generations
would rue the feud begun so gaily that day on the site of
the future Ticonderoga.

Upon the return of the victors to Quebec, the Algonquins tortured and burned the dozen Iroquois prisoners,
who endured the pain without flinching and regarded
their tormenters with an air of indifference and contempt.
To seal an alliance with the Algonquins, Champlain proposed an exchange of hostages. He accepted the chief's
nearest relative to live with him at Quebec, giving in exchange a highly intelligent man, Etienne Brule,* who took
up his residence in the midst of savages to learn their ways
and to learn more about the geography of the country.

As Brule trailed the forests with Algonquin companions,
his boots wore out and he donned moccasins. His coat
and trousers fell to tatters and he drew on a blanket and a
breech clout. His hat followed the trousers, and he wore
his hair long, plaiting it like the Indians and dressing a
scalp lock. At length he came to look so much like an
Indian and to act like one that when he came back to
Quebec, Champlain could recognize him with difficulty.
Brule learned Indian languages and dialects. He learned to
like Indian ways of preparing food. He learned to read

---

*Since the use of the grave and acute accent marks in an Eng-
lish text is optional, all such markings are omitted from this book.
For the benefit of the reader a glossary of proper names may be
found at the back of the book, with correct pronunciation indicated.

signs and to follow the trails without loss of direction even though his path led through the gloom of a forest on a cloudy day.

Champlain would have preferred to roam the woods with Brule, but his duty as governor engaged his time. An assassin killed King Henry, and Champlain had to hurry back to France to confer with the new king's regent and obtain a renewal of authority as governor. Many other times when he would have liked to travel in the forest and explore, he had to cross the ocean to report in Paris on the progress of his colony in Canada. The recurrence of scurvy each winter claimed his attention. Finally he conquered the disease by planting a garden of vegetables. Each fall he directed his men to store a supply of wild grapes and vegetables for use in winter. He also had his men gather spruce gum and drink spruce tea in winter. He sent them out to kill deer to provide fresh meat. All this brought health.

Champlain founded a second trading fort on the site of the present Montreal in 1611. He also built a third trading post at Three Rivers, midway between Montreal and Quebec.

Early in 1615 Brule came to Quebec to tell Champlain that he had heard the Indians speak of a very great body of water, which could be reached by way of the Ottawa River, a stream flowing into the St. Lawrence west of Montreal. From Brule's report, Champlain was convinced that the water was too large to be a mere lake. It must be the Pacific Ocean!

Accordingly Champlain and Brule set out with a few other Frenchmen and Indians in a fleet of birch-bark canoes. Birch bark is almost as light as paper and canoes made of that material can be carried readily by one man across a portage between streams and around falls or rapids. Until the white man came to America, he had never thought of making bark canoes. It was the Indian who invented this graceful and serviceable craft and taught the Frenchmen how to make it. It was the canoe that made possible Champlain's voyage into the West. He and his men never could have carried the heavy boats of European make around the many falls and rapids of the Ottawa River.

Westward paddled the adventurers up the Ottawa, until the Indians showed them a portage over which they could carry their barks to a westward-flowing stream, down which they floated to Lake Nipissing. They crossed the lake to its outlet and descended a stream called French River. Since French River flows west, Champlain was certain that he was on the Pacific slope and would soon arrive at the ocean.

One evening as the setting sun heightened the glow of his face, his eager eyes saw the shining waters he had travelled so far to find. Was it the Pacific which he had seen at the Isthmus of Panama during his Spanish service? The men paddled faster and faster, outrunning the river as it debouched into the bay. Westward across the water peered Champlain, shading his eyes against the setting sun. He could see no farther shore. Surely the water must stretch to China! Yet to an experienced seaman the water had the glint of an inland lake. He scooped up a drink in the hollow of his hand and sipped it. It was not salty!

If the governor felt a dashing of hopes, he gave no sign.

It was true that he had not found the ocean, but he had discovered a wonderful lake. No white man had ever before seen a greater one. In fact only two other lakes in the whole world can equal it and they were unknown to Europeans in 1615. Champlain gave the name Lake Huron to the great body of water, because the Huron Indians lived upon its shores. It is a curious fact that although both Ontario and Erie are nearer to Quebec than Huron, it was Lake Huron that Champlain first saw, due to the fact that he voyaged by way of the Ottawa and Lake Nipissing instead of by way of the St. Lawrence.

Champlain, while making friends with the Hurons and visiting with them, learned that they too were living in dread of the bloodthirsty Iroquois. Since it was summer, the Hurons were expecting a raid at any time. Once more Champlain proposed to carry the war into the enemy's country and the Hurons responded to the plan as eagerly as had the Algonquins six years before. Although the Iroquois numbered only 17,000 people, they were so well organized for war that they had no difficulty in terrorizing the Algonquins and Hurons, each of whom were more numerous.

The Iroquois confederation was composed of five tribes —Mohawks, Oneidas, Onondagas, Senecas and Cayugas, dwelling in the present state of New York and living in villages extending from Lake Champlain to the foot of Lake Erie. It was to an Onondaga village that the Hurons guided Champlain. Their journey led them southeastward along rivers and creeks from Lake Huron to Lake Ontario. Thus Ontario was the second great lake to be visited by Champlain. In frail canoes they paddled across Lake

Ontario and ascended a river to the village they sought. Upon his arrival Champlain saw that the village was too strongly fortified to be taken with his small force. A brook flowed on each side of the village; and to attack it, the invaders had first to cross the brook, climb a steep bank and then scale a palisade of upright logs which the Onondagas had erected for their protection.

Accordingly Champlain dispatched Brule to a nearby Algonquin village for help. The Hurons became impatient at the delay and began the attack contrary to Champlain's plan. In order to assist them, the Frenchmen erected a high wooden platform, from which Champlain was able to fire over the palisade into the Onondaga houses. His fire did great damage, yet it was useless, for it was impossible with his small force to scale the palisades and take the town. Whereupon the Hurons became discouraged and withdrew before Brule could come back with the Algonquins. They recrossed Lake Ontario, retraced their course to their villages and once more Champlain found himself on the shores of Lake Huron. After waiting all winter for word from Brule, he returned to Quebec without him in the spring of 1616.

In the meantime Brule was on an adventure of his own. Accompanied by a few Indians, he journeyed southward, discovered the headwaters of the Susquehanna River in what is now southern New York, built a canoe and floated down that stream southward across the present states of Pennsylvania and Maryland into Chesapeake Bay. This voyage was made twenty years before Lord Baltimore established the first English settlement in Maryland and sixty-six years before William Penn founded the

Quaker settlement in Pennsylvania. Returning north, Brule
was captured by the Iroquois and held prisoner for more

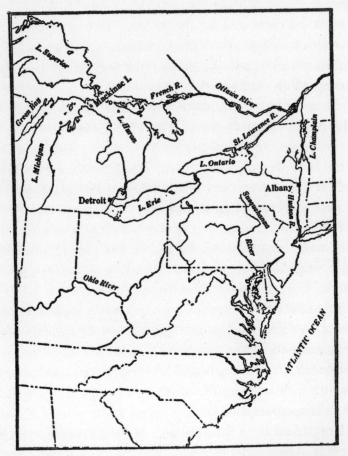

Region Explored by Champlain and His Woods Rangers

than a year. Eventually he escaped and in 1618 came once
more to Quebec.

Champlain's duties as governor prevented him from taking other long inland journeys. In 1620 he brought his
wife with him from France and did all he could to make
her happy in Quebec. He planted flowers in her garden

and grew exquisite roses for her. It was his hope that other women would come from France so that French families might help in the growth of the colony. A few women did come and in Champlain's time Quebec grew to be a small village. Madame Champlain, however, had no interest in America. Quebec was nothing but a rough trading town with almost no women for company. She cared nothing for the dirty Indians with whom her husband spent so much time. She longed for the beauty of Paris and for the music of the organ at church services. After four disagreeable years, she returned home where she saw Champlain only when business brought him there.

Since Champlain could no longer explore the country, he relied more and more on woods rangers, such as Brule, to discover new regions. It is probable that Brule discovered Niagara Falls and Lake Erie, but of that we are uncertain. He continued his woods ranging until 1632 when he was killed in a quarrel with a Huron Indian. By that time Champlain had other woods rangers in his employ. They married Indian women and lived in wigwams. Their half-breed children spoke both French and Indian with equal facility and knit the alliance between the French and the Indians more closely.

Most famous of Champlain's woods rangers was Jean Nicolet, who came to America in 1618 at the age of twenty and was sent by Champlain to the Hurons where he lived nine years. He helped the Jesuit priests to found missions there, and he helped the French fur traders to extend their business into Huronland.

Champlain also sent Nicolet to the Iroquois. He concluded a peace with those Indians so that they did not make war on the Algonquins and Hurons for a long time.

Until after Champlain's death, the Iroquois, Hurons and Algonquins all came to Quebec to trade furs for French goods.

After concluding the peace, Nicolet once more took up life in the Huron country. While there he learned of other large lakes to the west of Lake Huron. He also learned of a strange people living west of the lakes who differed in speech from the Indians he knew. He wondered if they were Chinese.

Champlain was now growing old and could not undertake the rigors of a long canoe voyage in quest of China, and so he fitted out Nicolet in the dress of a Chinese mandarin and gave him a grand robe of Chinese damask, embroidered with flowers and birds of many colors. Nicolet paddled westward in 1634 with seven Huron companions. He skirted the Lake Huron shore, crossed the Straits of Mackinac, paused at Mackinac Island and entered Lake Michigan. Coasting southward, he arrived at Green Bay in the present Wisconsin where he encountered the people he sought. Here he donned his damask robe, advanced toward the strangers with a pistol in either hand and fired the pistols into the air. The natives, startled and impressed, welcomed Nicolet and gave a feast at which they ate 120 beaver.

Instead of being Chinese, these strange people were Winnebagoes, a tribe of the Siouan family. Thus the French were visiting the Sioux in Wisconsin at the same time that the English were making the acquaintance of the Pequots in Connecticut. This explains why we spell the word Sioux in the peculiar French manner, although it is pronounced Soo. It also explains why several of the

Siouan tribes bear French names, such as the *Gros Ventres* (big bellies) and the *Bois Brules* (burnt woods.)

Nicolet spent two years in the West. He is credited with discovering Lake Superior as well as Lake Michigan. When he came back to Quebec in 1636, he brought samples of copper ore from the southern shores of Lake Superior. Champlain examined the samples and planned the opening of mines, which would add new wealth to France. But while his mind was as active as ever, his body could not respond. He died from paralysis that year on Christmas Day; and there was mourning in New France, for the colony had lost a leader who could not be replaced for a generation.

Even today, after three centuries, the people of Canada remember Champlain. In the city of Quebec there are paintings and statues at the parliament building to honor the discoverer of the Great Lakes and the founder of New France.

Nicolet survived Champlain seven years. Always ready to serve, he was a brother to everybody. One night there came to him a messenger to say that a party of Iroquois had taken an Algonquin as captive and were about to torture him. Nicolet made ready his canoe, intending to cross the St. Lawrence in an effort to save the life of the captive Indian. A storm was raging at the time and friends tried to dissuade him, for they felt no canoe could cross the river in that gale. But Nicolet, bent on his mission of mercy, did not hesitate. He pushed from the shore into the darkness where the wind-tossed waves wrecked his bark. The St. Lawrence enfolded him to her bosom and the storm sang his requiem.

CHAPTER III

WOODS RANGERS

For thirty years after Champlain's death the very life of New France was in constant peril. The peace which Nicolet had concluded with the Iroquois rested on the superior weapons of the French and not on the desire of the Indians. The peace would end as soon as the Iroquois could obtain guns. Even while Champlain was yet ruling at Quebec, a group of Dutch merchants founded the trading town of New Amsterdam on the site of New York City. From that seaport the Dutch ascended the Hudson River to the present Albany and there built Fort Orange.

Since the fort lay convenient to the Iroquois tribes, they ceased to bring their peltry to Quebec and, instead, carried it to Fort Orange. The loss of the Iroquois fur trade was keenly felt in Canada, but what was worse, the Dutch sold guns to the Indians. With guns in their hands these cruel warriors resumed their murderous excursions to the north.

They assailed the Indians of Huronland, who, being farthest removed from the protection of the French, were the easiest prey. The Hurons were a peaceful tribe, numbering about 20,000 people. Under the leadership of Jesuit missionaries guided to the region by Brule and Nicolet, many of the Hurons had accepted Christianity. They were far advanced in farming and were expert in the trapping of beaver, which they traded for French manufactured articles at Montreal. Although proficient in the arts of peace, they had no talent for war and did not know how to offer effective resistance to the Iroquois, who killed not only the Hurons but also the Jesuit missionaries. The calm courage with which the Jesuits remained to suffer martyrdom with their people, rather than to escape with their lives to Montreal, so moved the Iroquois to admiration that in some instances they tore out the hearts of the missionaries and ate them, hoping thereby to attain the same perfection in fearlessness.

Of the 20,000 Hurons not 500 escaped death. A few cowardly ones threw themselves upon the mercy of their enemies and offered to join them in hunting down other Hurons. Their craven offers were accepted and thereafter these renegade Hurons lived as Iroquois. A few hundred others escaped in canoes across Lake Huron and Lake Michigan to settle with the Winnebagoes west of Green Bay in the present Wisconsin. One white man, Medard Chouart, a servant at the Jesuit mission, hid in the forests by day and travelled by night to arrive at his home in Three Rivers where he told shocking tales of how the Iroquois had heartlessly destroyed not only men, but women and children as well, reserving the bravest to be tortured to death.

Having turned Huronland into a desolation, the Iroquois turned upon the Ottawas who lived near by. In a short time the Ottawas too were all killed except a few who escaped to live with the Huron refugees at Green

Bay. From then on the Iroquois came every winter to trap for beaver along the Ottawa and French Rivers and on the shores of Lakes Nipissing and Huron, and each spring they carried the peltry to Fort Orange. Step by step the French were losing all that Champlain had gained.

With the Hurons and Ottawas out of the way, the Iroquois lurked almost continuously around Montreal, Three Rivers and Quebec to waylay and destroy small parties of Frenchmen and Algonquins.

At that time there lived in Three Rivers, Pierre Radisson, an enterprising though heedless youth of seventeen, who, contrary to the warnings of his father and the pleadings of his mother, ventured with two companions from the village to hunt for deer in May, 1652. The three young men ventured into the gloom of a silent thicket where a dozen Iroquois pounced from the shadows upon them, took Radisson alive and killed his companions. With the two dripping scalps and with their captive the Iroquois departed for a Mohawk village on the Mohawk River not far from Fort Orange.

A warrior who killed an enemy and brought home his scalp was always honored by the Iroquois, but he who brought in a captive was even more highly esteemed, for a prisoner could be tortured before the eyes of all the people and the Iroquois regarded torture as the most thrilling form of entertainment. Accordingly, when the war party arrived with Radisson, the Mohawks howled acclaim and the people—men, women and even little children —came with clubs in their hands. They formed into two ranks between which Radisson was compelled to run while they clubbed him. As he raced to the end of the gauntlet and staggered, bruised and bleeding, past the last warrior, he was astonished when an old woman ran to him, threw her protecting arms around him and claimed him as her son. This woman had lost her boy a short time before and fancied that Radisson resembled him. She took him to her wigwam and bathed his bruises, while her husband demanded of the village council that the captive's life be spared. Since this man was a famous warrior, who had killed seventeen enemies in battle, the council permitted him and his wife to adopt the French youth.

For two years Radisson lived the life of a Mohawk. He learned their language and became as adept in woodcraft as the cleverest Indian. Once he escaped, and with a captive Algonquin, who fled with him, he made his way through 300 miles of trackless forest to arrive on the south bank of the St. Lawrence opposite Three Rivers. How his heart throbbed as he anticipated the delightful prospect of sitting beside his own fireplace with his parents and sister Marguerite. Searching on the river bank for material with which to fashion a craft to carry him across, he discovered an Iroquois canoe hidden in the weeds. Into it he leaped and paddled in impetuous haste to gain his beloved home. In his feverish eagerness he failed to note a party of Mohawks put out from the farther shore and drive straight toward him. They were upon him almost before he saw them, and he had no chance to escape. These Mohawks were in high good humor, for they had just killed eleven men of Three Rivers, including the mayor, and they amused themselves by permitting Radisson to examine the scalps in an effort to recognize the hair of his friends.

Back at the Mohawk village they put him to torture by fire. He was cruelly scorched and would have been burned to death had not his foster parents once again given their protection. Radisson appreciated the kindness of his Mohawk parents, but he was homesick for his own people. Escape a second time was more difficult, for now that the Iroquois knew of his desire to get away, they never let him depart from the village without the company of others. At length when Radisson could stand his homesickness no longer, he dashed from the village, running toward Fort Orange. The Indians gave chase, but he outran them and gained the fort where he begged for help. The Dutch commandant hid him behind a bale of furs and, when the next boat went to New Amsterdam, sent him along. From New Amsterdam Radisson travelled on a Dutch sailing ship to Holland, made his way to France and again recrossed the Atlantic to arrive at Three Rivers.

Here he found that in his absence his sister, Marguerite, had been married to Chouart, the former servant of the Jesuits. Chouart and Radisson became very fond of each other and from that day called each other brother.

At about the time of Radisson's homecoming several chiefs of the Onondaga tribe of the Iroquois confederation came to Quebec to seek peace. This tribe, living in the village south of Lake Ontario where Champlain had fought them forty years previous, was among the western Iroquois, and the chiefs professed that they were too far from Fort Orange to trade there. They begged the French to build a trading post at their village where it would be convenient to offer beaver skins for French merchandise.

The governor, delighted at the prospect of peace and also glad of an opportunity to regain a part of the lost beaver trade, sent men to build the requested trading fort. Since Radisson had lived so long with the Mohawks and could speak the Iroquois tongue, he was sent along as interpreter. The Frenchmen soon regretted that they had listened to the Onondagas. As soon as the trading post was well stocked with merchandise, the Onondagas broke the peace, apparently reasoning that it was foolish to go to all the trouble of catching beaver and trading for merchandise when it was so much more interesting to capture the things they wanted in war. The Indians surrounded the trading post and waited for the white men to come outside and fight or remain inside and starve.

One night, however, there came a terrific storm. Here then was a chance to slip by the Onondaga sentries in the blackness of night. Even if they should evade the sentries, possibility of escape was not great, for the Frenchmen were encumbered with their wounded, whom they had to carry. As soon as the Iroquois should discover that the fort was abandoned, they would most certainly take up the pursuit. Then one of the Frenchmen, perhaps it was Radisson, thought of a ruse to prevent the discovery of the escape. He had the others dress up billets of wood with coats and hats to make them look like soldiers. These were placed at the loopholes to stand guard. Then they caught a live pig, which the Frenchmen had been saving to kill and eat after all other supplies should be consumed. They placed the pig in a room adjoining the chapel and tied one end of a rope securely about the pig's body and the other end to the chapel bell. Having done this, the Frenchmen stole out into the black of the stormy night, eluded the sentries and were gone.

The next morning, the pig awoke, moved about and in so doing rang the bell. The Onondagas, hearing the sound, supposed that it was the morning call to worship. Several days passed and the Frenchmen were well on the way to Canada. Not until then did the Indians begin to wonder why the sentries at the loopholes were so motionless and why the bell rang in such a crazy fashion and at any hour of the day. They drew nearer, knocked over the dummy sentries, broke into the trading post and found all living things gone except the pig. How the Onondagas cursed the cunning of the Frenchmen and how Radisson laughed in many a winter camp as he, in later years, related the tale of the pig that rang the bell!

Once more the Iroquois hovered about the Canadian villages. They made war not only upon the French but upon all Indians who approached the villages for trade. They hid in the corn fields to shoot farmers who came to tend their crops.

Late in the spring of 1658 the Frenchmen were heartened by the arrival of a few Algonquins, who had slipped by the Iroquois and had entered Montreal with furs brought from Green Bay. The Algonquins told of a wealth of beaver to be found in the region of the Upper Lakes and proposed that the Frenchmen send a fleet of canoes with goods to trade with the Hurons, Ottawas and other Indians who would welcome them. News of the proposal of the Algonquins was carried by sailing ship to Three Rivers and Quebec, and the merchants of Canada provided a shipment of merchandise to be taken to the Upper Lakes by thirty traders accompanied by 140 Algonquins. Among the traders were Chouart and Radisson.

Although the party put out from Montreal at night, the Iroquois saw them and gathered at the *Long Saut* (long jump). At this point the Ottawa dashes down a long series of rapids, which forces travellers to land at the bottom of the *Saut*, unload their merchandise and carry it with the canoes to the upper end of the falls. When the traders and Algonquins arrived at the *Saut*, the Iroquois launched an attack in which they killed several men. Chouart and Radisson rallied their comrades and beat the Iroquois off. As soon as the battle was over, most of the traders got back into their canoes for flight to Montreal. Although they had beaten the Iroquois, they felt sure that the enemy had merely retreated upstream to the next portage, where, with a larger force, they would fight again.

In spite of all Chouart could say to hearten them, the other Frenchmen, with the exception of Radisson, turned back. And so only two white men were left to push on with the Algonquins for Green Bay. Chouart was perfectly familiar with the Ottawa River, for he had traversed it many times going to and from the Jesuit missions on Lake Huron. He, therefore, knew the most secure places to hide by day. They travelled only by night until they at length arrived at Lake Huron. Crossing the lake and travelling the Straits of Mackinac, they entered Lake Michigan, coasted down its western shore and arrived at Green Bay.

Here they found the Indians in a panic. For several years the Iroquois had been on murderous raids, killing the Indians living in what are now the states of Ohio, Indiana and Illinois. They had now entered the present Wisconsin to kill all Indians they might find there. Confronted with this new menace, Chouart and Radisson led the Indians on a night march, struck the Iroquois camp at dawn and wiped out the invaders as they rolled from their beds. Because of this act the brothers were hailed as deliverers, and their fame spread throughout the Northwest. The Indians of the Upper Lakes invited them to visit them and be their friends. The two travelled westward and possibly came to the Mississippi. They explored the shores of Lake Superior and ventured north of the lake to visit Indians who told them of Hudson Bay.

So absorbed were they in their discoveries, they spent not one winter in the region but two. Not until the spring of 1660 were they ready to embark for home. They had their Indian friends assemble all the beaver skins at Mackinac Island at the northern end of Lake Michigan where that lake pours its water into Lake Huron. Never before had the world seen such a great stock of beaver in one place. The packs of furs filled 250 canoes manned by 500 Indians. The fleet was about ready to start when word came that the Iroquois were gathered in force on French River, Lake Nipissing and the Ottawa. It would not be possible to go through to Montreal, some of the Indians said. But Chouart and Radisson addressed the council with a speech something like this:

"Did not we lead you safely at Green Bay? Now are we rabbits to sit here with these fine beaver peltry when they can be traded for manufactured goods, which you would like to have? Let *children* remain here. We invite *men* to go forward with us."

It was just the speech to stir the heart of a savage. With shouts of approbation the Indians followed to a man. They crossed Lake Huron and began the ascent of the French River. As they progressed, they found evidence that the Iroquois had been there, but they found nothing but cold ashes in the camps. On the shores of Lake Nipissing they found the same thing. Portaging to the Ottawa River, they cautiously began the descent. At the *Long Saut* they met a few Iroquois, whom they quickly defeated. Then they sped on to Montreal. After their long voyage they would have rested for a few days within the protection of the palisades of Montreal, but there they learned that at Quebec three ships were about to sail empty for France. It was very important therefore that they rush on to Quebec before the ships departed. Voyaging both day and night, they paddled down the St. Lawrence, pausing only for a few moments at Three Rivers for Chouart and Radisson to greet their families.

When at last they came within sight of Quebec, the watchmen on the heights above the town and the lookouts aboard the ships supposed they were Iroquois, coming to the long-threatened attack, and cried the alarm. Gunners primed their cannon and trained them on the approaching fleet, while the bells summoned the militia. But as the canoes drew nearer and the people could make out figures, they saw that the canoemen were Algonquins and that the men in the lead canoe were Frenchmen. At length one of the villagers shouted:

"It is Radisson! It is Chouart!"

Once more the bells clanged, but joyously. The men standing with their matches at the vents of the cannon now touched the fire to the charge, but to fire salutes. Governor D'Argenson came out of his mansion wearing his finest clothing and, as he hurried to the water front to greet the returning travellers, ordered his cooks to prepare a banquet with seven kinds of fish, fowl and meat and all the varieties of fruit and vegetables the colony afforded. That night the adventurers feasted like heroes of the Golden Fleece come home. And indeed they had the Golden Fleece! Their two years' work made them rich men. After paying liberal rewards to their faithful Indian allies, they also had a fortune for the merchants who two years before had supplied the goods for the venture. The governor, being one of the men who had furnished money for the goods, received a large share of the profit.

For the moment nothing was too good for the two men who called each other brother. D'Argenson ordered two sailing brigantines to carry them home so that they might arrive in Three Rivers in state, one riding in one boat and the other in the other. Once back with their families, the brothers were content to remain for a time, telling of the places they had seen and the wonders of the West.

After a year of that, idleness tired them. They called upon the governor to request a license for trading with the Indians of Lake Superior and for further explorations in the regions to the north of the lake. In those days the laws permitted no one to travel into the West or to hunt or trap or trade with the Indians without a license. This law had been made by the king to protect his political friends, who had the monopoly of all Canadian trade. The brothers knew of this law, but since they intended to trade on the shores of Lake Superior where the king's friends had never been and since they intended to discover new lands for France, they believed the governor would be glad to grant permission. The crafty governor, however, saw an opportunity to make himself rich without taking any hazards himself. He offered Chouart and Radisson the license on condition that they would repay him with one half of their profits.

In disgust the brothers spurned the proposition. Secretly they bought trade goods, stowed them aboard canoes, engaged Algonquin canoemen and slipped out of Three Rivers at night. D'Argenson was beside himself with wrath when he learned of their disobedience. But there was nothing he could do but speak contemptuously of them as outlaws and woods rangers, for they were beyond the reach of his hand.

The painted forests of October were in all their glory when the partners arrived on Lake Superior. There on the northern shore they built a log house and began to trade with the Indians for beaver. They also began their exploring expeditions. They discovered and explored Rainy River and Lake of the Woods. Venturing farther northward, they discovered an overland route to Hudson Bay and found its shores rich with fur animals. Until that time Hudson Bay had been reached only by sailors from sea, who entered by way of Hudson Strait and found the bay a cold, barren region.

For two years the brothers remained. They knew that D'Argenson had not been a popular governor, and they hoped that the king would recall him. Should he be recalled and a new governor sent to rule Canada, they felt it would be safe to return home. Unfortunately D'Argenson yet ruled at Quebec. When the adventurers came back to Three Rivers, he confiscated their cargo, valued at $300,000. With such a fortune he no longer cared to remain in America. He resigned his office and retired to Paris.

Chouart and Radisson journeyed to France to appeal to the king, but the king denied them a hearing. Angered at what they regarded an injustice, the brothers crossed the English Channel where they revealed to the English the secret of wealth to be obtained from furs on Hudson Bay. They helped the English to organize the Hudson Bay Fur Company, which, after almost three centuries, is yet one of the great fur companies of the world. The English could not reach the fur country by way of the St. Lawrence, for the French barred the way. They therefore entered through Hudson Strait by ships and on the southern shores of the bay built their trading forts.

It is probable that Radisson also influenced the English to seize the Dutch possessions on the Hudson River. While England and Holland were at war in 1664, an English fleet captured New Amsterdam, changing the name to New York. The English also took possession of Fort Orange, changing the name to Albany. Thus, at a double stroke, England took possession of valuable beaver country on both the north and south sides of the French, thereby placing Canada in the position of a nut between the jaws of a nut cracker, the upper jaw being on the Hudson Bay and the lower jaw on Hudson River.

The English were not the only ones to profit from the explorations of Chouart and Radisson. The merchants holding the monopoly of the Canadian trade sent woods rangers to Lake Superior and to Lake Michigan to trade with the Indians. They founded the settlement of Mackinac on Mackinac Island. This settlement became the headquarters for traders of the Upper Lakes. For more than one hundred and fifty years it remained one of the important fur-trading centers of the world. Jesuit priests also came to Mackinac to preach to the Indians and to help in the exploration of the West.

CHAPTER IV

AT THE *LONG SAUT*

We will now turn back to the year 1660 in which Chouart and Radisson were welcomed home with their great supply of beaver fur from the upper Lakes. It will be recalled that they met almost no Iroquois on the Ottawa River as they came down to Montreal. We will now explain why.

In the spring of 1660 the Iroquois decided to destroy Canada. The war council agreed to send 600 warriors from the Mohawk villages by canoes down from Lake Champlain to Montreal, where they were to join 600 other warriors, who had spent the late winter and early spring trapping for beaver on the Ottawa. The 1200 together would first capture and destroy Montreal, then Three Rivers and finally Quebec. At that time Canada numbered only 2000 white people. The Iroquois counted 17,000. How long could the few Frenchmen huddled in their three villages withstand the continuous onslaughts of so many?

The probability is that Canada would have been destroyed had it not been for the self sacrifice of seventeen bachelors of Montreal. As the two armies of Indians were converging upon the town, the seventeen bachelors met secretly and with clasped hands pledged each other to go out and fight to the death. Their captain, Dollard des

Ormeaux, believed that if they would sacrifice themselves, they would instill in the hearts of the Iroquois such a respect for French valor that the colony might be saved.

Southwestward the seventeen drove their canoes a few miles up the St. Lawrence until they came to the mouth of the Ottawa. Then they ascended the Ottawa about thirty-five miles to the *Long Saut*. Since the Iroquois in descending the stream would have to stop at the head of the *Saut* and unload their canoes for the portage, this was an ideal place for an ambuscade. In case the Iroquois should arrive a few at a time, Dollard planned to kill them as they came. In case they came in too great a number, he decided to retreat to the foot of the *Saut* where, on the south bank, stood an abandoned Iroquois palisade with twenty loopholes. Dollard ordered that all food supplies be stored inside the palisade to be available in case of siege. He neglected, however, to make any provision for water, and this neglect was to cause needless torment in the days just ahead.

The Frenchmen had just completed their arrangements when they were annoyed by the arrival of three Algonquin warriors and thirty-nine Hurons, led by a Huron chief, Annahotaha. These Indians had stopped in Montreal and there had learned of Dollard's mission. The three Algonquins had been accusing the Hurons of cowardice; and when Annahotaha learned about the plans of the seventeen bachelors, he dared the Algonquins to go with him and put the charge of cowardice to the test. How Dollard regretted that the secret of his expedition had leaked out in Montreal! He did not object to the help from the three Algonquins, but he did not trust the Hurons. Yet he dared not reject the proffered assistance. To send Annahotaha away might mean that he would carry information of the projected ambuscade direct to the Iroquois. And so, putting on a show of friendship, he invited the Indians to pitch camp and await the enemy.

A few mornings later, while the allies were preparing breakfast, the lookout sighted a canoe bearing five Iroquois coming down the Ottawa. Quickly all skulked to cover, primed their muskets and watched as the five approached the landing at the head of the *Saut*. Dollard cautioned his men not to fire until he gave a signal. But before he gave the signal, the Hurons fired a volley while the canoe was yet well out in the stream. Although their fusillade killed four Iroquois, the fifth, unhit, uttered a howl which reverberated between the forest walls on either side of the Ottawa, echoing and reechoing.

In response, a great flotilla of Iroquois canoes came from up the river around the bend like hornets in a rage. Dollard's men, the three Algonquins and a dozen of the Hurons fled headlong to the palisade, shut the gate and thrust their muskets through the loopholes to await the enemy. Twenty-seven Hurons remaining outside saved themselves by joining sides with the Iroquois.

It is not necessary to give details of this fight in which the few men inside the palisade held 600 attacking Iroquois at bay for eight long days. It is not necessary to describe how the defenders suffered from thirst or to tell how all of the Hurons inside the fortification, with the exception of Annahotaha, became so crazed with thirst that they leaped over the wall to join the Iroquois in fighting their former allies. What we wish to show is how Dollard's small band spoiled all the plan of the Iroquois campaign.

Instead of attacking and wiping out Montreal, the 600 warriors from the Mohawk joined the Iroquois on the Ottawa to attack the Frenchman in the palisade.

The *Long Saut* and Adjoining Territory

Not until the eighth day did the Iroquois hit upon a plan of successful attack. They split logs to serve as shields against the bullets and behind these shields they advanced right up to the palisade, taking position beneath the loopholes where the Frenchman could not shoot them. There they commenced to hack at the logs with axes. In a short time two logs fell away simultaneously to be followed by two more. Into the breach sprang the Iroquois. Dollard, spearhead of the defense, leaped to meet them, hatchet in hand. Skulls cracked as he swung his hatchet, but they shot him down. Others took his place. The Iroquois dead piled up and the living stood upon the dead to force the fighting into the palisade itself. Annahotaha and the three Algonquins died with their French brethren. When but five white men remained alive, the cry went up to spare them for torture. But there was no chance for torture. The Frenchmen forced the fighting in a last mad sortie until all were slain.

The Iroquois, cheated of their hopes for torture, turned upon the hapless Hurons who had deserted Annahotaha. Five of the Hurons escaped by flight and arrived at Montreal with the tale of what had happened at *Long Saut*. The others paid for their faithlessness in torture fires.

Records fail to tell how many Iroquois fell in those eight days; but the slaughter was so appalling that it caused the survivors to reason against their projected destruction of Canada. If a few men without water could wreak such havoc, what could Frenchmen do if fighting in their fortified towns of Quebec, Three Rivers and Montreal? Thus Canada was saved and although almost three centuries of floods have leaped over the rocks of the *Long Saut*, Dollard's men yet live in the bright light of immortal memory.

CHAPTER V

THE MAGNIFICENT MATCHMAKER

For more than half a century after the coming of Champlain to Quebec, Canada remained a mere fur-trading settlement ruled for the benefit of the king's political friends, who had the monopoly of all commerce. The entire white population in 1665 numbered only 2000, of whom less than 500 were women and girls. In that same year King Louis XIV of France, after noting the growth of Virginia, Massachusetts and other English colonies of the Atlantic seaboard, appointed Jean Talon, one of his most faithful subjects, as intendant of Canada. It was the intendant's task to represent the king's property interests in the colony, while the governor looked after the political affairs.

As Talon set sail, the king commanded that he find a way to make Canada grow. It did not take the faithful intendant long to discover why Canada remained a small colony. He wrote home that no country could prosper without women as well as men, and that Canada's greatest need was one thousand women for the colony's bachelors. He asked that the king send agents into the agricultural areas of France to seek girls of good character and without physical blemish, who would be willing to become the wives of farm owners in the New World.

Before attention could be given to Talon's proposal, the

king received a request from the governor at Quebec, asking for an army of 1200 men to chastise the Iroquois. The army was sent; and, guided by the Canadian woods rangers, it marched into the heart of Iroquoisland, defeated the Indians in battle, burned the Mohawk and Oneida villages and forced the warriors to beg for peace. The war over, the veterans marched back to the St. Lawrence, where they were discharged from service and each man was given a piece of wilderness land as a home and farm. Since the soldiers were single men, this added to Talon's perplexity; for instead of 1000 bachelors, he now had 2200.

Once more he requested a shipment of marriageable girls. This time the king responded by sending agents into the provinces. In those days the lands of France were owned by the nobles and the clergy, who lived in the cities, while mere tenants tilled the soil. At the prospect of becoming wives of land owners, almost one hundred girls volunteered to go to America with the first ship. They became known as the king's maidens, for Louis provided the funds to pay their passage. Ursuline nuns accompanied them to serve as chaperones on the voyage and through the time of courtship.

The crossing of the sea was made merry for the king's maidens by the presence on shipboard of a twenty-three-year-old bachelor, Robert de La Salle, a man of excellent education and good social rank, who was on his way to Canada to buy a wilderness estate. Since he was socially superior to the maidens, he had no thought of marrying any of them; but that did not keep him from singing and dancing with them.

JEAN TALON

Statue to Dollard des Ormeaux at Montreal

When the ship arrived in Canada, La Salle went his way while the king's maidens were sent to Quebec, Montreal and Three Rivers to await the courtship of the bachelors. They had not long to wait. Soon came the bachelors, garbed in the very best clothing they could afford. Rarely indeed has the world seen more speedy courtships. Since there were twenty suitors to every maiden, each man proposed marriage almost as soon as he was introduced. In a very short time every maiden had become a wife. Talon, pleased with the outcome of his efforts as a matchmaker, wrote for more king's maidens to be forwarded the following summer. Each summer more girls came to America until every bachelor who desired a wife was supplied.

While most of the bachelors were delighted at an opportunity for marriage, several hundred declined to marry any of the king's maidens. For them Talon had a remedy. He had the governor refuse any man of twenty a license to hunt, trap or trade with the Indians unless he was married. Further, he had the governor assess fines against all unmarried men of twenty. Fines also were levied on fathers whose daughters were not married at the age of sixteen. The only exceptions to the rule were the priests, whose vows did not permit them to marry, and citizens of high social rank, such as La Salle, who were not expected to marry beneath their station.

While the fines had the effect in many instances of forcing recalcitrant ones into wedlock, it drove others to seek refuge in the forests with the Indians or beyond the lakes to Mackinac, where they were safe from the intendant's power. There they lived with the Indians as woods rangers and hunted, trapped and traded contrary to the law. And

thus the name woods ranger, borne so honorably by Brule
and Nicolet, became a term of reproach and a synonym
for outlaw.

It must not be supposed that the king's maidens had an
easy lot in the New World. When they came to marry men
with farms, they pictured lands with houses similar to the
buildings of stone in which they lived in France. Instead
they discovered that their husbands owned uncleared forest lands and houses which were crude, floorless, log cabins.
But whether they felt they had made a bad bargain or not,
it was a bargain for life. There was nothing for them to do
but to make the best of it; for while the king paid their passage to America, he would not pay for their return voyage;
and they had to remain. While some of the women regretted their coming, most of them lived happy lives in
their log-cabin homes.

After having found wives for the men, Talon encouraged the couples to rear large families. In the king's name
he paid pensions to families with ten children and larger
pensions to families with fifteen.

Talon's next step was to teach the men how to be successful farmers in a climate which differed greatly from
that of France. He set an example by laying out a model
farm adjoining Quebec and operating it himself to show
that farming could be pursued profitably on the St. Lawrence. Following his example, others became successful
farmers. In the seven short years of his intendancy, Canada
changed her balance of trade. Instead of importing food-
stuffs as had been done from the time of Champlain, the
colony shipped wheat to France. Talon built flour mills.
He started ship building to give the farmers employment

in winter; and for the first time Canada became sea minded and developed sailors, one of whom, Iberville, became a great admiral. Talon encouraged fisheries and shipped to France oil rendered from porpoises caught in the St. Lawrence.

Canada grew! Talon found it a land of 2000 white people with almost no agriculture. Seven years later, when he was recalled to Paris, he left a rich farming land with 7000 people, a thousand of whom were babies. The growth begun in Talon's day has never stopped. Eighty years after his departure the population had increased tenfold, practically all of the increase being due to the birth of children; for after Talon's day very few Frenchmen migrated to Canada. Although the king no longer pays pensions for large families, the high birth rate of Canada has continued even to our own time. Today there are 2,500,000 French Canadians living in Canada and a million more in the United States, a total of 3,500,000, almost all of whom are descended from the original 500 women and girls Talon found in 1665 and from the king's maidens imported from France to become wilderness brides. Among the most famous of the descendants of the king's maidens are the Dionne quintuplets.

CHAPTER VI

THE AGE OF FRONTENAC

News that the king was about to recall Talon from Canada was whispered about the court at Paris even before Talon learned of it. Among the king's men who heard the report was Count Frontenac, a famous soldier, whose strategic defense at the Island of Crete against the Turks had made him a national hero. Since the war was over and no further adventure offered itself in Europe, he presented himself before King Louis to request that he be appointed to succeed Talon and also to be made governor of Canada, thereby combining both the offices of intendant and governor in one.

The request puzzled the king, for Frontenac was fifty-two years old, an age at which most men of that time were content to seek a life of ease in Paris. Then the middle-aged hero took the king into his confidence and confessed that although he had high regard for his wife and she for him, she nagged him all of the time he was at home. He wanted to get away from her. The king therefore appointed Frontenac governor, but he sent another to serve as intendant. This proved unfortunate, for the new governor and new intendant quarrelled continuously and this hampered Frontenac, who was a man of wide vision and wished to build a great New France in America. Frontenac arrived at Quebec in 1672 and began taking stock of able citizens on whom he might rely for patriotic service.

One of the men he met was a youthful trader, Louis Jolliet, a favorite of Talon, who spent his summers buying furs at Mackinac and on Lake Superior, but who generally came into Quebec each autumn to spend the winter.

Another was Robert de La Salle, who will be recalled as the scholarly bachelor who danced and sang on shipboard with the king's maidens. La Salle had bought the wilderness estate he sought. It lay at the foot of the great rapids in the St. Lawrence a short distance west of Montreal. This was the head of navigation for ocean-going ships, for they could not possibly ascend the rapids. Here La Salle laid out a palisaded village, where he rented land to farmers at a trifling payment of a few cents in coin and three capons a year. Inside the palisade each farmer was allowed to have a third of an acre for his house and garden and outside he could have as much land as he desired for farming.

La Salle seemed to be utterly fearless of danger. He visited the Iroquois, learned their language and won the friendship of the Seneca tribe of that confederation. The Senecas told him of a westward-flowing river, which La Salle thought must be the Colorado, shown on Spanish maps as being a very large stream emptying into the Gulf of California. Should it prove to be the Colorado, La Salle thought he could float down it to the Pacific Ocean opposite China and trade with the Chinese. First he explored the shores of lakes Ontario and Erie, then struck southward across the country and found the river he sought, which

he named the Belle River, but which we call the Ohio.* He
explored it to the falls of the present Louisville, Kentucky,
and returned home with great ideas of trading with the
Chinese. His neighbors laughed at him and his ideas and
nicknamed his estate *La Chine,* meaning China. It is from
that nickname that today we call the adjoining rapids the
Lachine Rapids.

One of the men who ridiculed La Salle was Charles Le
Moyne, whom Talon recommended to Frontenac as one
of the leading citizens of Canada. La Salle and Le Moyne
were alike in one thing and that was fearlessness. Le Moyne
spurned the idea of living securely behind the shelter of
the palisades of Montreal. Instead he moved to the south
side of the St. Lawrence opposite Montreal and there made
his home. Once the Iroquois captured him and held him
prisoner a long time. He learned their language and their
mode of life and, when the opportunity presented itself,
escaped. He built his house stronger, fortified it with palisades and was careful to prevent being recaptured. On his
farm he and his wife reared eleven children, every one of
whom became famous in American history.

There was another valiant man, Daniel Duluth, a fur
trader of the Upper Lakes, who came to America after
the arrival of Frontenac. Duluth built a trading post on the
northern shore of Lake Superior and also traded with the
Sioux in the vicinity of the present city of Duluth, Minnesota. Frontenac later appointed Duluth as commandant at
Mackinac. There in 1684 he demonstrated his courage and

---

*Whether or not La Salle was the discoverer of the Ohio has
long been in dispute, but we believe that the preponderance of
evidence shows that he did. See Parkman's, *La Salle and the Discovery of the Great West,* pp. 8–27.

resolution when two Frenchmen were murdered by Indians. Duluth had the slayers brought into an open court, where they were found guilty of murder, and he sentenced them to be hung. At this the friends of the Indians threatened revolt. Since they numbered 400 and were armed with French muskets, officers of Duluth's garrison, which was little more than a squad, counselled that Duluth accept a gift of beaver skins in place of the required hanging. But Duluth wanted to impress on the savages that no Frenchman could be murdered without equal retribution. His very coolness and determination to exact justice overawed the threatening tribesmen. Sullenly they witnessed the execution without an outbreak.

With such valiant men on whom he could rely, Frontenac's first duty was to establish safety on the St. Lawrence. Although the Iroquois had been chastised in 1666, the eastern tribes of the confederation had suffered the most. The western tribes—Cayugas, Senecas and Onondagas—yet continued their depredations. Frontenac directed La Salle, because of his friendship with the Senecas, to summon the hostile chiefs to a council at the foot of Lake Ontario. Using Le Moyne as interpreter, Frontenac spoke to them and addressed them as "my children," at the same time speaking of himself as their "father." He told them that he wanted to be friends with his children and had come all the way from Quebec to show his willingness to be a friend. But while wishing to be a friend, he explained that he was strong enough to take care of himself without their friendship; and that if they wanted war, he could give it to them. At his command men towed barges up the Lachine Rapids to Lake Ontario where they gave

a brilliant naval display. Before the eyes of the Iroquois
he had his men build Fort Frontenac on the shore of the
lake and mount guns upon it. He placed La Salle in command at the fort and instructed him to attack the Iroquois
the next time they made trouble on the St. Lawrence.

For ten years Frontenac ruled Canada and they were
years of peace and expansion. The fur trade of the Great
Lakes grew. Duluth advanced westward across the prairies.
Jolliet and La Salle explored the rivers to the southward.
But the tongue of the busybody is long. It reached from
Quebec to Paris and told the king how Frontenac did not
punish the woods rangers, how he advanced Duluth, how
he played favorites with La Salle and how he was unfair
to the Jesuit priests. In the end the busybodies won. The
king recalled Frontenac to Paris in 1682.

His recall was a severe blow to New France. Almost
at once the Iroquois resumed their hostility, using guns
supplied them by the English merchants of New York and
Albany. Although at peace with France, the English encouraged the Iroquois to raid the Canadian settlements.

In retaliation Iberville, the eldest son of Le Moyne, led
an overland expedition to Hudson Bay, captured the English trading posts there, warned the English they were trespassers on French territory and expelled them. The king of
France gave the forts back to the English and apologized
for the acts of Iberville so that nothing came of it, yet the
colony was kept in constant turmoil.

Finally in 1689, King William's War broke out between
England and France. The Iroquois gladly went to war on
the side of the English. They captured and burned La
Chine and tomahawked all the inhabitants. Elated with

victory, they swooped down upon the other French settlements. New France was about to be lost, when King
Louis suddenly remembered how ably Frontenac had ruled
his colony and how skillfully he had fought at Crete. Back
to Canada came Frontenac with viceregal powers.

He arrived none too soon, for an English naval invasion
of the St. Lawrence was imminent. An English fleet arriving before Quebec commanded the approaches to the
town and the sailors discovered a secret path leading up
from the river around to the rear of the town to a high
plateau, known as the Plains of Abraham. It was by this
secret path that the English General Wolfe, sixty-nine
years later, climbed to the rear of Quebec and effected the
conquest of Canada. But the discovery of the secret path
did the English no good in 1690, for Frontenac, now at the
age of seventy, was as alert as a fox. He beat off the enemy,
although it cost the lives of many of his men, among them
one of the gallant sons of Le Moyne.

While the English were fighting before Quebec, the
Iroquois plundered the outlying posts, destroying the
smaller settlements and driving the people to Montreal,
Quebec and Three Rivers for safety.

In the course of their plundering, they came to the little
palisaded village of Vercheres, twenty miles east of Montreal on the south side of the St. Lawrence. The Iroquois
bounded from the cover of the forest in broad daylight
to cut off and tomahawk the farmers at work in the field.
As their bloodcurdling war whoops sounded across the
growing wheat, Madeleine Vercheres, fourteen-year-old
daughter of the founder and commandant of the village,
was at the boat landing outside the palisades with an eighty-

year-old man, Viollette. She and the old man ran as fast as
they could to the village, slammed and barred the gate,
fired the cannon to make the Indians believe the village
was ably defended and then began to look for the soldiers
who had fled from their bastions.

There were but two soldiers at the village. Madeleine's
father had been summoned to Quebec with the other soldiers to defend the capital from the British. Her mother
was at Montreal on business. Since both soldiers had abandoned their post, the command then devolved on this
young girl. Entering the block house, she found the soldiers cowering in fear with the women and children. One
of the soldiers was in the act of hurling a firebrand into
the powder magazine, it being his intention to blow up the
block house and the people to prevent their falling captive
and suffering torture. Madeleine dashed the firebrand from
his hand just in time to avert the catastrophe. Seeing that
the soldiers were too craven to be of any service, she commanded them to stand guard within the block house;
where, in case the palisades should be taken, they were to
fight for protection of the women and children and to pray
for help to come from Montreal.

Then calling her two brothers, ten and twelve years
old, and to Viollette, she armed them with muskets, powder
horns and shot pouches and moved to man the defense of
the fortifications about the village. At each corner of the
four walls of the palisades stood a bastion thrust out beyond the walls in such a manner that a sentry atop the
bastion could shoot down any invaders who attempted to
approach the palisades and hack their way in.

Upon two of these bastions she posted her brothers and

From a statue in a niche of the Parliament Building at Quebec. By courtesy of the Library of the Quebec Legislature.

COUNT FRONTENAC

He broke the power of the Iroquois and brought
peace and security to Canada.

The Statue of Madeleine de Vercheres.

stationed herself and Viollette upon the other two. Through the day it was possible for two of the sentries in opposite corners to sleep while the other two stood guard; but after nightfall, it was necessary for all eyes to be on the alert. To insure that her brothers and the old man kept awake, Madeleine cried out at intervals through the night, "All's well." To her challenge her brothers and Viollette were required to respond, "All's well."

For seven nights and days the four sentries held the Iroquois at bay. Then toward morning after the seventh night, the time at which Indians are most accustomed to make their attacks, she heard a hail from a boat in the river. The voice was in French, but she feared that it might be the ruse of an Indian to throw her off her guard. After several calls, the man on the river persuaded her that he was a military captain from Montreal coming with forty men for her relief. At this she threw open the gate, welcomed the reinforcements, saluted the captain and, as she surrendered her command, remarked:

"It is time to relieve the sentries, sir. They have been on duty a week."

The heroism of the young commandant inspired all of Canada. Even today the people have not forgotten her. Especially is this true at the village she so valorously defended. There the people have erected a shaft of stone in a field of flowers; and atop the monument they have placed a bronze figure of the fourteen-year-old maid, who, with musket at the ready, stands alert on her bastion guarding the peace of Vercheres.

While Madeleine was doing her part at her village, Frontenac's troops beat off the British fleet. This accomplished, he replied to the raiding Iroquois by granting pardon to the woods rangers and inviting them to come home. From out of the forests they came; across the lakes and down the rivers they sped, the foam frothing from the prows of their birch-bark vessels. Leading them came Duluth and Henri Tonty.

It was high time they came, for Montreal was in a panic and Three Rivers was in despair. Despite the success of Madeleine at Vercheres, the people felt that the massacre at La Chine would be repeated in the larger places. Duluth entered the St. Lawrence from the Ottawa with twenty-eight men and, as he approached Montreal, saw several Iroquois craft approaching with twenty-two warriors. Giving orders to his men not to fire until he gave the word, he drove straight toward the Iroquois, who, becoming excited, opened fire before they were near enough for effective shooting. While they were reloading, Duluth's men came alongside and emptied their guns at the enemy. Eighteen Iroquois doubled up over their paddles. Three others were taken alive. One was permitted to escape and bear to his people the message of defeat. From that moment the tide of war turned.

Frontenac resorted to Champlain's strategy of carrying war to the enemy to keep him busy at home. Four expeditions were organized. Two raided New England with frightful ruthlessness. One, consisting of 114 Frenchmen and 96 Indians, was led by Sainte Helene, one of the sons of Le Moyne, into New York. These raiders carried no baggage and had no commissary. They subsisted for food on what they might find each day, and at night dug into the snow to the ground and built a fire around which they clustered for warmth. In the bitter cold of night they entered the unsuspecting town of Schenectady, killed and scalped sixty-three of the English, spared sixty old men and carried ninety young women and their children as prisoners to Canada. The captive children were parcelled out to various families to be reared as Frenchmen and to be brought up in the Catholic faith. One of these captives, Esther Wheelwright, became famous as mother superior of the Ursulines at Quebec. One of the boys became Bishop Plessis of Canada and lived to see the English masters of the St. Lawrence.

The eldest of the Le Moynes, Iberville, was placed in command of an expedition to the Hudson Bay forts. He marched overland, emerged from the forest and took the forts one at a time. Leaving a small command behind, he returned to Quebec to be promoted to the command of one of the ships built in the time of Talon. In this ship Iberville ravaged the coast of Maine. Turning north, he took St. Johns, Newfoundland. As a result of his naval successes, he was made an admiral and promoted to the command of five ships, with which he drove the English from the Gulf of St. Lawrence.

Then came news that the English had retaken the Hudson Bay forts by the aid of a fleet. Iberville departed with his fleet to recapture the forts. As he entered the bay through Hudson Straits, his ships encountered ice floes and were separated. Thus he was alone when he met three enemy ships in the summer of 1697. Despite odds in ships, guns and men, he maneuvered his vessel so skillfully that he sank two of the enemy, the third escaping by flight. Although victor in battle, he was defeated by storm. His battle-scarred vessel sank in shoal water and was rocked to pieces by the waves. The crew, escaping to land by wading, lived on sea moss until the other four ships of the fleet arrived. Then Iberville stormed and captured Fort Nelson, which commanded the control of the fur trade of the Bay.

Unfortunately for Canada, news of Iberville's victory did not arrive in Europe until after England and France had made peace by signing the Treaty of Ryswick. By the terms of the treaty England retained ownership of Newfoundland and her forts on Hudson Bay. The victory, however, made Iberville a hero in France. We shall hear again of him and also of other sons of Charles Le Moyne, among them Bienville, the youngest of the boys, who as a mere lad served with Iberville at the capture of Fort Nelson.

Frontenac led in person an expedition to the Iroquois towns. Twenty years earlier he had promised his children friendship if they kept the peace, and he promised the tomahawk if they wanted war. They had made the wrong choice and his vengeance was appalling. We would not care to give details of his frightful campaign as he took village after village. At first the Iroquois welcomed the invasion. They expected to cut off Frontenac's retreat and take his scalp and eat his heart. But after one half of the Iroquois nation had been slaughtered, the warriors pleaded with their father like punished children. Like a father Frontenac forgave them. Never again, except in actual wars between the French and the English, did the Iroquois harry the villages on the St. Lawrence. At last Canada became a continuous settlement with happy homes from Quebec to beyond Montreal, and no savages from the Mohawk molested them with the war whoop.

From ruin Frontenac brought Canada to security. Under his guidance the Great Lakes became French seas. With the end of the Iroquois menace the Algonquin tribes once more dared to resettle the Ottawa and Huron country. The Illinois became safe for Indians and the Shawnees moved from their hiding places to make their homes once more along the Ohio. With the restoration of peace, the French beaver market boomed once more.

Frontenac, however, was nearing his end. Only one year of life remained to him after the Peace of Ryswick. He died in Quebec in 1698 and among those who shed sincere tears at his bier were his children, the Iroquois.

CHAPTER VII

THE FIRST HOME IN THE WEST

ONE of the very last matters considered by Frontenac before his death was the founding of a settlement and trading post at a strategic point to serve the double purpose of increasing the Indian trade of the Great Lakes and of barring the westward expansion of the English from Albany. The man whom Frontenac selected as leader of this proposed settlement was LaMothe Cadillac, whose swashbuckling manner and sarcastic remarks directed toward those whom he did not like made him many enemies, but whose knowledge of the Great Lakes, unswerving loyalty to France and skilled swordsmanship commended him to the count despite other shortcomings.

Cadillac was born in France in the province of Gascony, a region noted for its boastful, swaggering soldiers of many moods; and he was a typical Gascon. Upon his arrival in Canada in 1683 as a subordinate officer in the Quebec garrison, he immediately quarrelled with most of his fellow officers and engaged in fights with them, both with fists and swords. Although he was a very poor man, he presumed to fall in love with Marie Therese Guyon, said to be one of the most beautiful of all the women in America. She was of good family, which had considerable wealth. He fought other officers who tried to pay court to her so that for several months he was in one brawl after another. He succeeded in his strange courtship and married Marie in 1687, just two years before Frontenac's return for his second service as governor. Frontenac found him a useful soldier and promoted him, in 1694, to be commandant at Mackinac. Cadillac accepted his promotion with ill grace, for Mackinac was a lonely spot in a land of Indians and woods rangers and to go there meant separation from his wife and children. But eventually he learned to enjoy his command in the wilderness. It was exactly the post needed to fit him for his greatest life work. His restless spirit did not permit him to sit idly at his office at the fort.

When not needed at Mackinac, he travelled with the woods rangers and familiarized himself with the Great Lakes. He made at least two journeys to Quebec every year to visit his family and to call upon the governor. In summer he travelled by canoe, but at least once every winter he walked the entire distance on snowshoes, travelling by day and camping by night in a hole dug in the snow to the solid ground. Like the canoe, the snowshoe was the invention of Indians; and Cadillac had ample cause to be thankful to the red men for devising such an aid to travel, by which he could skim over the fields of white instead of floundering through the deep drifts of the northern forests.

On his lonely snowshoe travels and on his long canoe voyages, he made a careful survey, mile by mile, of the watercourse through which the Upper Lakes debouch into Lake Erie. The woods rangers named this stream *Detroit* (the strait). Cadillac formed an intimate acquaintance with the rocks and headlands, the valleys and gullies. He came to know prominent trees. He learned the calls of the birds. He studied the soil and learned where it was the richest. At one place where the channel of the river is so narrow that a cannon could be fired across it, Cadillac landed on the southwestern bank and there made a study of the soil. It was rich and grew tall, straight trees which might serve in house building. Here, then, was the place for a settlement.

Cadillac discussed this situation with his wife and with Frontenac many times. This, so he determined, would be the best possible place to build a city. When the king ordered the dismantling of Fort Mackinac in 1698, Cadillac was ready to move at once to build a new fort and settlement at Detroit. The death of Frontenac, however, balked his plan, for the new governor was of narrow vision and foolishly imagined that a western settlement would impair the growth of Quebec and injure the profits of the fur-trading monopoly. Cadillac hurled scornful words at the governor and his associates. This did nothing but make enemies.

Then he sailed for France and presented his plan to the king and to his minister, Pontchartrain. He showed how the English were reaching westward from Albany to take the trade of the Great Lakes. Since the English merchants paid better prices for fur than did the French monopolists in Quebec and Montreal, the woods rangers made a practice of carrying their furs through the land of the Iroquois to Albany. This was made possible since Frontenac had humbled the Iroquois, for those savage Indians had to respect Frenchmen. A series of rivers extend from Lake Erie to the headwaters of the Mohawk River; and the woods rangers, by making several portages, could cross from the Lake Erie watershed to the Mohawk and arrive in Albany. Cadillac showed by a map how he would mount cannon at Detroit and with those cannon force every woods ranger to bring the furs to him for reshipment to Montreal. He also showed how Detroit could attract the trade of the Shawnees living on the Ohio River and secure their trade for France instead of permitting the Shawnees to carry their peltry the long, weary trail across the Alleghenies to the English traders of Virginia or Pennsylvania.

The king and Pontchartrain approved the plan and appointed Cadillac as commandant with a force of fifty soldiers. In June, 1701, Cadillac, accompanied by his twelve-year-old son and by Alphonse Tonty, a cousin of Duluth, as lieutenant, departed with fifty soldiers for Detroit where they built Fort Pontchartrain, a stout structure of logs, and adjoining the fort built a cluster of log houses, surrounding them with a palisaded wall for protection from the Indians.

Late in the summer Cadillac and Tonty wrote to their wives in Quebec that all was ready for them to come and join them. These were to be the first women to live in the West, of whom we have any record. It was Cadillac's plan to bring his own and Tonty's wife as an example for the soldiers' wives. He realized that no settlement can grow and prosper without wives and children. All previous French settlements had begun as bachelor towns. Cadillac did not intend to make any such mistake at Detroit.

When Madame Cadillac received the letter, her friends wept over her and told what a terrible calamity it would be for her to go into the wilderness where no woman had ever been. She, who had been born in Quebec, and who had spent her entire life among friends, would suffer untold hardship and live in a log house. They made scathing remarks about her swaggering Gascon husband for expecting her to make such a sacrifice. To their advice Madame Cadillac replied:

"A woman who loves her husband as she should has no stronger attraction than his company wherever he may be. Everything else should be indifferent to her."*

She put two of her older daughters in the Ursuline school at Quebec and set out with Madame Tonty and five of her children in canoes for the West. It required a month for the boatmen to bring her to Detroit. They ascended the St. Lawrence to the Lachine Rapids, portaged around the rapids, crossed Lake Ontario, portaged around Niagara Falls and then crossed Lake Erie. The same journey can now be made by train in less than a day.

At length they entered the Detroit River and the *voyageurs* told her that on the next day they would arrive at Fort Pontchartrain. Accordingly both Madame Cadillac and Madame Tonty dressed themselves in their most becoming frocks. The children, too, were attired in their gayest suits. Thus they arrived at the settlement garbed in the latest styles from Paris and fit for presentation to the royal court.

The arrival was a triumph. Indians who had never been to Montreal or Quebec and had never before seen white

*The quotations from the Cadillac letters are reprinted from translations in *Cadillac,* by Agnes C. Laut, copyrighted 1931, and used by special permission of the publishers, The Bobbs-Merrill Company.

women were awestruck at the beauty and richness of the apparel they wore. The soldiers were delighted. Cadillac and Tonty were almost ready to burst with pride. The men doffed their hats and cheered, and the cannon in the fort barked a thunderous salute suitable as a welcome for a queen.

We may judge how Detroit appeared to Madame Cadillac from a letter written that September by Cadillac to King Louis.

"The shy stag," he wrote, "the wild turkey hen, the strutting woodcocks, the quail, the partridges are in greater numbers than in a private park of France and as unafraid of man. The wild fowl are in continuous flocks and kind— the goose, duck, teal, bittern, heron, loon, wood pigeon and song birds, among them the tanager, cardinal, blue bird, robin, thrush. As for the trees there is every kind which French parks are importing from all over the world."

Writing further, he tells of wild grapes so fruitful the vines cannot bear their load, of hazelnuts, chestnuts, walnuts, wild plums and cherries, more than man can gather.

Although Madame Cadillac and her children had to live in a log house, the walls of which were chinked with moss and the floors of which were nothing but hewn logs, yet those rough floors were carpeted with rich rugs of the finest fur, and the tapestries of the walls were of like material.

At Tonty's log house, which was furnished in the same style as that of the Cadillacs, the first white baby of Detroit was born that winter. The Tontys named her Therese in honor of Madame Cadillac. So far as we have any record, Therese was the first white baby born west of the Alleghenies and east of the Spanish settlement at Santa Fe. In later years several babies were born to the Cadillacs. They had thirteen children in all, five of them being born after they came to Detroit.

Fortune smiled on the venture of Cadillac. The fur business proved profitable, and by the next season Madame Cadillac ordered silver plate and linen from Paris. She always kept in touch with Paris fashions and ordered the most stylish and beautiful clothing for herself and her children.

The example of Madame Cadillac and Madame Tonty in coming to the West resulted in the arrival of a number of the wives of the soldiers the following summer. By the second winter Detroit had thirty families and at the end of three years numbered eighty homes. Indians came in great throngs from Mackinac to trade. Not only did they come from Mackinac, Shawnees came from the Ohio, Illinois from the Mississippi, Osages and Missouris from the Missouri, and Sioux from the northwestern prairies. Here too came the woods rangers, wearing bright-colored coats, which to this day are called mackinaws, for mackinaw is merely another way of spelling Mackinac and Mackinac was the chief *rendezvous* of the woods rangers. Sometimes as many as 7000 Indians were camped at Detroit at a time. Although they were often from warring tribes, Cadillac so managed them that when they neared Detroit they buried the hatchet.

For three years Cadillac prospered at Detroit and the merchants at Montreal and Quebec prospered too as he shipped them annual consignments of furs in ever increasing quantities. But the merchants, instead of being thankful for what he sent them, became jealous. They trumped

Arrival in Detroit of Marie Therese Cadillac and Madame Tonty
with their children

A BASTION

Detail from Fort Dearborn showing how a bastion was thrust out at the corner of the palisade so that the sentry had an unobstructed view of the outside walls.

up charges against the master at Detroit and had him haled before the governor at Quebec. Although nothing could be proved against him, the governor kept him there under arrest for two years. When Cadillac departed from Detroit, he turned affairs over to Tonty, who was a faithful subordinate but lacked the ability to rule as commandant. The governor therefore replaced him with Etienne V. de Bourgmont, an officer in the garrison at Quebec.

Bourgmont had fought against the English and Iroquois under Frontenac and appeared to be an able man, but his lack of understanding of Indians was soon demonstrated. While holding a council with a group of Ottawa warriors, Bourgmont's dog, taking a dislike to one of the Indians, bit him in the leg. The warrior, angered, struck the dog with a club. Thereupon Bourgmont beat the warrior severely. It would have been no worse had Bourgmont killed the Indian outright, for the Indians regarded it as a terrible disgrace for a man to be beaten. War followed, and Fort Pontchartrain was besieged, until the old men of the Ottawas counselled the warriors to remember that the French had always been the friend of their tribe and to cease fighting.

Upon being rebuked by the governor for his mishandling of affairs, Bourgmont deserted his post, wandered through the present state of Ohio with a group of other soldiers, collected furs from the Indians and sold them to the Iroquois, who in turn sold them to the English at Albany. This desertion alarmed the governor, who feared that Detroit might fall into the hands of unfriendly Indians. He cared nothing for Detroit, but he realized that the king would blame him.

He therefore restored Cadillac to his post in 1706. Arriving at Detroit, Cadillac dispatched soldiers to arrest Bourgmont and the renegades who were with him. Bourgmont escaped but three of his followers were brought back to Detroit, convicted of desertion and one of the three was executed, in accordance with the cruel practices of the time, by having his head broken on a wheel. Bourgmont, not daring to return home, fled to the west of the Mississippi, where for a dozen years or more he lived with the Missouris. In the state of Missouri there is today a dashing river, which tumbles impetuously down from the Ozarks to wind in and out among rugged hills to flow into the Missouri River. This stream is called the *Gasconade*, a name given to it by the early French adventurers. It is probable that it was Bourgmont who first called the river by that name, because it reminded him of Cadillac, the swashbuckling Gascon.

The return of Cadillac brought back confidence and prosperity to Detroit. Business boomed. The farming community prospered. Cattle, hogs and sheep grazed on the meadows and grain grew in the fields. Orchards yielded apples, peaches and pears. In fact, some of the orchards planted in the time of Cadillac were yielding fruit until a few years ago when they were cut down to make room for the growing city. As for Cadillac, he reaped a fortune. It has been estimated that his income became equivalent to $25,000 a year in modern exchange. All the riches in fur which came to Detroit found its way to Montreal and Quebec. No longer did beaver from the Upper Lakes pass through the Iroquois country to Albany and New York.

Thereupon the English authorities bought the site of Detroit from the Iroquois. Of course the Iroquois did not own the site of Detroit and the bill of sale was a mere scrap of paper, but the time would come when England would flaunt that scrap of paper in the face of the French rulers and would go to war for possession of the land they had bought from the Iroquois.

Had Cadillac been allowed to remain at Detroit as he wished to do, it is possible that he would have built such a strong western settlement that the English could never have taken it. In that event the language spoken in Detroit today would be French instead of English. But Cadillac had worse enemies than the English. The merchants of Montreal and Quebec sent letters to Paris praising Cadillac and pointing out that he was too great a man to be wasting his talents in a backwoods settlement like Detroit. They recommended him for the post of governor of Louisiana, where a vacancy existed, and did this, not because they wished to see Cadillac promoted, but because they desired to gain control of Detroit themselves.

The king, not being wise enough to see their plans, commanded Cadillac to proceed at once to Mobile and take charge as governor of Louisiana. Royal commands are given to be obeyed, but Cadillac had the temerity to protest to the king. By writing letters, he delayed his removal for a year. But in 1711 there came an order from the king dismissing him as commandant at Detroit.

Thus did the French politicians and monopolists bungle affairs. With the recall of Cadillac, Detroit fell upon evil days. For a long time it struggled for existence. But the site was too well chosen for the town to die entirely. Despite political mismanagement, it grew. When the English soldiers finally arrived in 1760 to perfect their title received from the Iroquois, they reported that the settlement numbered 2500 people.

CHAPTER VIII

JOLLIET AND MARQUETTE

THE secret that a vast, fertile valley lay hidden in the mystic region west of the Alleghenies was kept from Europeans until long after the St. Lawrence, the Hudson, the Amazon and the Plata Rivers had been explored and settlements were flourishing upon their banks. True, Spanish mariners had sighted the Mississippi Delta, from which radiated silt-laden streams. True, the ill-fated DeSoto and his men had reported stumbling upon a river so wide that a man could scarcely be seen on the farther shore. True, the woods rangers came swaggering into Mackinac with tales of having stood at the headwaters of a mighty river to the west. But DeSoto's tale had been forgotten, the writings of his men had been locked in the archives of Madrid, and nobody believed a woods ranger.

There is a good reason why the Mississippi remained unknown. Unlike the St. Lawrence, the Amazon and the Plata, which invite ships to enter through their wide estuaries, the Mississippi spreads fanwise at its mouth into a series of smaller rivers and rivulets pouring off the sides of a muddy, mosquito-infested delta, thereby repelling rather than inviting the explorer. Thus it came about that the world's longest river, with its 100,000 miles of tributaries draining the most productive valley on earth, was explored, not by mariners from seaward but by inland boatmen, portaging their canoes on their shoulders from the watershed of the Great Lakes.

Foremost among these boatmen was a tall, slender, handsome fur trader, whose gentle fingers played the white keys of the grand organ at Quebec on Sundays and whose sinewy arms guided the birch canoe through the treacherous rapids on week days. He could read the New Testament in the original Greek, could converse with the learned priests in Latin, and on the wilderness trail could speak to Algonquins, Iroquois, Hurons or Ottawas, each in his own guttural tongue.

Louis Jolliet's father, a Quebec wagon maker, died while Louis was yet a lad; and his mother, consecrating him to the priesthood, placed him in the Jesuit seminary at Quebec. Being studious of habit, he advanced rapidly in scholarship. One evening in 1665 there came into the seminary chapel the newly appointed intendant, Jean Talon, to address the students. As the intendant concluded his speech, the other novitiates pushed forward twenty-year-old Louis Jolliet as best fitted of their number to make the response. This was done with such logic and eloquence that it went straight to the heart of Talon, who made the young man his protégé, persuaded him to secure his release from the Jesuit orders and sent him to Paris for a year's study in science.

Upon his return to America, Jolliet entered the fur trade at Mackinac and on Lake Superior, serving the merchants who held the monopoly of Canadian commerce. On his travels into the West, he was ever alert for information, which, whenever he came to Quebec, he poured into the intendant's ears. Jolliet thus became Talon's eyes and pictured the West by maps and by eloquent words.

His ready mastery of many languages enabled him to perform a distinguished service in a dramatic manner in 1669 at Sault Ste. Marie, where a roving band of Iroquois and another of Ottawas were about to engage in battle. Jolliet thrust himself between the contending warriors, shouting alternately in Iroquois and Ottawa, until he settled the matter in dispute and persuaded the chiefs of opposing sides to clasp hands. Among those to admire Jolliet's skill and courage on that occasion was Jaques Marquette, newly arrived in the Lake Superior region, who had been commissioned by the Jesuit order to serve as missionary at Sault Ste. Marie. Marquette invited Jolliet to his home and the two became as brothers. It was natural that these two men of high intelligence and excellent education should become keenly interested in reports brought by woods rangers of a southward-flowing river, which the Indians called the Mississippi.

Since the Indians declared it to be the largest of all rivers and since no maps showed any large stream emptying into the Gulf of Mexico, Jolliet and Marquette concluded that it must be the Colorado, shown on Spanish maps and flowing southward into the Gulf of California. Both Jolliet and Marquette were fired with ambition to follow the stream to the Pacific; and Jolliet, at his next visit to Quebec, requested Talon for permission to explore it. Talon was already preparing to leave for France; but he introduced and recommended Jolliet to the new governor, Frontenac, who, after catching the young fur trader's enthusiasm, gladly commissioned him to explore the mysterious Mississippi in the name of France.

Bidding good-by to his mother, Jolliet departed from Quebec in October, 1672, and arrived at Marquette's mission in early winter. There he remained until spring, trapping beaver and trading with the Indians. Of course it was understood from the beginning that Marquette would be a member of the exploring party. In addition Jolliet selected five woods rangers, each of whom was an expert canoeman. The party carried no baggage except manufactured articles to serve as gifts to the Indians, a strongbox to safeguard maps and journals, and a little dried meat and corn to supplement the fare when hunting was difficult.

Following directions given by the Indians, they voyaged to the head of Green Bay and entered the Fox River, a turbulent stream, where they had to portage their canoes again and again around boisterous rapids. After days of arduous canoeing, they came to the site of the present Portage, Wisconsin, so named because at this place they needed to portage their canoes only 2700 paces to the Wisconsin, a broad, island-studded, westward-flowing stream abutted by forested bluffs. For seven days they floated down this enchanting river, but their big moment came on June 17, 1673, when they rode with the current into the immense, southward-flowing flood they were now to explore. That evening they camped on the bank of the Mississippi and feasted on a sturgeon caught in its waters. The next morning they crossed the river and coasted along the west bank. There followed days of exquisite delight as they glided without effort between ranks of picturesque bluffs, broken occasionally to admit views of extensive grasslands, to which they gave the French name of *prairie*, meaning meadow.

At length they came to a flotilla of empty *pirogues*, or dugout canoes, fashioned from single cottonwood logs, sixty and seventy feet long. The presence of the flotilla indicated Indians were at hand. Drawing alongside, Jolliet and Marquette left the woods rangers to stand guard at the canoes, while they followed a path through the green forest to the village. Approaching confidently, yet wondering how they would be received, the two men gave the peace sign with uplifted hands and proffered gifts. It chanced that this was a village of Illinois Indians, a tribe related to the Algonquins of the St. Lawrence. While their language differed, there was a similarity of words, which the skilled ear of Jolliet quickly detected; and soon he was conversing readily with these brothers of the wilderness. Although no white man had ever come that way before, the Illinois had heard of the Frenchmen. The chief thought to compliment them by shading his eyes as though their appearance dazzled him.

"How bright the sun shines now that you have come!" he exclaimed.

Into his wigwam he invited his guests and there spread a four-course feast, the first course being pounded hominy served on a great wooden platter, the second a serving of fish, and the third a steaming platter of dog. At sight of the dog Marquette explained that it was not customary for white people to eat that animal. The Indians therefore, out of courtesy to their guests, removed the dog and brought the fourth course, consisting of roast buffalo.

The Illinois had once been a populous tribe living on the banks of the Illinois River, but the Iroquois had destroyed the majority of their warriors, and for that reason the survivors had fled to the west of the Mississippi. We will recall that this was 1673 and that Frontenac had not yet beaten the idea of peace and brotherhood into the minds of the Iroquois. From the Illinois, Jolliet obtained information concerning the geography of the Mississippi and also learned of the courses of the Missouri, the Illinois, and the Ohio and learned of the various tribes on the banks of various rivers as far south as the mouth of the Arkansas, where dwelt the Arkansas tribe. The descriptions given were accurate, as Jolliet's maps reveal. As the explorers took leave of the Illinois, the chief, to show his affection, presented Jolliet with a boy of eight, captured in a raid against a tribe of prairie Indians to the west. Jolliet accepted the little captive, resolving to enter him in school at Quebec. The boy was intelligent and quickly mastered the French language, much to the delight of Jolliet and Marquette. That the explorers were enchanted by the lands through which the Mississippi flows is evident from this description penned by Jolliet:

"I have seen nothing more beautiful in France than the number of prairies that I have admired here, nothing so pleasing as the variety of groves and forests, where they gather plums, apples, pomegranates, lemons, mulberries and several small fruits that are not known in Europe. In the fields one scares up quail, in the wood one sees parrots, in the rivers one catches fish that are unknown for their taste, form and size.

"For nourishment the savages do not prize the deer.

They kill buffaloes that go in herds of thirty and forty (I have counted even as many as 400 of them on the banks of the river) and the turkeys are so common there that they set no value on them."*

Southward voyaged the adventurers past awesome Pictured Rocks just above the present Alton, Illinois. Here a change came in the course of the Mississippi. Instead of rushing southward, it described a half circle eastward, being pushed from its course by a mightier river, whose violent roar could be heard even before it could be seen and which filled the woods rangers with apprehension that they were approaching a cataract. In describing this second river, the Missouri, Jolliet wrote that it carried "an accumulation of large and entire trees, branches and floating islands and so great was the agitation that the water was very muddy and could not become clear."

At the point where the Missouri and Mississippi unite, the travellers camped for the night and discussed the immensity of this stream from the west, which convinced them that it must drain a large basin. This was of great consequence, for the volume of the water indicated that the Pacific Ocean was farther removed than had been imagined. Jolliet believed, however, that by ascending the Missouri, he could come to the Pacific, for the Spanish maps depicted America as being much narrower than it really is and gave no hint of the presence of the intervening Rocky Mountains.

*This translation from Jolliet's own narrative as well as other translations from the same narrative on pages 77 and 83 are reprinted by permission of the publishers, The Arthur H. Clark Company, from Francis Borgia Steck's *The Jolliet-Marquette Expedition of 1673*.

The day after the discovery of the Missouri, the travellers resumed their journey, noting, as can be observed to-

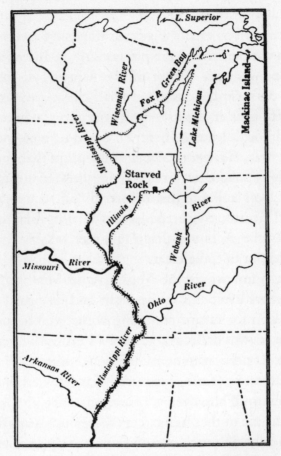

The Route of Jolliet and Marquette

day, a distinct boundary line between the currents of the two rivers even after they flow side by side in the same channel, one stream being yellow with mud and the other being comparatively clear. After several miles the waters

mingle and thereafter the Mississippi takes on the muddy
character of the Missouri. Voyaging southward, the explorers passed the mouth of the Ohio and finally came to
the Arkansas, where the Arkansas Indians proved hostile
and were won to friendship with much difficulty.

Although the Arkansas River cannot compare in volume
with the Missouri, the quantity of water it discharges
into the Mississippi is so great that it proved to Jolliet and
Marquette that it drains a great area to the west. They
therefore lost all hope of arriving at the Pacific, for they
realized that the combined expanse of the Missouri and
Arkansas drainage basins meant that the Pacific Ocean was
very far away and that the Mississippi must empty into the
Gulf of Mexico. Since Spain claimed the Gulf, and im-
prisoned foreigners venturing upon it, Jolliet felt that he
should return to Canada to report what he had discovered
rather than run the risk of capture, which might mean that
France would lose the information he had obtained. Another reason for return may have been the illness of Marquette, who was suffering seriously from tuberculosis and
was in no condition to continue the adventure.

Pointing their canoes upstream, they retraced their route
to the mouth of the Illinois River, which joins the Mississippi in the arc of that half circle where the Missouri thrusts
the Father of Waters toward the east. Entering the Illinois, as they were advised to do by friendly Kaskaskia Indians, they ascended to its headwaters and near the site of
the present Joliet, Illinois, portaged to the Chicago River,
and arrived once more beside Lake Michigan. [It will be
noted that Joliet, the city, is spelled with a single "l." This
is the common English spelling, but in this book we have

used the "double l" for Jolliet himself signed his name that way to letters and to maps.]

The voyagers, skirting the western shores of Lake Michigan, came to a Jesuit mission on Green Bay, where they spent the winter. They had completed a circuit of 2500 miles, covering the entire distance in frail canoes. Any person who has paddled a canoe as far as a single mile against the current of the Fox, the Mississippi or the Illinois can appreciate their accomplishment.

As soon as spring warmth thawed the ice from Green Bay, Jolliet took leave of Marquette. It was the last time the two friends were to meet. Marquette's subsequent history is soon told. He descended the Illinois River that summer and preached to the Kaskaskia Indians, but his health was failing rapidly, and he died in 1675. Cities in Michigan, Wisconsin, Iowa, Nebraska, and Kansas have been named in his honor.

It was May when Jolliet left Green Bay accompanied by the Indian boy given him by the Illinois chief, and by two able canoemen. Eager as he had been to commence the expedition, he was even more impatient to return and relate the story of his adventures. He and his men passed the straits of Mackinac, descended Lakes Huron and Erie, portaged around Niagara Falls and descended Lake Ontario almost to where it debouches into the St. Lawrence, where they were astounded to behold, rising from a hill adjoining the lake, a stout, log fortress with a French flag floating from the highest bastion. That fort had not been there at the time of Jolliet's departure. Landing at the foot of the fort, they were welcomed by La Salle, master at La Chine. What a tale each man had to relate! We can well imagine how each shouted questions to the other, until Jolliet learned how Governor Frontenac had over-awed the Iroquois and had built Fort Frontenac to menace and control them, placing La Salle in charge as comman-dant. We are certain that La Salle, eager as he was to open trade with China by way of the Ohio, listened with bated breath as Jolliet gave details of his adventures on the Mississippi.

One other person who spent that memorable night at Fort Frontenac must have gaped in amazement at the sights he saw. This was Jolliet's Indian boy, now a year older than when the Illinois chief gave him away. The boy had come far since his capture from his native village on the western prairies. He had seen much to astound, but we can guess that nothing in all of his nine years had awed him as much as the great log fort, the sentries pacing their posts, the blare of trumpets at the mounting of the guard, and the bellow of the cannon at sunset.

La Salle would have detained Jolliet as long as he cared to remain and rest, but the next morning he was impatient to be away. Down the St. Lawrence he guided his canoe to the verge of the treacherous Lachine Rapids. Here cau-tious boatmen unload and portage their cargoes. But Jol-liet, excited in anticipation of his near approach to Mon-treal, took a chance, the results of which are best described by himself.

"The good fortune which had always accompanied me on this voyage," he wrote, "failed me a quarter of an hour before arriving at the place where I set out. I had escaped the dangers of savages. I had passed forty-two rapids. I was ready to disembark with all the joy one could have over the success of so long an enterprise when my canoe capsized, whereby I lost two men and my strong-box in the sight and at the entrance of the first French houses which I had quitted nearly two years ago."

Not only did his two canoemen drown, the little Indian boy was dashed to death among the jagged rocks. Jolliet himself was in the water four hours, until rescued by a group of fishermen at the risk of their own lives. Naked, without a single map or journal, he came from his 4500-mile, round-trip canoe voyage. At Quebec he reported to Frontenac, who directed that he immediately write from memory another account of his exploration and also re-draw the lost maps.

In reading this report today, one cannot help but note that no mention is made in it concerning Marquette. Jolliet had a reason for this omission. Upon his return and before seeing the governor, he had learned that Frontenac and the Jesuit priests were hostile to each other. The governor wished to extend the settlements of New France westward to include the Upper Lakes and the Mississippi Valley, while the Jesuits hoped to restrict the westward advance of white men and to create a spiritual state in the heart of America, of which they would be the rulers. When Jolliet learned of the clash between Frontenac and the Jesuits, he withheld from mentioning, either in his conversation or in his written report, that the Jesuit priest, Marquette, had been a partner in the exploration of the Mississippi.

Frontenac, however, discovered the fact later and fearing that Jolliet, who had begun his career as a Jesuit noviti-ate, was too much under their influence, denied him permission to return to the Mississippi Valley and engage in the fur trade there. The king, however, at Frontenac's recommendation, granted Jolliet the ownership of Anticosti Island, a vast stretch of land 30 miles broad and 130 miles long and situated in the St. Lawrence estuary. Jolliet married and moved to the island, where he engaged in fur trapping and in fishing, and there he reared four children.

Although denied the right to return to the river he had discovered, he continued his explorations. He explored and mapped a large part of Labrador and on another occasion traced a way from Montreal to Hudson Bay by a more direct route than the one followed by Chouart and Radisson. Jolliet died in 1700 at Anticosti Island. He had so conducted his life that every man he knew counted him as a friend.

CHAPTER IX

LA SALLE AND TONTY

La Salle's dream of paddling down the Ohio to the Pacific, there to engage in trade with China, was shattered by Jolliet's discovery that the Ohio was merely a tributary of a river emptying into the Gulf of Mexico. But La Salle never mourned over shattered dreams. Not many days after Jolliet had written his report to Frontenac, La Salle was in Quebec, seated at the governor's table outlining a plan to convert Fort Frontenac into a trading post to develop the commerce of Lake Ontario and Lake Erie.

The governor approved the plan, wrote a letter of recommendation to the king, and sent La Salle to Paris where he could obtain final sanction. This was a new role for the man who had danced with the King's maidens, had fraternized with Iroquois, had explored the Ohio valley and had commanded woods rangers in the wilds; but he felt himself able to meet on equal terms even the Grand Monarch, Louis XIV, most gorgeous of all men on earth, who required two valets to help him don his shirt, another to manicure his nails and a private hair dresser to curl his locks. Bearing Frontenac's letter, La Salle entered the royal presence, bowed with the air of a practiced courtier, and proposed to rebuild Fort Frontenac with stone at his

86

own expense and to man it with soldiers in his own pay. In exchange he desired the right to use the fort as a trading post and to engage in trade, the profits of which would be used for the expansion of New France. La Salle must have presented his arguments ably, for the king agreed. To obtain money for his new venture, La Salle sold La Chine and borrowed from his relatives. Success came immediately, and La Salle was paying off his debts and also making a profit for himself, when news came to him that Jolliet had been denied the right to open the fur trade of the great valley he had made known to France.

Here then was an opportunity for greater things than Fort Frontenac offered. Unlike Jolliet, who was partial to the Jesuits, La Salle opposed them with as much vehemence as did Frontenac. At his fort he recognized no priests but the Recollect friars. Calling upon the governor, La Salle gained his approval and another letter of recommendation to the king. Once more he crossed the ocean, once more bowed at the feet of royalty, and once more presented his plan acceptably. The king appointed him commandant on the Mississippi with exclusive right to trade with the Indians there, so that he might make money to finance the occupation of the valley. La Salle agreed on his part to complete the exploration of the Mississippi to the Gulf, to fortify the river at strategic points against both the English on the east and the Spanish on the south and to maintain the forts at his own expense.

He returned to America jubilant, little concerned that his achievement would breed a pack of enemies already jealous of his success at Fort Frontenac. First the merchants of Montreal were in a fury. They feared that the bringing of furs from the Mississippi to the Paris market would result in an oversupply and reduce prices. Likewise the woods rangers opposed him, because they were already trading in a small way with the Indians of the Mississippi without license. The coming of a well-organized trading concern meant the end of their illegal business. The Jesuits opposed him for the same reason that they opposed Frontenac. Already their missionaries had followed the trail of Marquette to preach to the Indians of the valley, and they wished to exclude the white men from the Mississippi country. That his enemies would go to any length to block him out of the valley La Salle soon learned. On two different occasions they bribed his own men to poison his food and both doses almost brought death.

Disregarding his enemies, La Salle borrowed money from his relatives and friends, mortgaged Fort Frontenac for all he could borrow on it, arranged for supplies to be brought from France and proceeded to his task. At Niagara Falls he built a fort to protect his men as they transported goods from Lake Ontario around the falls to be launched on Lake Erie for shipment to Lake Michigan. Above the falls he built the *Griffon*, a vessel of fifty tons capacity and the first sailing ship to navigate the Great Lakes above the falls. Upon her he loaded cordage, sail cloth and iron to be transported to the south end of Lake Michigan, whence it was to be transported on men's backs to the headwaters of the Illinois, where he intended to build a second ship for the exploration of the Mississippi to the Gulf and for shipment of furs to Europe.

The *Griffon* sailed to Green Bay and here La Salle loaded her with a cargo of furs, which he shipped to Fort

Niagara, the object being to raise needed money. As the ship sailed toward the Straits of Mackinac, La Salle proceeded with thirty-three men in boats to the southern end of the Lake, where the men unloaded a forge and other equipment and carried it by man power to the headwaters of the Illinois, down which they floated to Lake Peoria. There they erected Fort Crevecœur early in 1680. The men felled trees, sawed lumber by hand and built the hull of a second ship. In the meantime no news came of the *Griffon*, and La Salle needed the cordage and other material for the superstructure of his ship. He sent messengers to Lake Michigan to look for her, but all reported the ship had disappeared and that no one could give information of her. La Salle became alarmed, fearing that his enemies had sunk her. His enterprise required that he remain at Crèvecœur, yet it was imperative that the *Griffon* be found if she was afloat.

It now became apparent to La Salle that his own men were turning against him. He thought they were under the influence of his enemies, but it is more likely that he was his own worst enemy. His haughtiness of manner and his harshness toward those under his command tended to convert his employees into foes. In fact he could rely on only a few in his command.

One of these was Henri de Tonty, brother of Alphonse Tonty, and a cousin of Duluth. Henri Tonty had lost his right hand in the Sicilian Wars, and in its place wore an iron hand with hooked fingers, which he usually concealed under a glove. This hand served him amazingly well and once saved his life. When threatened by a group of Iroquois warriors with death, he struck one of the chiefs in the mouth with his gloved hand, knocking his teeth into his throat. Since the Indians did not know that the glove concealed a hand of iron, the Iroquois opened their mouths as an expression of admiration, and murder vanished from their hearts. That gloved hand became known and respected from the Lakes to the Gulf in the years that Tonty followed La Salle, and in the years following La Salle's tragic end. Although Tonty was slight of frame, he never seemed to grow tired. La Salle, who seldom paid tribute to any man, once wrote of Tonty:

"Perhaps you would not have thought him capable of doing things for which a strong constitution and the use of both hands seemed absolutely necessary. Nevertheless his energy and address make him equal to anything; and now, at a season when everybody is in fear of the ice, he is setting out to begin a new fort."*

Another devoted follower was Nika, a Shawnee hunter, so skilled not only with the bow and arrow but also with the musket that no one lacked for meat when he was along.

When it became imperative for La Salle to go in quest of the *Griffon*, he placed Tonty in command at Crève-cœur and shortly thereafter instructed him to build a second fort at Starved Rock, a much superior point for defense. He also directed Michael Accau to proceed with two other men, one being Louis Hennepin, a Recollect friar, to explore the Mississippi above the mouth of the Wisconsin. Having given instructions, La Salle departed.

Upon arrival at Fort Niagara, La Salle learned that the

*This translation is reprinted from Francis Parkman's *La Salle and the Discovery of the Great West* by permission of the publishers, Little, Brown & Company.

Griffon had disappeared. Not a man of her crew survived to tell where or how she sank and no wreckage of her was ever found. After more than two and a half centuries, the loss of the *Griffon* remains one of the mysteries of Great Lakes navigation. The loss of the ship with her cargo was a severe blow to La Salle, for he had gone deeply into debt to build her.

From Niagara he hurried to Quebec to meet the ship coming from France. There he received news of a second disaster. The ship had been lost in the Atlantic with all her crew and her valuable cargo. He had scarcely recovered from the shock of loss when there came a letter from Tonty.

Tonty had gone to Starved Rock in accordance with instructions to survey the place with a view of building a fort there. During his absence those remaining at Fort Crevecœur stole all the supplies they could load into canoes, destroyed what they could not carry and fled to Lake Michigan. There they found a shipment of furs consigned to La Salle. These they stole and proceeded to Fort Niagara, which they looted. La Salle, upon receipt of the letter from Tonty, hastened to capture the renegades; but only eight of them fell into his hands to be turned over to Governor Frontenac for punishment. The rest escaped to Albany, where they sold their stolen goods to the English.

More difficulties beset Tonty. A war party of Iroquois swept westward to attack the Illinois, who had dared to return from the Mississippi to their old home on the Illinois River. Hostile woods rangers told the Illinois that La Salle had equipped the Iroquois and had sent them to wipe the Illinois off the face of the earth. This seemed plausible, for

La Salle had long been friendly with the Senecas and had traded with the Iroquois at Fort Frontenac. In their wrath the Illinois sank the hull of La Salle's ship and threw his forge into the river. They would have killed Tonty and three loyal companions who had not deserted La Salle's cause; but Tonty was equal to the occasion. To prove his friendship for the Illinois, he offered to fight for them. He soon realized, however, that fighting was out of the question. The Illinois were no match for the Iroquois, armed as they were with swords and English muskets. Tonty therefore laid his weapons on the ground and advanced toward the Iroquois, demanding to know why they were making war upon the Illinois, who were under the protection of Frontenac.

Before Tonty could make himself heard above the howling of the Iroquois, one of the warriors rushed upon him and stabbed him in the breast. Others, however, fearing the wrath of Frontenac, agreed to a truce, which lasted long enough to enable the Illinois to launch their boats and escape. The Iroquois went in pursuit, but a few of the chiefs tried to make friends with Tonty by presenting him with six packs of beaver furs. Tonty, however, upon learning that they intended to continue their pursuit of the Illinois, spurned their gift by kicking the packs away from him. There was nothing left on the Illinois to keep Tonty longer. With his followers he made his way to Lake Michigan and eventually rejoined La Salle.

Accau's expedition fared no better. He ascended the Mississippi to the Falls of St. Anthony, where he and his two followers were captured by a band of wandering Sioux Indians, who stripped Father Hennepin of his sacred vestments and wore them on their own bodies. The three Frenchmen were detained as prisoners for several months, their release finally being effected by Duluth, the Lake Superior fur trader, who came upon them by accident. This chance encounter of two parties of Frenchmen far out in the northwest, in a land which Accau and Hennepin had fondly supposed they had discovered, reveals the extent of the wanderings of the woods rangers. Duluth took the refugees back to Green Bay, travelling by way of the Wisconsin and Fox Rivers. Hennepin returned to Europe to win fame as the author of the first book describing Niagara Falls, the Great Lakes and the Mississippi.

Despite disaster La Salle was able to organize a party of thirty Frenchmen and a hundred Indians. They sledged supplies on the ice from Lake Michigan to the Illinois and down that frozen stream to Lake Peoria, arriving there in January, 1682. Below the lake the ice had broken up and in the ice-cold water the men launched canoes for a descent to the Gulf. They arrived at the Mississippi on February 6, 1682, passed the Missouri, the Ohio and the Arkansas, confirming all of the descriptions Jolliet gave of that region. Warmer and warmer grew the sun. The land of the elm, oak, sycamore and hickory gave way to a land of liveoaks, magnolias and cypresses. A stream thick with red mud poured in from the West. The Frenchman named it *La Rouge* (the red). South of the Red River La Salle noted that the slowing of the Mississippi current resulted in the stream dropping loads of suspended silt to the river bed, thereby building up the bed until the river was higher than the surrounding country. No longer did new tributaries flow into the Mississippi. Instead channels and bayous burst out from the main stream to right and left, diminishing the volume of the river as it neared the Gulf.

La Salle saw alligators floating like logs. He saw birds with ungainly long legs wing their way athwart his course. He saw festoons of vines and moss draping the cypress trees. Supplies ran low. Nika killed an alligator and the men found the meat good. On and on they travelled. The river seemed unending. Mosquitoes swarmed at noon. The days grew hot. La Salle, who dressed in velvet in the wilderness as he did when calling upon King Louis, was bathed in his own sweat.

The explorer has the joy of seeing new lands and new sights, but he also has tedious days and weeks of travel, wondering when his boredom will end. It was on April 9, two months and three days after they entered the Mississippi, that the men smelled salt water. Then a sudden break in the swamp forest showed them the open sea. The sight put strength into the muscles of the canoemen. They burst into song. The prows of their birch canoes frothed in response to the exuberant calls of the *voyageurs*. And thus they came to the muddy bank that angled between river and sea.

Exulting, La Salle sprang to the point of mud between the muddy water of the river and the salt of the sea. He had his men hew a wooden cross upon which he erected the arms of King Louis XIV. Off came hats. Master and *voyageurs* bowed heads. The priest read mass. The prayer ended, La Salle raised his sword and with dramatic eloquence claimed on behalf of his king and France, the Mississippi, her 100,000 miles of tributaries and her 1,244,000 square miles of valley.

"Long live the king" burst from the lips of the *voyageurs*. The cypress forests echoed the outcry, startling ibis and egret. Having added an area six times as large as France to their king's realm the men sat down to a feast of roast alligator, while La Salle busied himself with observations. From the sun that day and the stars that night he reckoned the latitude of the mouth of the Mississippi with fair precision; but unfortunately he had no accurate chronometer for calculating longitude. At the moment he thought little of the lack; yet the day would come when his inability to be certain of the river's longitude would conjure up hunger and rags, homesickness, desertion, insubordination, mutiny, degradation and death.

La Salle, like other men, could not foresee the future and on April 9, 1682, his spirit knew no trouble. He visioned a mighty realm, loyal to the monarch in whose honor he named the dominion of the Mississippi Valley—Louisiana. He dreamed of the capital he would found on the Illinois River, which he would name St. Louis for the patron saint of the king. Nothing could quench his ardor as his *voyageurs* paddled northward the following day on the tawny current. Eventually they came once more to the Illinois, up which they forced their canoes. At the eminence of Starved Rock, about six miles from the present city of La Salle, he built Fort St. Louis. This rock was chosen as the citadel of his capital, because it rises sheer on three sides and is approachable only from the fourth direction. At its face it overhangs the Illinois, and a plummet dropped from the edge measures 125 feet to the river below. At the summit of this rock Tonty and La Salle directed the clearing of a space an acre in extent and here built a palisaded fort of logs. Certainly the lonely fort in the wilderness was as secure against the raiding Iroquois as the rocky heights of Quebec.

Word of the building of the fort spread among the Indians and soon they began assembling to the number of 4000, all looking to La Salle for protection. Here came the Illinois, at last convinced that La Salle was their friend. Here came refugees from the Indian wars of Virginia, and lonely survivors of King Philip's War of New England. There were Abenakis from Maine, Shawnees from the Ohio, Kaskaskias from the Mississippi's banks, Miamis, Wyandottes and Ottawas.

They brought furs to trade for anything La Salle had to offer, and he had little enough. Visioning an opportunity to make enough money to pay his debts and proceed with his colonization of the Mississippi, he sent a shipment of furs to Canada to buy more merchandise; and with his messengers he sent a letter to Frontenac. It was in this year, 1682, that Frontenac was recalled to France, and the greedy, officious LeFebre de la Barre sat in the governor's hall at Quebec. He threw La Salle's messengers into prison and confiscated the furs as he might have those of any unlicensed woods ranger, leaving La Salle to wait in vain for a reply. Other messengers and other furs were sent. These too were seized. Months passed before the news came to Starved Rock that Frontenac had been removed.

La Salle could ill afford to leave Fort St. Louis. His long experience with the Indians made it seem almost imperative that he remain to command the colony. But how can a man rule a country with a mere twenty men and a mere five pounds of powder to the man and with his supplies cut off? Placing Tonty in command, La Salle proceeded to Canada. At Quebec he quickly found that he could expect no consideration from the governor, who already had written to the king, poisoning his mind against La Salle, whom he denounced as a fool. And so the man branded as a fool and a dreamer took ship for Paris, taking with him as his companion the faithful Nika, his Shawnee hunter.

Once more La Salle appealed to the king in person, answering the charges brought against him by La Barre. Once more he told of a realm with a valley larger than the St. Lawrence, with a climate milder than that of Canada, which was to be lost through the policy of a disgruntled governor. La Salle never failed to stir the king, who dictated a stern rebuke to La Barre, which must have made that official tremble in apprehension. In no uncertain language the king directed that La Salle was not to be molested, that his supplies were to be forwarded, that his furs were to enter the French market without seizure. But as La Salle, clad in velvet scarlet and gold braid, stood in the presence of the king, he was practically penniless. His creditors were clamoring for payment and he could get nothing to supply the thousands of Indians in the Illinois valley, all asking for merchandise in exchange for their beaver peltry.

La Salle knew that as soon as he left the presence of the king and could no longer defend himself, his enemies would once more gain the ear of the monarch. And so La Salle proposed a daring plan. He asked for a ship to carry him and a colony to Louisiana by sea. He proposed to take the colony to the mouth of the Mississippi, open communications with Tonty at Fort St. Louis, and bring out furs without the risk of encountering his enemies on the St. Lawrence. His plan was fraught with hazard, for the Mississippi, since it empties into the Gulf, was regarded by Spain as her private water; and woe to the foreign ship that flew a flag there! The king approved the idea, for at the moment he was quarrelling with the king of Spain, although not at war. He ordered not one ship but four to be placed at La Salle's disposal and assigned officers and crew to sail wherever La Salle directed. Of the four ships, the king gave one, the *Belle,* as an outright gift.

The fleet weighed anchor without La Salle supplying the captain with the longitude of his destination. We know, of course, that La Salle did not know the longitude; but the captain, who resented being placed under orders of a landsman, thought the explorer was merely withholding his confidence. The fleet had not left land before there was bickering between the naval commander and La Salle and they quarrelled throughout the entire voyage.

At La Salle's direction they passed along the southern shore of Cuba, entered the Gulf through the Channel of Yucatan and steered toward the northwest. Not a man of the fleet had ever been in that forbidden water before. Each day the captain took his bearings from the sun and each night from the stars so that he might enter the latitude and longitude in the log. He knew where he was but did not know where he was going. At length they came to the coast of the present Texas, and La Salle directed that they cruise westward to find the mouth of the Mississippi. They coasted as far as the present Corpus Christi. Then, since the coast line continued to veer ever southward, La Salle had

n a French painting.

ROBERT CAVELIER, SIEUR DE LA SALLE

From a contemporary sketch in Hennepin's "A New Discovery of a Vast Country in America."

La Salle landing on the Texas Coast

to admit he was approaching Mexico. He ordered the fleet to turn about and cruise eastward. Day after day they anxiously gazed ashore in vain for the mouth of the Mississippi.

When they came to Matagorda Bay on the Texas coast, La Salle pretended to believe that a channel of salt water pouring out with the tide between two coastal islands was the Mississippi. He certainly knew better, but he seems to have come to the conclusion that the fleet must have passed the mouth of the Mississippi in the night, and that he could find it by marching along the shore. He felt that he must get rid of his captain, who continually found fault. After the ships had lightered their cargoes, La Salle dismissed them, keeping only the *Belle*. Here on Matagorda Bay he founded the first white settlement in the present state of Texas. It numbered 180 persons, 7 of them women.

As a safeguard against Indians, La Salle directed the building of a palisaded fort, which he also named St. Louis. He gave directions for the laying out of fields and gardens. He directed herders to watch the pigs, goats and chickens, which now were turned loose to range the prairies and to reproduce their kind for the future needs of the colony.

Having established the colony, he appointed Henri Joutel as second in command, placed him in charge of the post and set out himself with a few companions to rediscover the Mississippi. First he marched eastward. He was gone for months and discovered the Colorado, Brazos and Trinity Rivers. Then coming to the conclusion that the fleet must have passed the Mississippi west of Matagorda Bay, he returned to St. Louis and marched west. He discovered more rivers, but was hundreds of miles from the great stream he sought. He once more came back to St. Louis and decided to board the *Belle* and coast the shore in quest of the Mississippi; but before he could launch on the voyage, his men ran the *Belle* on a reef and the waves pounded her to pieces. For a year and a half he kept up his fruitless quest.

His men grumbled. Some decided that he was mad. All became desperately homesick. Many sickened and died. A few deserted to live with the Indians. Among the deserters was Jean Grollet, who married an Indian maid and became an important man in an Indian village. Of 180 colonists landed in 1685 less than 50 remained to celebrate Christmas in 1686. After a forlorn Christmas celebration, La Salle took his leading men into his confidence and admitted that he could not find the Mississippi. He announced that he would march with seventeen men, including Joutel, and would proceed northeastward to Canada. He knew that if worst came to worst, he would arrive at the Alleghenies, which, with Nika to aid him, he could follow northward to the St. Lawrence. As he parted from those left at Matagorda Bay, he promised to send a ship for them as soon as he could get back to France. He warned them to be friendly with the Indians, but never to permit any of them to enter the palisade.

Northeastward marched the seventeen. Each day La Salle shaved himself and dressed with meticulous care. Always he wore his scarlet coat with gold braid, for he had learned that it never failed to impress strange Indians. It also marked him as the commander. The men, however, felt that he was a peacock in the wilderness. January and February passed as they marched northeast and ever north-

east. March came and they were somewhere in northeast
Texas. Buds were swelling; birds were singing; Nature was
vibrant with the hope of a new season. Yet there was no
hope in the hearts of his followers. Three in particular were
oppressed with discouragement, homesickness and a hate
of their master—a hate so savage that it has perpetuated
their names—Duhaut, Liotot and Hiens. Behind his back
they muttered imprecations, and the more they muttered
the greater grew their hate. They spread discontent among
the others and plotted mutiny.

It was one thing for Duhaut, Liotot and Hiens to plan
mutiny. It was something else to muster the courage to
challenge their commander to his face. One afternoon nine
of the seventeen were about six miles from camp butchering buffalo, which Nika had killed. In the party were the
three conspirators and three others whom they had won
over to hostility against La Salle. In command of the butchering detail was La Salle's nephew, Morganet, who was
hated even more than his uncle, because of his arrogant at-
titude toward those under him. The three conspirators resolved to kill Morganet, but had not the courage to do it
by daylight. They therefore dawdled with the butchering
so that night fell before they had finished their work of
cutting up the meat. This necessitated their spending the
night at the spot instead of returning to La Salle at the
main camp.

Even with darkness they lacked the courage to act. The
three therefore volunteered to stand watch. Nika, sus-
pecting nothing, fell asleep. He had killed the game. He
had done his share of the butchering. He was tired and
welcomed rest. Nika was, of course, loyal to La Salle and

the conspirators determined to kill him with Morganet. While they were about it, they decided also to put an end to Saget, who also was faithful to his master. When the three victims were asleep, Hiens gave the signal; and the three assassins leaped to their task. Morganet and Saget awoke at the onslaught, but they were killed after a short struggle. Nika never stirred as the knife struck home. The Shawnee hunter, who had never wronged a single member of the party, died peacefully without a murmur.

Back at the camp, La Salle spent an anxious night. He knew of the grumblings of the conspirators and feared for his nephew. It did not occur to him that Nika and Saget also were in peril. He lit signal fires to guide the party back to camp, but no one arrived. Early in the morning he set out with a priest to find the hunters. It was not difficult to follow their trail; and after almost two hours of walking, he came to where he could see the strips of meat set on the drying racks. But where were the men?

These six men, three of whom had had no part in the murder of the night before, but who had been won to the side of the conspirators, should certainly have had no fear of La Salle. The priest, who accompanied him, went unarmed. Yet with the odds of six to one, the conspirators dared not face La Salle. And so they skulked in ambush. They realized, however, that La Salle might suspect something if no one was visible. They therefore persuaded Jean L'Archeveque to serve as a decoy. L'Archeveque had come to Matagorda Bay as a fifteen-year-old youth. He was now seventeen. Left to himself, he would have followed La Salle faithfully, but he had imbibed the poison of hate from the others.

La Salle, seeing L'Archeveque, hailed him. To this the youth paid no attention but stood immobile. La Salle drew nearer, rebuked L'Archeveque for his failure to reply and for failing to remove his hat in salute to his master. At this L'Archeveque gave an insolent and meaningless reply and backed off. La Salle called harshly to give an account of the men. The youth continued to back away, and La Salle followed toward clumps of grass and brush where Liotot and Duhaut lay concealed, their fingers itching at the triggers.

Suddenly blazes of flame and puffs of smoke burst from the thickets. The woods echoed the bark of muskets. Taint of gunpowder hung in the air. La Salle pitched to the ground and lay still. Out from ambush leaped Liotot like an Indian about to strike a fallen enemy.

"There you lie, you great Bashaw," sneered the murderer.

Before his accomplices could come running up, Liotot stripped his master of his scarlet coat and sword and appropriated them for his own. The others stripped the body of the remaining clothing and left it naked. The priest, who would have spoken the last rites for the dead, was ordered back to camp. Not so much as a whispered prayer accompanied La Salle on his voyage to his Maker. No stone was raised to mark his resting place. Only after man had gone did the coyotes slink to the body and howl a requiem.

Back to camp marched the mutineers. Liotot, seemingly because he was wearing La Salle's coat and bearing his weapons, assumed his authority. Joutel feared for his life as the mutineers disarmed him and as Liotot strutted about the camp. But there was no reason for fear. Hiens, who had been a buccaneer, coveted the scarlet coat with gold braid and felt that he could better command than either Liotot or Duhaut. He killed Liotot and donned the coat, while another killed Duhaut. Hiens gave permission for Joutel and six other men, including the two priests, to proceed toward Canada, while he led the mutineers to a Cenis Indian village, where they married Indian women and where Hiens, because of his fine coat and superior weapons, was regarded as a chief.

Joutel led the other six toward the northeast. One of his followers was drowned while crossing a stream, but the others stumbled on for week after week. They came to rivers and prairies. They plunged through forests. There was nothing left for them to do but to keep marching. On a hot day in midsummer they arrived at a wide river flowing eastward. Gazing across, they were dumbfounded to see on the farther side a log hut and in front of the hut a wooden cross. They had no idea where they might be, but that rude hut and rough-hewn cross meant only one thing. It meant that white men and Christians had been there. Like doomed men receiving an unhoped for reprieve, Joutel and his five followers threw themselves on their knees and devoutly thanked God. They were yet kneeling when two men came out of the hut, cupped their hands to their lips and shouted in the French tongue.

The two launched a canoe, crossed the river and transported the six ragged, barefoot travellers to the hut. This hut was on the Arkansas River just a few miles above its junction with the Mississippi. It was standing on a point later to be named Arkansas Post and was the first white settlement in the present state of Arkansas. It was long a

Photo by Haller, LaSalle, Illinois.

STARVED ROCK

Fort St. Louis the first white settlement in the Mississippi Valley, was built in 1682 by La Salle and Tonty atop this rock, which rises 125 feet above the surface of the Illinois River.

ARKANSAS POST

This is now a state park. The log house is a restoration, not of the log hut built by Tonty's men but by men during the later American period. Below is a view of the park across an elbow of the Arkansas River.

---

noted trading post and was the first capital of Arkansas Territory. Today it is a state park.

It was the loyal Tonty who had set up this post in the wilderness for the aid of La Salle. It was a poor post indeed, but it was all that Tonty could afford. For many months he had waited at Starved Rock for the coming of La Salle. Not hearing from him, he descended the Mississippi in 1686 and stood once more at the wooden cross at the river's mouth. Except for the cry of the swamp birds and the ripple of the water before the snout of an alligator, all was solitude. Unable to discover any sign of his master, Tonty made his way to an Indian village, where he wrote a letter to La Salle and asked the chief of the village to deliver it to the first white man who should pass that way. On his way back to the Illinois, Tonty paused at the mouth of the Arkansas to visit an Indian village a short distance up the stream. Here he built the hut and left six volunteer woods rangers to trade with the Indians and to await tidings from La Salle. Had the post been a few miles up the Arkansas or only a few miles down the Mississippi, the refugees from Matagorda Bay would have missed it entirely. Did blind chance lead Joutel to that very spot?

After resting at Arkansas Post, Joutel and his men proceeded to Starved Rock, where they arrived in September, 1687, having been nine months on the tragic trail from Matagorda Bay. From Fort St. Louis the refugees proceeded to Canada and to France.

The king, upon learning the fate of his colonists, heartlessly abandoned the survivors. When the question came up regarding La Salle's trading rights on the Mississippi, the king forgot all La Salle had told him of the great possibilities of the valley and erased the Mississippi from his memory. Later, after Frontenac had been reinstated as governor of New France and after Tonty had served Frontenac with valor in the Iroquois wars, the governor persuaded the king to give orders that Tonty should succeed La Salle as commandant at Fort St. Louis. The order, however, permitted Tonty to ship only two canoe loads of furs a year. Tonty remained on Starved Rock, traded with the Indians and became the first white citizen of the Mississippi Valley.

Although the king forgot his Texas colonists, Tonty was of different stuff. In an attempt to rescue the remnant at Matagorda Bay, he ventured with one French companion and one Indian to ascend the hitherto unexplored Red River across the present Louisiana to Texas. He then travelled afoot to the Cenis village where Hiens had last been seen strutting about in La Salle's scarlet coat with the gold braid. There Tonty learned that Hiens had been so overbearing that he had been killed. L'Archeveque and the others could not be found. Unable to find anybody who could lead him to Matagorda Bay, Tonty was forced to give up the quest and returned to Starved Rock.

As for the survivors at Matagorda Bay, as soon as La Salle's guiding hand was gone, they grew careless. In an unguarded moment they permitted the Indians to enter the palisade. A massacre followed and all were killed except five children, whom the Indian women saved and adopted. Two others survived the massacre, due to the fact that they were absent at the time. These were L'Archeveque, who had decoyed La Salle to his death, and Grollet, who had married an Indian.

In the meantime the Spaniards had heard of the French colony, and the viceroy of Mexico sent Alonso de Leon with a military force to destroy it. Leon arrived after the massacre by the Indians. He found skeletons of the slaughtered people and reported finding more than 200 books, a number which astonished the Spaniards, who had never seen so many in one place before. Leon found the five white children, whom he ransomed from the Indians, and also found L'Archeveque and Grollet, whom he arrested for trespass. The children were taken to Mexico and adopted by Spanish families. One of them, a girl, Magdalene Talon, was taken to Spain, where she grew to womanhood and married a Spaniard. Her two brothers, Jean, age ten, and a younger brother, Robert, were sent to sea as cabin boys and grew up to be Spanish sailors. Subsequently their ship was taken by a French man of war and they were restored to their home country. L'Archeveque and Grollet were sentenced to the mines for trespass, but later were offered freedom if they would take the oath of loyalty to the Spanish king. This they did willingly. Grollet, a deserter, would have been shot had he returned to France; and of course L'Archeveque, an accomplice in the slaying of La Salle, would have been executed, despite the fact that he was only seventeen at the time of the murder and was a tool of older men.

These two men proved valuable in the Indian trade of New Mexico. From their life with the Indians, they understood Indian character and took readily to the trader's life. L'Archeveque changed his name to Juan de Archebeque to give it a Spanish form. He married a Spanish woman and lived in Santa Fe, where he amassed some wealth. He became a citizen of such consequence that when his first wife died and he married again, his second wedding was one of the events of Santa Fe; and the brother of the governor served as best man.

His French love of adventure led him on distant trading expeditions to the plains a full 400 miles beyond Santa Fe. He established a trading post at a pueblo, El Quartelejo, in the present Kansas. There he learned of the steady advance of French traders westward from the Illinois country up the Missouri River, and he reported this to the Spanish authorities at Santa Fe.

An expedition to drive out the Frenchmen was organized by the governor at Santa Fe in 1720. First command was given to Pedro de Villazur, a Spanish officer, but second command fell to Archebeque. It was now thirty-three years since the La Salle tragedy. Archebeque was fifty years old and in the height of his influence. He guided the Spaniards and their Indian allies into the Pawnee country of what is now western Nebraska.

But as La Salle was decoyed into ambush by L'Archeveque thirty-three years before, so did Archebeque now lead himself and his followers into a trap. While encamped at night on the South Platte, the Spaniards and their allies were surrounded by Pawnees armed with French muskets and doubtless aided by French woods rangers. The slaughter of the British under Braddock on the Monongahela River thirty-five years later was here rehearsed. The Spaniards were wiped out to the last man. Only a few of the Indians' allies escaped to carry the news of disaster to Santa Fe. Archebeque, the sole survivor of those who had conspired to slay La Salle, was shot as his servant was bringing him his horse. Like La Salle's, Archebeque's body lay stripped without burial. Wind and snow toyed with his bones on the treeless plains, and the Pawnees dried his scalp in the smoke of their wigwams.

We have advanced thirty-three years ahead of our story. We have not yet told who these Frenchmen were that alarmed the Spaniards by advancing among the Pawnees. La Salle was dead. The king had forgotten Louisiana. Who was it that through these years kept the dream of La Salle alive?

Let us go to the log fort atop Starved Rock and find Tonty as he sits beside the commandant's desk. Tonty is writing a letter to Pontchartrain, the king's minister; and since he is right handed and wears a hook in place of his right hand, writing is to him a laborious task. But there is no one to whom he can dictate, for his woods rangers are unlettered Canadians, brought up in a colony where it was thought that none but priests and gentlemen and king's men needed to know how to write. And so Tonty does his own writing.

As he writes, he describes the wonders and resources of the Mississippi Valley. He tells of his own adventures. He describes the mouth of the Mississippi, so that if other Frenchmen should come by sea, they might be able to know it by its appearance. He relates the story of his own voyages up and down the river, and he tells of the letter he wrote and left with an Indian chief to deliver to La Salle. He pleads for Pontchartrain not to forget the valley which La Salle claimed for his king. In describing the lower Mississippi, he writes:

"The river is only navigable for large vessels as far as the village of the Natches, for above that place the river winds too much; but this does not prevent the navigation of the river from the confluence of the Ouabache and the Mississippi as far as the sea. There are but few beavers, but to make amends, there is a large number of buffaloes, bears, large wolves—stags and hinds in abundance—and some lead mines, which yield two-thirds of ore to one of refuse. As these savages are stationary and have some habits of subordination, they might be obliged to make silk in order to procure necessaries for themselves; bringing to them from France the eggs of silkworms, for the forests are full of mulberry trees. This would be a valuable trade."*

When the letter arrived in Paris, Pontchartrain became very much interested. King William's War was raging at the time, however, and the king's minister filed the letter away for future inspection.

*This translation is reprinted from Volume I of the *Illinois Historical Society Collections* by permission.

CHAPTER X

THE FOUNDING OF LOUISIANA

Shortly after the close of King William's War, an English publisher brought out a new edition of Hennepin's book concerning the Mississippi. This contained not only an account of Hennepin's own adventures in America but also those of the priests who had accompanied La Salle to the Gulf, the latter being garbled to make it appear that Hennepin was writing from first-hand experience. No one read Hennepin's new book with greater interest than the London proprietors of the colonies of North and South Carolina, who claimed all the land westward from the colonies to the Pacific under a sea-to-sea grant from the English king.

It was not long until the French minister in London informed Pontchartrain that the Carolina owners were planning to send colonists to occupy the Mississippi. Thereupon Pontchartrain remembered Tonty's letter and read it with greater interest. He felt that if the Great Valley was desirable for the English, it must be equally desirable for the French. And so he began to wonder which of the soft-handed political favorites in Paris he should name as governor to found a colony. It did not occur to him that Tonty was the one best suited for the post.

Just at this juncture Iberville, whose father had been

one of the enemies of La Salle, arrived in Paris. Iberville
was the hero of the hour. All France was talking about his
three successful campaigns against the English on Hudson
Bay. It had been his ambition to found a colony on the
bay, but the Treaty of Ryswick had restored the region
to the English. Blocked in accomplishment of his ambition
in the northland, Iberville presented himself at the office
of Pontchartrain to apply for authority to head a colony in
Louisiana.

It was this same Pontchartrain who granted to Cadillac
authority to found Detroit. He was a good judge of men
and quickly saw that Iberville was the man to lead a colony
into the wilderness. With one hundred sailors and ninety
colonists, including two of his brothers, Iberville sailed
for America, entered the Gulf of Mexico through the
Straits of Florida, cruised along the coast near enough to
view the newly founded Spanish colony at Pensacola and
continued westward. He admitted to his sailors that he did
not know the longitude of the Mississippi, but he was certain that he could discover it. He permitted the fleet to
sail only by day, thereby avoiding the chance of missing
the stream in the night. Each night he directed a few men
to camp on shore and look for Indians. When Indians were
seen, the men gave presents and inquired by signs for the
mouth of the river that had eluded La Salle.

On the first day of March, 1699, the lookout shouted
from the mast that he could see a muddy headland thrust
into the sea. The ship drew alongside and Iberville believed
this must be the Mississippi delta described by Tonty. The
following day the lookout discovered issuing from the
delta a channel, which carried such a flood of water that

Iberville knew it was no ordinary stream and felt that it must surely be one of the mouths of the Mississippi.

Giving orders for the ship to remain off shore, Iberville ordered that two sea boats be lowered. He took command of one himself and placed his eighteen-year-old brother, Bienville, in command of the other. This was Iberville's youngest brother and his favorite. During King William's War, Bienville had enlisted as a cabin boy aboard one of his brother's ships and at the age of fifteen had commanded a squad of men under Iberville's eye at the Battle of Fort Nelson on Hudson Bay. For many days Iberville and Bienville voyaged with their crews up the channel of the river, looking in vain for proof that they were on the Mississippi. They could not find the wooden cross erected by La Salle, but they realized that floods might have washed it away. Once they came to an Indian village and saw one of the Indians carrying water in a glass bottle. But the bottle proved nothing. It might have been obtained from the Spaniards at Pensacola. Although he could find no proof that he was on the Mississippi, the river fitted the descriptions of Tonty and was so large that Iberville continued voyaging northward, hoping to find conclusive evidence that he was on the water he sought.

Eventually he came to a point of high ground, which he named *Baton Rouge* (red rod) from the fact that he saw a tree there with a red trunk. Here he determined to return to his ship. To Bienville he gave instructions that he return down the same channel up which they had come. As for himself, he entered a bayou leading out from the river and descended the Ascontia River. It empties into a large salt-water bay, which Iberville named Lake Pontchartrain in honor of the king's minister. Crossing the lake he eventually returned to his ship. But where was Bienville? Iberville, having taken a new route, had travelled farther than Bienville and had expected to find his brother at the ship.

Bienville was travelling slowly so as to observe the river bank for something that might prove he was on the Mississippi. He found nothing unusual until one day he spied a narrow footpath leading from the river's brink back into the swamp. It was such a narrow path that other men might have passed it by, but Bienville sprang to shore, directed some of the crew to remain and guard the boat and others to follow him. As the party advanced into the jungle to discover the people whose feet had worn the path, clouds of stinging insects assailed the Frenchmen. Snakes wriggled from underfoot. Thorny brambles scratched their faces and hands. They persevered despite the discomfort, until the trail led them to higher ground above flood level and there they found an Indian village.

The Indians were startled for a moment at the sudden appearance of white men, but they quickly regained their composure and advanced with extended hands, indicating to Bienville that they had met white men before and had been treated well by them. An old chief welcomed the boy commander. Then he hastened to his lodge and brought forth a piece of paper.

Imagine Bienville's astonishment at receiving a letter in the swamp! He saw at once that it was addressed to La Salle! This, then, was the letter written thirteen years before by Tonty! Here was the proof indeed! The river was the Mississippi!

Presenting the chief with a hatchet to reward him for de-

IBERVILLE

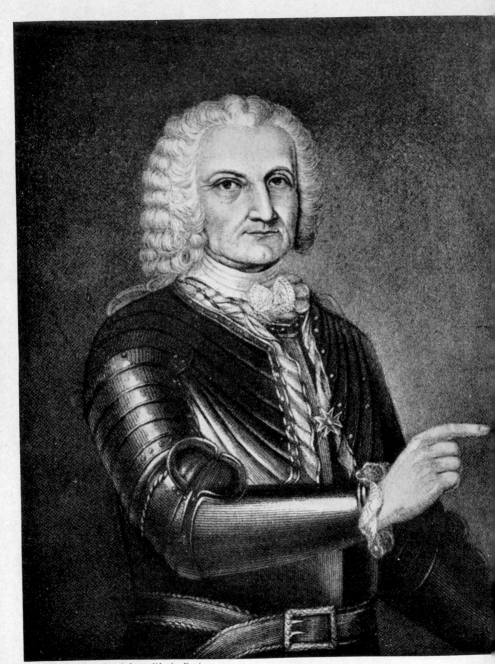

BIENVILLE

He was the founder of Mobile and New Orleans and the builder
of the colony of Louisiana.

livery of the letter, the young captain almost ran as he hurried back through the swamp to his boat. No longer did he voyage leisurely along the river's banks. He drove his boatmen as though they were racing at a regatta. Out of the channel of the Mississippi into the Gulf sped the boat until it came alongside the ship. Here the exultant Bienville ran up the ship's ladder to deliver the important letter to his brother.

Iberville's next move was the selection of a place of settlement. Bienville favored building the city far up the Mississippi at a place where they had landed and which is today the site of New Orleans. Iberville, however, vetoed the proposal. He preferred a place looking toward the sea. He would have built his capital at the mouth of the Mississippi, but the delta was too muddy for consideration. And so he chose a sandy beach on the coast to the eastward in what is now the state of Mississippi. This he named Biloxi for the Biloxi Indians living near by. It is not far from the present city of Biloxi. Here the men erected a fort and around it built cabins to house the colonists—ninety souls —all men. Iberville named Sauvole as acting governor and placed Bienville as second in command. He then sailed for France to bring out more colonists.

Little did the governor think, when he sailed for France, that his lonely, wilderness colony would be visited by white men during his absence. But in the summer there came two French priests and twenty woods rangers from Canada. They had come down the Mississippi to preach to the Indians and had been escorted as far as Arkansas Post by Tonty. On the lower Mississippi they had been told by the Indians of the colony at Biloxi and had come to visit it.

After a few weeks of rest, they returned to the Mississippi and once more ascended the river. Upon arrival at Starved Rock they reported to Tonty their discovery of the French colony named Louisiana.

While Sauvole directed operations at Biloxi, Bienville ranged the forests. He made friends with the Indians, marched to Pensacola and inspected it from the jungle, without permitting the Spaniards to know of his presence. He proceeded northeastward to visit the Chickasaw Indians, who he found were trading with the English colonists in the Carolinas. Turning westward, he travelled by boat to Lake Pontchartrain, traversed it to the westward shore and once more landed on the site of New Orleans. The object of this voyage is not made plain. Possibly Bienville wanted to inspect the spot once more with a view of urging upon his brother the removal of his colony. He found that the site of his proposed city not only faced the Mississippi, but it also could be reached by boat from Lake Pontchartrain, which is only five miles from the Mississippi. The situation at Biloxi had proved to be very bad. Soon after Iberville's departure, several of the colonists became ill, apparently from malaria caused by mosquitoes coming from an adjoining swamp.

Whatever Bienville's purpose, the expedition proved to be a very important one, for after he had portaged his boats from Lake Pontchartrain to the Mississippi and was descending that stream toward the Gulf, he encountered an English ship, commanded by a Captain Barr, whom he recognized as an officer Iberville had captured at the Battle of Fort Nelson. Running the risk of being made prisoner, Bienville boldly drew his boat alongside, clambered up the ladder and, standing on the Englishman's own deck, warned him to withdraw from French waters. He told Barr that the French had prior rights from the explorations of La Salle, from the building of Fort St. Louis on Starved Rock, from the building of Arkansas Post and from the colony at Biloxi.

Barr haughtily answered that he was a representative of the proprietors of the Carolinas, that the English king had given the Carolinas all the territory from the Atlantic seaboard from the thirty-first to the thirty-sixth degree and all land westward from sea to sea. The captain had a ship full of colonists, whom he said he intended to settle on the river.

Bienville noticed that some of the colonists were speaking to each other in French. He approached them and one of the men replied that he was a native of France; but because of differences of religion, he had been expelled. He said that he was one of 400 French Huguenots living in the Carolinas. He proposed to Bienville that he and his fellow co-religionists, not only in the Carolinas but also in Europe, be allowed to settle in Louisiana as loyal subjects of France. We can but wonder what would have been the result had King Louis been gracious enough to permit the entrance of the Huguenots to Louisiana. There were many thousands of them, driven from France because of their religious beliefs. In England the king permitted persons of opposite beliefs to migrate to America, but the French laws strictly forbade Huguenots entering the king's American colonies. As a result these people, who might have come to Louisiana in great numbers, found a refuge in the English colonies instead and, in the wars between France and England, served loyally in the English armies. Bienville, of course, could not admit the Huguenots and told them to depart with the English ship.

Captain Barr blustered. He declared that Bienville was a trespasser and that he should get out. But despite his bravado, Barr turned about and sailed for the Carolinas. From his turning about, the point is still shown on charts of the Mississippi River as English Turn.

Iberville was back in Biloxi in December, bringing with him sixty Canadian woods rangers and one man of a socially prominent family in Canada. He was Louis de St. Denis, a young man of gracious manners, whose international love affairs will be discussed in the next chapter. Iberville listened gravely to Bienville's report of the claims of the Carolina English. He ordered Bienville to build a fort on the Mississippi about fifty miles north of the mouth of the river.

The young commander began at once to build the fort. Working on the palisades one afternoon, he saw a fleet of canoes approaching from the river. In the leading canoe stood a slender middle-aged man, who hailed Bienville in French and saluted with a gloved right hand. It was Tonty. His license permitted him to ship only two canoe loads of furs annually to Canada, but there was no barrier to trade with Louisiana, and Tonty had brought all the furs his canoes could carry.

Bienville dispatched him to Biloxi, where he arrived just as Iberville was preparing to depart for France. Iberville bought all the furs Tonty had to offer. He also invited Tonty to make his home in Biloxi, take charge of the fur trade there and serve as advisor to the colony. Tonty accepted and Iberville, pleased with Tonty's able assistance, sailed for France.

Without any effort on Iberville's part, his colony began to grow far up the river. In the year 1700, two Canadian priests, Jacques Gravier and Gabriel Marest, opened a mission at the Kaskaskia Indian village on the Mississippi in the present Illinois. It was to these same Indians that Marquette had preached the Gospel the year prior to his death. Shortly after the founding of the mission, several Canadian woods rangers arrived to marry Indian wives. They built cabins near the mission and thus the town of Kaskaskia began. Shortly afterward a second town, Cahokia, was founded near at hand. The woods rangers left by Tonty at Starved Rock abandoned that point to make their home at Kaskaskia. This little settlement became the outfitting point for trappers and traders on the Illinois, the Upper Mississippi and the Missouri. Encouraged by Tonty, they no longer tried to ship furs to Canada, but brought them to Biloxi. Before the winter was over Bienville saw more fleets, bearing peltry, float past his fort on the Mississippi with cargoes for Biloxi.

Kaskaskia and Cahokia were more than fur-trading towns. As they grew in size, white women eventually came from Detroit with their husbands to make their home. Farms were laid out adjoining the villages. Here the Frenchmen raised livestock and wheat and soon were shipping wheat to Louisiana.

During the summer of 1701 Iberville failed to come from France. King Louis had joined with Spain in an unfortunate war with England, known in American histories as Queen Anne's War. Iberville, being an admiral in the

French navy, had to neglect his colony to participate in the war. In the meantime Sauvole died at Biloxi from fever. This raised Bienville, at the age of twenty, to the rank of acting governor of the colony. He had never approved the selection of Biloxi as the capital. But since Iberville did not approve of New Orleans, Bienville moved the colony to Mobile Bay, not far from the present city of Mobile, Alabama. Here he directed his nephew, Pierre Boisbriant, who had studied architecture in France, to build a fort. Bienville named the new capital Mobile, from the Mobile Indians.

Iberville took time from the war to visit his colony once more in 1702. It was to be his last visit. He remained long enough to approve the selection of Mobile, to take on board the furs in the warehouses, to unload a cargo of merchandise and then he was gone. Illness prevented his return that year and by the following year the war again required his services. The king dispatched him to take command of the West Indian fleet, with which he harried the commerce of the English colonies for three years. His career was cut short in 1706 when he died in Havana of yellow fever.

During the years he was serving in the navy, he thought much of his colony. Once he arranged for a shipment of a number of girls to Mobile to become the wives of the woods rangers there. These were the first white women of Louisiana. Their arrival was just three years after Madame Cadillac and Madame Alphonse Tonty came to Detroit. Unfortunately the ship on which they sailed stopped at Haiti, where yellow fever was raging. The ship carried the infection to Mobile and this resulted in much sickness and loss of life. Among those to die in the epidemic was the gallant Tonty. The loss of Tonty in 1704, followed by that of Iberville, was a severe blow to Louisiana.

Bienville continued to manage affairs of the colony as acting governor. His was a position of great responsibility and of danger. An English fleet hovered about Mobile Bay and at the mouth of the Mississippi for several years. Once the English were about to capture Pensacola, and Bienville hurried with a force of men to help the Spaniards repel the British. Through the twelve years of the weary war Bienville served with great ability. During all of that time he had the title merely of acting governor. With the close of the war in 1713, he had hope that the king would recognize his services and appoint him governor in his own right. The politicians in France, however, had other plans.

CHAPTER XI

CADILLAC RULES LOUISIANA

IT WAS a sad day for Louisiana when King Louis blundered into war with Queen Anne of England. To carry on the war, Louis borrowed from Antoine Crozat, a French money lender. It was a sad time for Crozat too, for as the war continued through twelve years, it became evident that the king could never repay his loans. Crozat was therefore a willing listener when Cadillac came from Canada with a plan for recovery of the debt.

Although Cadillac had declined the governorship of Louisiana in 1710, he felt differently after the king had removed him from the command at Detroit. He studied maps of the Mississippi Valley, saw how the trade of the valley naturally flowed with the river to the Gulf, and concluded that Mobile could be developed into a greater city than Detroit. Calling upon Crozat, he persuaded him to cancel the king's debts in exchange for the monopoly of the trade in Louisiana. Cadillac offered to go to Mobile and take charge as governor, while at the same time he would be a business partner of Crozat. The selfish king, without any consideration for Bienville and others in Louisiana who had served him so well, accepted Crozat's offer, and, at the money lender's request named Cadillac as governor of Louisiana, a realm which included not only the entire Mississippi Valley but also the Gulf coast from Florida to Mexico. Bienville was retained as assistant to Cadillac.

Cadillac felt kindly toward his assistant, now a thirty-two year old bachelor; and soon after his arrival in Mobile with his family, proposed that Bienville marry the eldest of the Cadillac daughters. Bienville, however, affronted the governor by rejecting the proposal, not because he did not like the girl, but because he did not want Cadillac for a father-in-law. Bienville had been angered when the king failed to promote him to the governorship, and since he had no means of showing his displeasure to the king, he hated Cadillac, whom he regarded as a supplanter. Since Mademoiselle Cadillac was of high social position, there were but two men in Mobile of sufficient rank to marry her. One was Bienville and the other St. Denis. Of the two, Bienville was regarded as the better match, for St. Denis had no money. From the time of Bienville's rejection, Cadillac disliked him with all his heart.

Other matters, however, engaged the attention of both the governor and his assistant. In order to increase the trade of his colony, Cadillac sent out expeditions of traders to set up forts for trade with the Indians. The first was built at the Natchez Indian village on the site of Natchez, Mississippi; the second on the Tennessee River at the present Nashville, capital of Tennessee; the third on the Red River at Natchitoches, Louisiana. The founder of Natchitoches was St. Denis.

Suddenly an illiterate trapper came to Cadillac's office in Mobile to conjure up visions of great wealth without the bother of trading with the Indians. This trapper thought that he had found a silver mine on the Upper Mississippi.

From his descriptions, the silver lay in great abundance; and there was enough of it to provide unbounded wealth for Crozat, for Cadillac and for the trapper himself. When the governor asked the trapper why he had not brought samples of the silver with him, the man answered that when he discovered it, he had not known it was silver, because he had never seen silver before. But upon coming to Mobile, he had seen silver. He said that it was whitish in color, that it came in cubic crystals and that it was heavy to lift.

In a fever of excitement, Cadillac accompanied the trapper on a two months' voyage up the Mississippi, until they arrived on the site of the present Galena, Illinois. Here the trapper took him to the mine and showed him the metal he had found. It was nothing but lead. Disappointed, Cadillac returned to Mobile, and it is quite likely that Bienville smiled at the governor's failure.

Another of Cadillac's ventures was an effort to open trade with Mexico. Crozat had told him to carry on trade legally if he could and by smuggling if it could not be done legally. Already traders were smuggling French goods into the Spanish port of Pensacola, for while Crozat's prices were high, his was a mild monopoly as compared with the exactions of the merchants who had the monopoly of the Spanish king to trade with his overseas colonies. For his mission to Mexico, Cadillac selected St. Denis, commandant at Natchitoches. Possibly Cadillac wished to give St. Denis a chance to make himself rich in the Mexican trade so that he could afford to marry Mademoiselle Cadillac. Perhaps he chose him because he was trading with the Indians on the Red River and had some knowledge of Texas.

In fact there was no one better suited for the post than

St. Denis, for he and the men at his post were familiar with the use of horses. Until the time of his expedition to Mexico, Frenchmen had generally carried on explorations by canoe. But now France had advanced from the region of rivers and forests into the sunlit prairies of the West. From now on her explorers would mount horses rather than crouch over a paddle.

As guides for his expedition St. Denis engaged Jean and Robert Talon, who will be recalled as two of the boys saved from massacre by the Indian women when La Salle's colony at Matagorda Bay was destroyed. The Talon boys, after service in the Spanish navy and after their return to France, were now residents of Mobile. Although they had been with La Salle, the oldest was a mere lad of ten at the time of their rescue by General Leon. Of course, they were of small use as guides, for neither one had any idea of the immensity of Texas, which is greater in length from its eastern boundary to the western tip than is the distance from its eastern boundary to Lake Michigan.

Ignorant of the distance he had to travel, St. Denis bought horses from the Indians, packed goods upon them and marched for the west. He could travel only about fifteen miles each day, for the horses had to be unpacked so that they might graze. He and his men swam their horses across the Sabine, the Trinity, the Brazos and the Colorado. He forded the Nueces and had not yet sighted the Rio Grande. Well could he sympathize with La Salle, lost in the expanse of Texas. Months passed before St. Denis came to a trail leading to a wide, sandy bed down which meandered the glistening Rio Grande. On the banks of the river stood the tiny mission of San Juan and around the mission were a few huts. Out of the huts swarmed a rabble of Spaniards and half breeds, wondering at the strangers from the East. A husky officer, Don Diego Ramon, shouldered the rabble aside to welcome the visitors with traditional Rio Grande hospitality.

"My house is your house," he exclaimed in words which the Talon brothers translated for St. Denis. "Enter! Eat! Rest!"

Had this meeting occurred at Mexico City, the women of the household might have observed the gallant Frenchman through latticed windows, but he never could have had a glimpse of them. On the Rio Grande, however, houses were small and the rooms few so that the women had to occupy the same rooms as the men. Thus it came about that St. Denis met Manuela Maria de Sanchez, granddaughter of Ramon. All writers agree that she was beautiful, good, and resourceful. To St. Denis, deprived for fourteen years of women of his own social rank, she was ten times beautiful. To Manuela, who was threatened with marriage to a fat widower as soon as the loose earth should settle on his first wife's grave, St. Denis was a prince out of a fairy tale.

In the meantime Captain Ramon pondered the problem of the pack-train of smuggled goods. His people needed the goods and he would have been glad to pay for them in silver, yet he dared not admit them to the province without the consent of his superior officer. This officer was Governor Gaspardo de Anayas of Coahuila, the fat widower who was seeking Manuela's hand in marriage. Ramon dispatched a messenger to the governor to ask what should be done regarding the foreigner and his goods.

It is quite likely that Anayas would have been willing to accept the goods had it not been for the messenger, who was a gossipy soul and who reported that St. Denis and Manuela had done nothing since his arrival but look into each other's eyes. This roused the jealousy of Anayas, who directed the messenger to invite St. Denis to come in person with his pack train to Coahuila.

Without realizing that Anayas was a rival suitor, St. Denis took leave of Manuela and hastened with his pack train to Coahuila. There Anayas seized him, confiscated his pack train and threw him into the *calabazo*.

Manuela, upon hearing the news, swore that Anayas was the worst scoundrel unburied and that she would not marry him if he were young, slender and opulent. She rode to Mexico City where she pleaded with the viceroy for the release of St. Denis. The viceroy granted her plea and commanded that the Frenchman should be released from the *calabazo* and that his property should be restored. Manuela arrived home before St. Denis had returned. The day after her return a host of Indian warriors surrounded San Juan and lay siege to it. There St. Denis discovered them a few days later. He called the warriors to his camp, presented each with a handsome gift and explained that the Spaniards were his friends. At his request the Indians withdrew. Ramon hailed St. Denis as a deliverer and was glad to sanction the marriage of the Frenchman to his granddaughter.

St. Denis quickly found a market for his goods, loaded his horses with silver and returned to Natchitoches and Mobile. Cadillac sent him west a second time with a larger pack train of goods. This time Anayas knew better than to put the Frenchman in jail himself. Instead he arrested him and sent him with his pack train of goods to the viceroy at Mexico City. This time it was the viceroy who threw St. Denis into prison.

Upon the pleadings of Manuela the viceroy at length consented to release her husband on the condition that he lead a Spanish expedition eastward across Texas. He also confiscated all of the smuggled goods, which he kept for his own. Taking his wife with him, St. Denis marched eastward once more, guiding the Spanish soldiers. He showed them the site of San Antonio, where they built a mission and presidio, and also pointed out the site of Nacogdoches, where the Spaniards built a second post. For a hundred years the post of Natchitoches, founded by St. Denis, and Nacogdoches, selected by him for the Spaniards, faced each other across a neutral strip between French Louisiana and Spanish Texas. One was the farthest west Louisiana town and the other the farthest east Texas town.

The trail marked by St. Denis on his homeward march with the Spaniards became famous as *El Camino Real* (the King's Highway). During the Spanish regime in Louisiana, the trail was extended across Louisiana to unite Mexico with the Spanish possessions in Florida.

While the adventure of St. Denis extended man's knowledge of geography, it failed to provide a husband for Mademoiselle Cadillac and it proved a financial loss to Cadillac and Crozat.

Even before St. Denis returned home, Crozat saw that he was losing money in Louisiana. He realized that it would take many years before his monopoly there would yield him a profit. He therefore surrendered his monopoly to the king in 1717. At the same time he brought charges of misrepresentation against Cadillac and had him removed as governor of the colony.

Cadillac was willing to be recalled. Louisiana had brought him nothing but disappointment. He took his family to Quebec, where he placed his eldest daughter in a convent. He then returned to France and accepted the governorship of a small province in southern France, where he spent the remainder of his life.

CHAPTER XII

BIENVILLE THE BUILDER

Although Crozat failed to win fortune in Louisiana, others were willing to try their luck there; and the French government soon granted the monopoly of Louisiana trade to John Law, a Scotch gambler. To understand how France permitted a gambler to take over the mastery of one of her colonies, we must consider the unhappy affairs in that country.

Louis XIV died in 1715, leaving a staggering debt to his great-grandson and successor, Louis XV, a boy of five. Since the young king was not old enough to rule, the Duke of Orleans served as regent. Among the boon companions of Orleans was John Law, a fugitive from Scotch justice, who had killed a rival in a love affair; and while the killing had been accomplished in the course of a duel, the jury held that the duel had been unfairly conducted and that Law must die for murder. It required all the money he had to escape from Scotland, and he came to Paris without funds. He was twenty-three, reckless and willing to try anything.

Since he had no skill at honest employment, he opened a gambling bank where the rich of Paris came to play faro. It was not long until he had amassed two million francs. The novelty of faro attracted many of the men and women from the king's court. In this way Law became acquainted with Orleans. The regent was greatly worried about the kingdom's debts. This gave Law an opportunity to suggest a way of paying the debts by having the government printing presses print paper money. The printing of so much money caused prices to rise, whereupon Law suggested a scheme by which both of them could make a fortune by speculation in currency. Law bought property with his own money and with money advanced by Orleans. Then Orleans issued a great deal of paper money, which once more caused prices to rise. Law then sold the property at the advanced prices and divided the gains with Orleans. Since no one but Law and Orleans knew in advance of the proposed inflation of currency, they alone could reap a benefit from the rising market.

Orleans was grateful to Law for helping him to this dishonest wealth, and when Law asked for the monopoly surrendered by Crozat, the regent was glad to award it to him. At that time the South Sea Company of England was enjoying the height of its boom, and Law decided to organize a similar company for Louisiana—the Mississippi Company. He began a fraudulent advertising campaign, conducted exactly like the campaign of the South Sea Company in England. He exhibited a gold bar in his bank with the statement that the gold had been extracted from the sand of the Mississippi delta. He displayed diamonds, which his advertisements declared had been solidified in a single night from the nectar of a certain flower that bloomed only in Louisiana. His advertising told of the fertility of the soil, of the wealth of fabulous mines and of the multitude of beaver.

Only one voice was raised against Law's fraud. Cadillac,

fresh from Louisiana, denounced the advertising. For his temerity in telling the truth about the boon companion of Orleans, both Cadillac and his eldest son were cast into prison and detained there until they promised to say nothing more against the Mississippi scheme.

When the books of Law's company opened, the credulous public, eager to make a great deal of money in this get-rich-quick scheme, flocked to the bank to buy stock. Those who had nothing begged to be taken to Louisiana where they could pick up gold and silver and diamonds and could live without work. For three years the company prospered. Money poured into Law's bank and filled his vaults with gold and silver. Only one thing was wrong with Law's scheme and that was the failure of Louisiana to produce the wealth it was supposed to yield. The stockholders became suspicious and wanted to collect dividends.

Then in 1720 the South Sea Company failed in London. When news of the failure arrived in Paris, the stockholders of the Mississippi Company became alarmed and offered their shares for sale. When everybody wanted to sell and nobody wanted to buy, the market value dropped rapidly until the stock was utterly worthless. In a rage the investors sought to kill John Law, who managed to escape with his life.

Since the Mississippi Company was bright and shiny on the outside like a lovely soap bubble reflecting the colors of the rainbow and since inside it was nothing, the people called it the Mississippi Bubble. When the company failed, it again reminded the people of a bubble, for a bursting bubble amounts to nothing. After John Law's flight, the directors of the company tried to make a success of the company. They continued to keep the monopoly of the Louisiana trade until 1731, when they surrendered it to the king.

Although John Law was a swindler of the worst sort, he did one useful thing in that he had Orleans appoint Bienville to the governorship of Louisiana to succeed Cadillac.

No sooner was he governor in his own right than Bienville moved the capital of his colony from Mobile to the Mississippi River, building it on the very site, between the river and Lake Pontchartrain, which he had recommended to Iberville. This city he named New Orleans in honor of the ancestral city of the Duke of Orleans. He laid out streets and built a palisade to protect the city in case of an attack. As protection against floods, he had the town ditched so that flood water would drain back to Lake Pontchartrain. He planned the system of levees, which today protect the city in time of high water, and he also planned the building of a great spillway north of the city to drain floods of the Mississippi to Lake Pontchartrain before they reached New Orleans. This spillway was not built for more than two centuries, but today it safeguards the city founded by Bienville.

To the Jesuits the governor granted a tract of land fronting 3600 feet on the Mississippi and extending all the way back to Lake Pontchartrain. Here the Jesuits laid out a model farm and cultivated the fig, the orange and the indigo, which they imported. They also cultivated the native myrtle bush and operated an experiment station.

Bienville also made a grant to the Ursuline nuns, who came to the city and opened a girls' school and hospital in

1727. To one of these nuns we are indebted for a description of the new city. This is contained in a letter written by a nun to her father. In it she declares that in New Orleans one could see as much refinement and politeness as in Paris, that gold and velvet were commonly worn, and that the people feasted on cornbread, watermelons, potatoes, pineapples, figs, pecans, walnuts, hickory nuts, pumpkins, swans, hares, chickens, ducks, teals, pheasants, turkeys, partridges, fish of every variety, venison, buffalo steak, chocolate, coffee, milk, boiled rice, and bread of rice and flour.

While giving much attention to building his new city, Bienville had to find locations for colonists sent him by John Law. Among these were 200 Germans, who settled first near Arkansas Post and later on the Mississippi in the present Louisiana. The Germans were disappointed when they were unable to find any flowers that yielded diamonds; but after recovering from their disappointment, they became successful farmers. Their descendants still live in Louisiana.

Bienville was constantly on the alert for the progress of agricultural districts on the Upper Mississippi, for it was through them that New Orleans obtained bread and pork. In 1720 he dispatched his nephew, Boisbriant, to build Fort Chartres on the Mississippi, sixteen miles from Kaskaskia. After building the fort, Boisbriant remained to rule as commandant.

During Bienville's time an important settlement arose on the Wabash River. Woods rangers from Detroit and Mackinac came there to trade with the Indians. Unfortunately, they did not know whether they were under the rule of Canada or of Louisiana. Eventually Louisiana, claiming possession of the region because it was in the Mississippi Valley, sent Francis de Vincennes, a native of Canada, but a resident of New Orleans, to command the Wabash and all the district of the Ohio. He build a fort on the Wabash, and around the fort there grew a farming community, rivalling the settlements at Kaskaskia, Cahokia and Fort Chartres. The village took the name of Vincennes and is today the oldest city in the state of Indiana.

Bienville was so engrossed with the affairs of his colony that he paid no attention to operations of the Mississippi Company or the bursting of the Mississippi Bubble. In France, however, the victims of the swindle, chagrined that John Law had escaped their hands, clamored for some one to be punished. Their demands were so persistent that the Duke of Orleans saw that unless he provided a victim he might be punished himself. And who was a more likely victim than Bienville? Orleans had the governor removed from authority and brought to Paris to face charges. Several years were required before Bienville could clear his name of guilt.

During his absence matters were mishandled in Louisiana. The Natchez and Chickasaw Indians, armed with English weapons, attacked and destroyed Natchez and massacred the inhabitants. The situation became so serious that the king's government restored Bienville to the governorship.

He came back to New Orleans to find the population in a panic of fear, but his coming restored confidence. He organized the colony for defense and in 1736 led a military expedition in person to punish the Indians. Bienville's great-

ness lay in his ability as a colonial organizer and not as a
military commander. He approached the enemy with a
divided force, one section of his army being commanded
by Vincennes, who had come with an army of woods rangers and Miami Indian warriors. At a critical moment the
Indians abandoned the field, leaving Vincennes to face
the enemy alone. In the ensuing battle he was slain and his
woods rangers defeated. Having turned back the threat of
Vincennes, the entire Indian host attacked Bienville. His
army was also beaten and escaped slaughter only by a retreat to Mobile. Of the men with Vincennes, seventeen
were captured alive and burned at the stake by slow fire.
It was several years before Bienville could raise a second
army to invade the Indian country. This time he marched
with all of his troops in a compact body, intending to spread
havoc through all the Natchez and Chickasaw country.
The Indians, awed by his advance, begged for peace. Bienville, believing that it would be better to grant peace than
to wage a costly war, accepted the proposals of the Indians
and marched back home.

The king's ministers, after learning how Bienville had
accepted a peace without victory, sent him a stinging rebuke, charging him with mismanagement of the entire campaign. Bienville waited two years in angry silence before he
replied. In his answer he explained every detail of his campaign. To this the ministers sent a scathing denunciation.

For a long time Bienville nursed his wrath. He felt that
the king's government never had been fair to him. They
had replaced him with Cadillac. They had accused him of
guilt in connection with the bursting of the Mississippi
Bubble. They had restored him to authority only after the

Natchez massacre. Now after he had restored order, had exacted a peace from the Indians and was once more bringing the colony back to prosperity, he was scolded like a bad boy.

Without telling any one of his intentions, he began selling his property in Louisiana. Several years were required to dispose of everything. When all was sold, he sent his resignation to the king in 1742. With the exception of the time he was in Paris clearing his name of the charges growing out of the Mississippi Bubble collapse, he had lived in Louisiana continuously since 1699. He was one of the founders of Biloxi, and had founded both Mobile and New Orleans. He had found the lower Mississippi region a jungle and had been the leader in converting it into a center of civilization. New Orleans was in tears as he departed for Paris, where he spent the remainder of his life.

One who came to bid him farewell as he boarded the ship at the New Orleans levee was St. Denis, hero of the international romance on the Rio Grande. St. Denis was now a prosperous citizen of New Orleans. His marriage to Manuela had been a happy one. They had five daughters and two sons, all of whom mourned as Bienville resigned the governorship.

CHAPTER XIII

THE HORSEBACK MEN

Bienville had just succeeded Cadillac to the governorship of Louisiana when St. Denis came home from his second Mexican expedition. In that remote era, when the geography of Texas was less familiar in Louisiana than is the map of Kamchatka today, the returning traveller was a welcome guest at every home, for he was the only link with the foreign world. We could better understand the welcome of a traveller in old Louisiana, if we could do away with radio, motion picture, telegraph and telephone, daily mail and all magazines and newspapers for one year. Then if we could do away with the automobile, train, airplane and ship so that we could not travel anywhere ourselves, we too would crowd around a traveller to learn what he had seen.

It will be recalled that when St. Denis set out for Mexico, he bought horses from the Caddo Indians. When he marched westward, he had opportunity to see galloping herds of fleet horses running wild on the Texas plains. The horse was unknown to the Indians until introduced into America by the Spaniards, and this accounts for the fact that there were no wild horses except on the western plains and mountains adjacent to the Spanish settlements. From the Spanish ranches of Coahuila and New Mexico and from trading and exploring parties, a few animals escaped to form wild herds. These herds increased in numbers through two centuries, until they made the earth tremble beneath their flying hoofs.

Indians who caught wild horses no longer plodded the weary trails afoot or labored against swift currents in a canoe. Instead they sat proudly astride their mounts to journey without effort in quest of buffalo. Of course St. Denis knew nothing of the origin of the wild horse. But he did tell in New Orleans how horses could be had merely for the catching or how they could be bought for a trifle from the Indians. The horse solved the problem of exploration of a region beyond the navigable rivers.

Acting on this information, Bienville sent three successive horseback expeditions to explore the plains north of Texas. One under Bernard de la Harpe proceeded from Natchitoches in 1719 westward up the Red River valley to south central Oklahoma. Then turning northward, La Harpe explored the present eastern Oklahoma and returned to Arkansas Post and New Orleans with descriptions of a beautiful country, where dwelt Indians eager to trade buffalo robes and beaver furs for articles of French make.

Claude Charles du Tisne, a resident of Kaskaskia, ascended the Missouri to the land of the Osages in the same year. He bought horses from the Osages and marched west and south across the present western Missouri, southeast Kansas and northeast Oklahoma to discover a Wichita Indian village on the Arkansas. Du Tisne met with much difficulty on his journey. First the Osages objected to his going to the Wichitas, and then the Wichitas blocked travel toward the Comanches. The opposition of the Osages was overcome, but the Wichitas feared that Du Tisne would carry firearms to their enemy, the Comanches. The Wichitas were a peace-loving people dwelling in grass houses and cultivating gardens. On the other hand, the Comanches were roving hunters dwelling in skin teepees and looking with contempt upon their sedentary neighbors. Realizing that if the Comanches could buy firearms they would turn them upon all other tribes, the Wichitas forbade Du Tisne to proceed farther. Balked of progress, the explorer returned to the Missouri River and to Kaskaskia.

At about this time there came into New Orleans from the Missouri River country Etienne de Bourgmont, the deserter from his command at Detroit. For thirteen years he had been hiding on the Missouri to escape having his head broken on a wheel for desertion. Just how Bourgmont learned that he no longer was being sought for his crime and that it would be safe to return to the cities of Frenchmen, we are unable to state. We can well understand that since Bienville detested Cadillac, he willingly would condone an offense which Cadillac sought to punish. But it appears that even Cadillac forgave him.

It has been said that Cadillac permitted Bourgmont to escape in the first place out of gratitude, because it was Bourgmont's desertion that resulted in Cadillac returning to the command of Detroit. It is also possible, although there is no evidence to substantiate it, that Cadillac and Bourgmont met on the occasion of the Gascon's expedition to the fabled silver mines of Galena. It is possible that Bourgmont was able to do a valuable service for the governor on that occasion.

Laying conjecture aside, we do know that in 1706

Bourgmont found a safe refuge with the Missouri Indians, that he ranged the country with them and became familiar with the river and the tribes dwelling upon its banks as far as the mouth of the Platte, known to the Pawnees as the Nebraska River. Other woods rangers coming to the country regarded him as their chief, and they lived a wild life with the Indians, with whom most of the woods rangers formed marriage alliances. In their travels on the Missouri, the rangers used *pirogues;* for the frail canoe, which had served the French explorers on other streams, could not live on the raging Missouri, where it might be ripped wide open by a torn tree snag submerged in a sifting sand bar and hidden by the dirty water.

Like the canoe the *pirogue* was an invention of the Indian and was used by him on both the Mississippi and Missouri. It was built of cottonwood logs, hollowed by fire and streamlined by pointing at either end. Two such logs, placed side by side and lashed together, constituted a *pirogue*. Since cottonwood trunks grow straight, tall and thick, logs would be found three and four feet in diameter and as much as seventy-five feet in length. When well seasoned, the cottonwood is not only tough but buoyant. The largest *pirogues* could bear ten or fifteen tons burden. On such vessels was transported the commerce of the Missouri from the day of Bourgmont until after the Louisiana Purchase, a period of a century.

As an outlaw Bourgmont dared not sell furs at New Orleans. He could, however, dispose of them on the same basis as an Indian to licensed traders. In all probability he sold furs to Du Tisne at Kaskaskia.

After Bourgmont learned that Cadillac had been recalled

and that Bienville was governor, he came to New Orleans where he offered his services to the authorities in extending the fur trade of Louisiana. It was at this time that the Spaniards at Santa Fe, learning of the operations of Bourgmont on the Missouri and of the explorations of Du Tisne and La Harpe, dispatched the ill-fated Villazur expedition to drive them out of a region claimed for the Spanish king. As has been related, Villazur and his followers were destroyed by the Pawnees.

Information of this disaster came to Bienville, who obtained a captaincy for Bourgmont and directed him to build a fort on the Missouri to be garrisoned by soldiers of the king. This fort was erected in 1723 near the mouth of the Grande River in the present Missouri and was named Fort Orleans to flatter the king's regent. In 1724 Bourgmont advanced with a king's commission and at the king's expense on a horseback expedition to visit a strange people living "600 leagues" to the west of the Pawnees. A curious letter telling of these people was written from Dauphin Island, situated at the entrance to Mobile Bay, by Sieur Presle.

He stated that they were little people with "large eyes, an inch apart from the nose, dressed like Europeans, always with boots, wearing spurs and some placques on their buskins, very well lodged around a great lake distant from the Pawnees by 600 leagues and always occupied by some beautiful work. One says there is much gold there within that country and some rubies. One believes that there are some Chinese."*

*This translation and all other direct quotations from the original French in this chapter are by Miss Beatrice Paddock for the Wichita City Library.

Whether Presle obtained his information from Bourgmont is not explained, but the letter does reveal the imper-
fect geographic knowledge of that time. Except for the
Spaniards, Europeans knew nothing of the Rocky Mountains which walls eastern America from the Pacific. Likewise the world's knowledge of the North Pacific was
equally hazy; for it was not until 1728, or four years after
Bourgmont's westward march, that Vitus Bering discovered that North America was separated from Asia by a
body of water. When Presle wrote from Dauphin Island,
he was ignorant of the existence of Bering Strait and Bering
Sea and was yet under the influence of geographers who
imagined that a land bridge joined Asia to North America.
Presle probably believed that a man needed only to walk
far enough from New Orleans to arrive at China. The fact
that discoveries of Frenchmen revealed that North America was broader than had been supposed tended to confirm
the land-bridge theory.

Bourgmont's instructions from Bienville, however, con-
tain no hint of the Chinese village where the people had
"eyes an inch apart from the nose." From childhood Bienville had been taught by his father, Charles Le Moyne, that
there was no easy road to China, for it was this same Le
Moyne who had sneered at La Salle's estate and had called
it in derision *La Chine*. Bienville directed Bourgmont to
advance westward until he met the Padoucas—our modern
Comanches. He was to establish peace between the Padoucas and the tribes of the Missouri, invite the Comanches
to trade at Fort Orleans and learn from them all he could
concerning the Spaniards at Santa Fe.

Among Bourgmont's subordinate officers on this expedi-

Early Settlements on the Mississippi and on the Gulf Coast

tion was a young Canadian, Louis St. Ange, who is mentioned here because this was the beginning of his career as one of the useful army officers of Louisiana. He served at Fort Orleans, at Fort Chartres and, after the death of Vincennes, commanded for twenty-eight years at Fort Vincennes. He later commanded for eighteen months at Fort Chartres and was the first acting governor at St. Louis of Upper Louisiana.

On this particular expedition Bourgmont's most valuable subordinate was Sergeant Dubois, whose knowledge of the Indians was second only to that of Bourgmont himself. As a preliminary to the march Bourgmont bought Padouca captives from the Osage and Kansas Indians. This was a wise policy and one often adopted by Frenchmen when moving to visit a new people. Bourgmont could use the captives as interpreters. Further, he could establish friendship by restoring them to their home tribe. Transferring a cargo of the king's gifts from a *pirogue* to horses bought from the Kansas Indians, Bourgmont advanced from the Kansas village situated on the site of the present Doniphan, Kansas, westward with a large convoy of Kansas warriors with their entire families. A thousand Indians were included in this strange exploring expedition, which feasted on the fat of buffalo brought in daily by Indian hunters. On the way Bourgmont fell ill and was forced to return to Fort Orleans. Dubois completed the journey, found the Padoucas, restored the captives to freedom and promised the chiefs that Bourgmont would come later with appropriate gifts.

In October Bourgmont was well enough to return to the plains and to enjoy the Indian summer under cloudless skies in a land where no forests obstruct the view. Following are excerpts from his journal, revealing the enthusiasm of this French explorer as he progressed across what was the greatest game country of the earth:

"October 11—There are quantities of roes, of deer, of turkeys, of buffalo and cows without number.

"October 13—We have seen today more than thirty herds of buffalo and cows; they are so numerous it is impossible to count them. We saw some herds of deer near the same. Our hunters killed as many as they wished and chose the fattest for eating, and others taking the tongues.

"October 14—we have passed quantities of sources of beautiful clear water which formed some brooks and some small rivers."

Bourgmont arrived at the Padouca teepee camp in the Smoky Hill Valley of what is now western Kansas on October 19. After an oration of the type calculated to please savages, he presented them with gifts, some of which were useful and some of which could be used for adorning the faces by painting. In his list of gifts we find the following:

Guns, swords, pickaxes, hatchets, powder, bullets, Limbourg red, Limbourg blue, mirrors, Flemish knives, chemises, scissors, combs, gun flints, worm screws, vermilion awls, beads large and small, brass wire, rings, and vermilion boxes.

He showed the wonders of the musket by riding alongside a buffalo and shooting it dead by aiming in the ear. The Padoucas wildly acclaimed the performance, for no Indian had ever killed a buffalo by shooting it in the head. They had always shot between the ribs, for the skull of the buffalo is so thick that it readily turned arrows and even turned bullets. Eager to show their own prowess, the Padoucas displayed their skill at horsemanship. It was Bourgmont's turn to grow enthusiastic, for the Padoucas were the most skilled horsemen in the world.

Acting as mediator between the Padoucas and the tribes from the Missouri, Bourgmont concluded a peace between them. He invited the Padoucas to bring their buffalo robes to Fort Orleans for trade in exchange for manufactured articles similar to the ones he had given them. Nothing came of the invitation, for after the return of the Frenchmen to Fort Orleans, war again broke out between the Indians of the plains and those living along the Missouri. In this war, the Missouri River Tribes, armed with French muskets, had all of the advantage.

Bourgmont returned to France in 1725, taking with him the daughter of a Missouri chief and a train of eight feathered warriors. Sergeant Dubois accompanied him on his voyage and on the way across the Atlantic improved the time by wooing the Missouri maid. Bourgmont approved the match, and they were engaged to be married.

The arrival of the Indians provided a diversion for the French nobility, whose time was devoted to leisure and entertainment. Bourgmont showed not only that he knew the art of winning the hearts of simple red men, but that he could win the favor of King Louis XV himself. Selecting a royal hunting park, stocked with wild game animals, Bourgmont staged the first wild west show. He had his Indian followers strip to breech clouts. He mounted them upon fleet ponies and had them demonstrate the buffalo chase by shooting down stags with bows and arrows. The nobles acclaimed the show and the king thought that this former deserter was a capital fellow.

Bourgmont, however, had to share the spotlight with the daughter of the Missouri chief, whom the ladies of the court styled "The Princess of the Missouris." This illiterate girl has the distinction of being the first Missouri lady to be presented at court. Parties were given in her honor and the women showered her with gifts when they learned that she was to marry Sergeant Dubois. The king, upon learning of the engagement, promoted the sergeant to the rank of captain so that he might be eligible as consort for a princess. She was baptized in the cathedral, after which the king and queen and the men and ladies of the court attended her wedding.

If any other Missouri girl has ever had a grander wedding, it has not come to our attention. Her girlhood had been spent in a dirt-floored wigwam. She was married in a lavishly adorned cathedral. In her childhood the only music she knew was the rattle of a gourd, the beat of the tom-tom and the plaintive strains of the Indian wood flute. At her wedding the bishop's organist played her bridal march on as perfect an organ as the skilled artisans of that day could contrive. In her home village the people wore hides of buffalo, sometimes adorning their dress with colored stones or the quills of porcupines. Her wedding guests came in silks and satins embossed with gold and with ropes of pearls about their necks and with jewelled bracelets and rings.

Dubois returned to the Missouri after the wedding. He and his bride lived for a time at Fort Chartres and at Fort Orleans. He escorted the eight Indians back to their home where as long as they lived they told incredulous listeners of the marvellous splendor of the king of the Frenchmen.

Bourgmont, having won the favor of the king, remained in Paris. The king granted him a title of nobility as a reward for his explorations. Endowed with the title and famed for his exploits, he entered fashionable society. He married a widow and the rest of his life was spent in luxury and ease.

While these three official explorers sent out by Bienville advanced far on the plains, it remained for eight Canadians, strangers to the west, to go farther than any of them. In some roundabout way the information came to Canada that the Spanish city of Santa Fe was so rich in silver that men wore silver buttons on their trousers and women wore solid silver heels on their slippers. It even was said that rich merchants put silver tires on the wooden wheels of their *carritas* and that silver was cheaper than iron.

Accordingly Pierre and Paul Mallet, brothers, and six others determined to run the risk of being punished for entering Spanish territory. The boldness of the Mallet brothers and of their six companions is such that we will record the names of all of them. The six were Philippe Robitaille, Louis Moreau, Michael Beleau, Joseph Bellecourt and Manuel Gallien, natives of Canada, and Jean David, native of France. They bought a supply of trade goods, voyaged by way of the St. Lawrence, the Great Lakes and the Illinois River in canoes, transshipped to a *pirogue* to ascend the Missouri and came to the Nebraska River, the name of which they changed to the Platte, because they said it was shallow like a plate.

They bought horses from the Pawnees and from them obtained instructions regarding the route to Santa Fe. On the way southwestward across the plains, they lost a part of their merchandise while crossing the Smoky Hill River at flood time, but aside from that disaster, they encountered no difficulties which they thought worthy of mention. They must have suffered thirst on the long marches between streams, yet the novelty of travelling where none of their friends had ever travelled before was so pleasurable that they never complained.

They had a spirit-stirring experience early in July when the snow-capped Spanish peaks, which the Pawnees told them stood just north of Taos, greeted their wondering eyes. At last Frenchmen had come the entire distance across the plains to the snowy, shining mountains of whose existence Jolliet and La Salle had never dreamed. In later years other Frenchmen coming to those peaks named them *Les Montagnes Roches*, which we have translated into the Rocky Mountains, so called because their stony, naked peaks pierce the sky above timber line in contrast to the Alleghenies, decked in forests to their highest ridges.

So true was the adherence of the Mallet brothers to the course laid down by the Pawnees that it required only six weeks from the time they left the mouth of the Platte until they had arrived at Taos. Their departure from the Platte's mouth was June 2, 1739. They were at Taos on July 15. This was indeed rapid going when we consider the delays and hardships suffered by Santa Fe traders of a later century. Not only did the Mallets travel without loss of time, they made their journey without incurring hostile Indian attacks such as American traders were to suffer. Truly the Frenchman had the knack of making friends with his red brother.

The Mallets found Santa Fe a city of 600 Spanish and half-breed families and so far removed from the rest of New Spain that it was meagerly supplied with merchandise from the outside world only once a year by a mule caravan, which had to pass over an Apache-infested trail from Chihuahua. So scarce were articles of manufacture that common cotton cloth sold for three dollars a yard and a man would gladly strip the silver buttons from his breeches to trade them for a knife. In spite of Spanish laws forbidding foreign trade, the people welcomed the Frenchmen as brothers and paid for their merchandise in shining metal at prices ten times those prevailing in Canada.

The governor was eager to have the Mallet brothers come every year with merchandise from Canada. He wrote to the viceroy at Mexico City, asking for permission to make Santa Fe a port of entry so that the goods might be received legally. The request was carried south by muleback over a highway on which travellers today make the journey in a motor car in a few days, but it was nine months before the answer came back by mule train from the viceroy. In the meantime the homes of Santa Fe were thrown open to the visitors. Parties and dances were given in their honor. Moreau fell in love with a Spanish *señorita* and married her while the Frenchmen awaited the reply from Mexico. In the spring of 1740 the long-expected reply came. The governor, seated at his desk in the one-story palace of the governors, summoned the Mallet brothers to him.

"I am sorry," he said in Spanish, "but his excellency, the viceroy, wishes you to get out of New Mexico as quickly as possible and never to return. As for Moreau, since he has married one of us and is willing to become a subject of our king, he may remain."

The seven Frenchmen took leave of the people who had treated them so kindly, bade farewell to Moreau, and rode eastward through Glorieta Pass to the old mission of Pecos and then turned northeastward. They took note of two rivers, one of which the Spaniards called the Colorado and the other the Cimarron. The name Colorado was given the stream because the Spaniards believed it to be the head-water of the Red. The names Red, *Rouge* and *Colorado* mean the same thing, depending on whether we are speaking in English, French or Spanish. The Mallets doubted that it was a branch of the Red, but thought that possibly it was a tributary of the Arkansas. It was not until seventy-nine years later that Stephen H. Long, American army officer, discovered that the Mallets were correct.

Passing the headsprings of the Cimarron, the Frenchmen ascended Raton Pass, a region then famed for its numerous Rocky Mountain sheep. Coming to the Purgatory River, they followed it to the site of the present Las Animas, Colorado, where the Purgatory empties into a larger stream, which the Spaniards called Rio Napesi. Since it was larger than any other rivers on the plains, the Mallets concluded that it must be the Arkansas and resolved to explore it to its junction with the Mississippi. Thereupon Bellecourt, Gallien and David protested. They wished to return to the Missouri River by the shortest route and go to their homes in Canada. Robitaille and Beleau, however, agreed to go with the Mallets. Consequently the party broke company on the high, treeless plains in a region where in later years Americans dared to venture only in large companies for mutual protection from Indians. The three returned to the Missouri River and to Canada without any serious incident.

The other four rode horseback along the banks of the river until they arrived near the present Oklahoma-Kansas line, where they found slippery-elm trees, from the bark of which they fashioned canoes. Abandoning their horses on the bank, they glided downstream. In time they came to the point where the Cimarron entered the Arkansas and identified it correctly. Later they came to the junction with the river which the Spaniards mistakenly called the Colorado. Once more they identified it correctly.

Later Frenchmen named this river the Canadian, probably in honor of the four Canadians who discovered it, but possibly in honor of some other Canadians. Some gazeteers tell us that the Canadian is so named from a Spanish word, *"Canada,"* meaning canyon. This is incorrect. The Spaniards always called the river *El Colorado*, a name by which it was known in New Mexico until after the United States took possession of that country. On the other hand the French of Louisiana called it the Canadian and passed on that name to Lieutenant James Wilkinson, who visited it in 1806 and was the first American army officer to report it to American authorities.

We cannot be certain that the river was named for the Mallets, for a group of Canadian hunters from Arkansas Post was a short distance below the river hunting when the Mallet brothers came by in their elm-bark canoes. The two parties hailed each other and joined company. The hunters assured the brothers that they were on the Arkansas. All proceeded together to Arkansas Post.

The unexpected appearance of the Mallets at the post aroused great interest, for these four men had explored a wider region than either Jolliet or La Salle. They brought to Louisiana the first accurate information concerning the extent of the Great Plains. They were the first to return across the plains from the rugged peaks of the Rockies. They had completed the exploration from the Rockies to the Mississippi of the third longest river of North America. What stories these travellers could tell! The men of Arkansas Post urged them to make themselves at home. Evidently they enjoyed their welcome, for they remained there hunting, trapping and fishing until the next year, when in March they rode down to New Orleans with the spring fur cargo.

There they reported to Bienville the story of their adventures. This decided him to send one of his own officers in an attempt to open trade. For this mission he appointed Andre de Bruyere, while the Mallets, Robitaille and Beleau agreed to accompany him as guides. We are unable to state whether Bienville intended to try to smuggle merchandise into Santa Fe or whether he thought Bruyere would succeed where the Mallets had failed. We do know that he filled a *pirogue* with merchandise such as was desired by the New Mexicans and sent the party up the Mississippi and Arkansas until it arrived at the Canadian. Here the Mallets declared they were certain that they were almost in the same latitude as Santa Fe and that they believed they could come almost to the Spanish city by ascending the branch stream.

At this juncture Bruyere conferred the name of St. Andre upon the Canadian River in honor of himself and his patron saint. The party proceeded by *pirogue* only a few days before Bruyere noted that while the river is as wide as the Mississippi in some places, it is often only an inch deep, due to the fact that like many other western streams much of the water flows under the sand. Soon the *pirogue* was grounded. Thereupon the Mallets recommended that they buy horses from the Osages and pack their merchandise to Santa Fe. Bruyere was unused to horses and vetoed the plan. Apparently he feared that his uniform would become wrinkled if carried in a pack. The

Mallets went so far as to offer to carry it in a chest so that it could be folded flat and be in perfect condition when Bruyere was ready to wear it in Santa Fe. Even then the commander declined to ride a horse. An entire winter was lost while the party waited an expected spring rise, which did not come. At last Bruyere abandoned the project, laid the blame for failure upon the Mallets and returned to New Orleans. The French pioneers soon forgot that the river ever had been called the St. Andre. To this day it is called the Canadian. The Mallets returned to Canada and disappeared from Louisiana history.

But the stories they told of Santa Fe lived on and fired the minds of woods rangers with a desire to see the city with its silver and its hospitable people. In succeeding years the lure of Santa Fe drew several parties to the Santa Fe Road. Most of the authors of books on the Santa Fe Trail have ignored these Frenchmen of the trail, despite the fact that they inspired later Americans to rediscover the way to the Spanish city. One reason so little credit is given to the Frenchmen is that most of them could neither read nor write and have left us no record. Even those who could write did not dare do so, for they were unlicensed woods rangers, entering Indian country without permit. Spanish records at Santa Fe give us the best information regarding them.

Three deserters from Arkansas Post arrived in Taos in 1749. Spanish records list them as Luis Febre, Pedro Satren and Joseph Riballo. None of the three could read or write and the spelling of their names is necessarily Spanish. Their depositions taken by Santa Fe authorities reveal that they ascended the Arkansas to a Wichita Indian village, then visited the Comanches, and finally accompanied the Comanches to the Taos fair. They had no difficulty in disposing of the few articles they had brought to trade, and the authorities permitted them to depart with the Comanches.

The following year there came Pedro Sandoval of New Orleans, who travelled by way of Arkansas Post and the Wichita village where, according to the Spanish records, he reported that there was a French trading post with a French flag flying. The location of this village and post cannot be given with certainty; but a few years ago Joseph Thoburn, then curator of the Oklahoma Historical Society, directed the excavation of an old French trading post south of the Oklahoma-Kansas line near the banks of the Arkansas. This ruin may have been the post described by Sandoval. At the Wichita village Sandoval met two French deserters, with whom he travelled to Santa Fe. The three were hospitably received, permitted to trade their possessions and allowed to return to Louisiana.

A different fate met Jean Chapuis and Luis Feuilli, who came overland from the Kansas village on the Missouri, following very nearly what later became the Santa Fe route of history. They brought a considerable quantity of trade goods to Pecos. No doubt they intended to smuggle the goods to the people without reporting to the authorities, for they lingered at Pecos. The arrival of so many different parties of Frenchmen alarmed the Spanish authorities, who confiscated their goods and sent them to prison at Mexico City. At intervals others passed over the trail until the Louisiana Purchase made Louisiana a part of the United States, and trade over the Santa Fe Trail became regularly established.

While various horseback expeditions were plodding across the Southwestern Plains, the French of Canada were advancing over another route into the Northwest. Among these westward-travelling men were Pierre de la Verendrye and his three sons. The elder Verendrye, while yet a boy, became ambitious to explore the West. He was born in Three Rivers where old men and women told him of the exploits of Radisson and Chouart. War, however, prevented him from doing what he desired. While little more than a boy, he was fighting the English in New England. Later he fought in Newfoundland, whence he was transferred to Europe. Nine times he was wounded on European battlefields and finally was sent home to die. Instead of dying, he found employment with the Montreal fur monopoly and went to a far western trading post as a clerk.

He was promoted from time to time and became one of the well-known traders of the West. At length he proposed a plan for extending the French fur trade northward toward Hudson Bay. The plan was accepted and with his three elder sons, eighteen, seventeen and sixteen years old, he built trading forts on Rainy River, Lake of the Woods and Lake Winnipeg. This latter post brought to the French trade which formerly had gone to the English of Hudson Bay.

In 1739, the same year in which the Mallets discovered a trail to Santa Fe, Verendrye and one of his sons explored an overland route to the Mandan Indian village on the Missouri River fifty miles above the present Bismarck, North Dakota. In 1742 two of his sons, Pierre and Francis, rode horseback from the Mandan village through the present Montana and Wyoming and explored the Yellowstone, the

Big Horn and the Powder Rivers. They spent the next winter with the Crow and Bow Indians west of the Big Horn range and in the spring came to the Rocky Mountains. They returned to the Mandan village in 1743.*

Other Frenchmen followed the Verendrye trail and a regular trade grew up between the Indians of the Upper Missouri and Canada.

Farther north the Verendryes discovered the Assiniboine and Saskatchewan rivers and explored the plains area of Canada to the foot of the Rockies. They built a trading post near the present Calgary, Alberta.

While the Verendryes explored a large part of the northwestern plains country and brought large supplies of furs to Montreal, their masters never appreciated their services. Verendrye was interested in finding a short route to China and that annoyed the merchants. He never was paid adequately for his services. He died in 1750. Five years later came the French and Indian War, which ended explorations of his sons. During their time on the western lakes and prairies, the Verendryes explored a region greater than the entire area occupied by the English in all the thirteen colonies with Newfoundland and the Hudson Bay region added.

*In this account we have followed the generally accepted belief that the Verendryes visited the Rockies. Some authorities believe they ventured only to the Black Hills. See Orin G. Libby, *Some Verendrye Enigmas* in *Mississippi Valley Historical Review*, Sept., 1916, pp. 143–160; Dec., 1916, pp. 369–399, who favors this latter viewpoint.

CHAPTER XIV

THE WAR FOR BEAVER

WHILE Frenchmen were threading every shadow-flecked stream from the Alleghenies to the Plains and riding their sun-splashed way over the Plains to the Rockies, Englishmen were building thirteen agricultural colonies upon the Atlantic seaboard. Unlike the French, the English had no vast waterways like the St. Lawrence or the Mississippi to invite adventurers into the heart of the continent. Instead, the Indian-infested Alleghenies walled them from the West. The Indians, who loved the brotherly French, were a menace to westward exploration of the English, whose pride of race restrained most Englishmen from marrying Indian women and accepting Indian men as brothers.

All this tended to keep the English colonist at home where he tilled his crops. More than a century elapsed after the first English settlement in 1607 before English frontiersmen had penetrated far enough inland to discover the headwaters of the Ohio. When they did cross the mountains to the Ohio Valley in the present Pennsylvania, they encountered French traders, who had been trafficking for years with the Indians and harvesting a fortune in beaver. This roused the English to remember long-neglected claims. The Virginians, most aggressive of the English colonists, recalled that the British royal grant gave their colony all territory west and northwest from the Atlantic to the Pacific. The Pennsylvanians also recalled that they too had been granted land to the westward. The New Yorkers remembered that they had bought the West from the Iroquois.

There was a flaw in all of their titles, for none of the colonies had occupied the land given them. Not until one hundred and nine years after the first Virginia settlement did the westward-looking Governor Alexander Spotswood organize a horseback party of fifty Virginians to cross the Blue Ridge, which he firmly believed to be the continental divide. On that horseback march he discovered the Shenandoah, named it the Euphrates and reported it as flowing into Lake Erie. It was twenty years after Spotswood's discoveries before Colonel William Mayo explored the Potomac to its headsprings, passed over the Alleghenies and came to the Monongahela, a tributary of the Ohio. Following Mayo came traders and trappers. Some daring Virginians even travelled down the Ohio as far as the Mississippi.

In comparing the Virginians with the French explorers, we find that in 1716, when Spotswood was discovering the Shenandoah, St. Denis was crossing the Texas plains a second time and Bourgmont was living with the Missouris. When Mayo was discovering the Monongahela in 1736, Vincennes had completed his career in the Ohio Valley and was dying in the Chickasaw campaign. When the Virginians were organizing the Ohio Company in 1749 with a view of taking possession of the Ohio Valley, the French

MODES OF TRAVEL

The lower picture shows the portaging of a birch-bark canoe, and the upper one depicts snowshoe travel, important factors in the fur trade.

A NEW ANIMAL

This quaint conception of the North American bison appeared originally in Hen
pin's *A New Discovery of a Vast Country in America*. It was often reprinted

had been to Santa Fe and were trading with the Mandans on the Upper Missouri.

Turning to the explorations of the Pennsylvanians, we find that in 1718 Governor Keith had learned from Pennsylvania traders that the Indians of the mountains were trading with the French on the Ohio, which La Salle had explored fifty years before.

The New Yorkers had engaged in the beaver trade with the Indians more systematically than had the Virginians or Pennsylvanians, but even the New Yorkers depended largely on furs brought to them by the Iroquois. Fort Oswego, the farthest west outpost of the New Yorkers, built in 1727, was yet a long way from Lake Erie, where the French had been trading since 1673.

The English had one claim, however, more potent than exploration or occupation. That claim was a tide of humanity rising from the Atlantic seaboard and sweeping inland mile by mile as new-born sons grew to manhood and took up lands to the west of the farms of their fathers. As this tide of white people rose, it swept the Indians backward out of the valleys up the slopes of the mountains and through the Allegheny passes into the Ohio Valley.

Contrary to popular belief, the English made a practice of buying from the Indians the lands they coveted. The idea of buying land did not originate with William Penn, who did not buy from the Indians until 1682. Before Penn was born, Roger Williams had bought land from the Indians of Rhode Island; Lord Baltimore from the Indians of Maryland; the Dutch from the Indians of New York; the Hartford settlers from the Indians of Connecticut. It is true that the poor Indian never understood the significance of a land sale. He always regretted his bargains later, but the English drove him out. Since the English did not live with the Indians and invariably drove them farther west, they were able to build solid settlements of white men. Single colonies of Englishmen therefore were more populous than all of New France.

By the year 1754 approximately 1,000,000 people were living in the English colonies. This was ten times the number of the French, who counted about 70,000 on the St. Lawrence and 30,000 more scattered about the Great Lakes, along the rivers and south to Mobile and New Orleans. Unlike the English, the French had no frontier, but lived in settlements in the midst of the Indian country. In some ways this was a weakness, but it also was a source of strength, for the French could call upon their Indian neighbors in time of war, while the English could depend on no Indian allies with the exception of the Iroquois and sometimes on the Chickasaws.

As the English trappers and traders began trickling through the mountain passes, the governor of Canada ordered the building of a chain of forts from Lake Erie south to the Ohio. At the present Erie, Pennsylvania, his men built Fort Presque Isle. Farther south on French Creek they raised the bastions of Fort Le Bœuf. Still farther south on the Allegheny River they erected Fort Venango. Trappers carried news of these operations back over the mountains to the settlements, causing Governor Robert Dinwiddie of Virginia to dispatch George Washington to warn the French to withdraw. Although Washington was but twenty-one, the governor chose him rather than an older man, because no older man in Virginia had the combination of

qualities possessed by him. He was a member of a distinguished Virginia family and from childhood had been
taught to observe the rules of common courtesy. Not only
was he polite, circumstances had made him a frontiersman.
Owing to the death of his father, he had been thrown on
his own resources and from the age of sixteen had made his
own way as a land surveyor, much of the time in the Shenandoah Valley, where he had associated with Indians and
frontiersmen and had become inured to wilderness hardships.

Washington knew how to make a comfortable bed in a
snow drift. He knew how to track a deer and kill it and
roast it over a fire built of wet wood on a rainy day. He was
six feet two inches in height, of perfect athletic build, the
champion broad jumper of his colony and the best horse-
man in Virginia. He had an unerring sense of direction and
could travel through trackless forests and twisting mountain ravines without losing his way. What better man could
the governor find for his mission?

Across the Alleghenies rode Washington accompanied
by Christopher Gist and a few other rough frontiersmen.
They proceeded northwestward down the Monongahela
to where it unites with the Allegheny to form the Ohio.
Today the traveller can follow Washington's trail in the
month of December in an enclosed car. Upon arriving at
the forks of the Ohio he can dine in a cafe and sleep in a
luxurious hotel, for the city of Pittsburgh rises on that spot.
But when Washington rode horseback to the site of Pittsburgh, there was no resting place except the dreary forest
through the branches of which pelted the snow of a mid-
December storm.

Washington took note of the fact that this inhospitable wilderness spot was a strategic site for a fort. A few cannon placed in the angle of the rivers could control the passage of boats of the Ohio, the Allegheny and the Monongahela.

Several days later the party came to Fort Venango, learned that the commandant of the region was at Le Bœuf, rode to that fort and presented the message from Governor Dinwiddie. The commandant was courteous to Washington. He gave the Virginians comfortable quarters, had them dry their clothing before the fire, fed them well and entertained them for three days while they rested for their return journey. But despite his courtesy, he sent word back to Dinwiddie that the French had come to the Ohio first and were determined to remain. Washington further believed that the French officer sent an Indian after him to murder him.

On the way home, a murderous Indian raised his musket and fired at Washington at close range. The bullet whizzed by Washington's face. So near was the Indian that Gist was able to capture him. Gist wished to kill the man, but Washington spared his life and let him go with a warning.

Upon arriving in Virginia, the young messenger reported to the governor and recommended the building of a fort at the forks of the Ohio. Dinwiddie accordingly sent forty men under Captain William Trent to build the fort. Several weeks after Trent had gone, Dinwiddie dispatched Washington with a second small force to follow him. The folly of not sending both parties together so that they could support each other soon became apparent. Woods rangers swarmed down the Allegheny from Venango and Le Bœuf in canoes, surrounded the forty Virginians at the fort and

forced them to surrender. Then advancing up the Monongahela, they met Washington. After two forest skirmishes
in which lives were lost on both sides, they secured the surrender of Washington also. Since England and France were
not at war, the French released both parties and sent them
back to Virginia.

As soon as news of this wilderness engagement reached
London and Paris, declarations of war were promptly
made. It was to be the fourth war between England and
France since the outbreak of King William's War in 1689.
It began as a war for the Ohio but spread until it became a
titanic struggle for the possession of North America and
even for the possession of India.

Having ousted the Virginians, the French examined the
forks of the Ohio, noted the point Washington had selected
for a fort and there began the erection of a fort of their
own. They built it of square-hewn logs. At each corner
they erected a bastion and equipped each bastion with cannon. One side of the fort was washed by the Allegheny,
the other side by the Monongahela. On the third side of a
triangle, they dug a deep ditch extending from one river
to the other. The ditch too was filled with water and was
spanned by a drawbridge. The French named it Fort Duquesne in honor of the governor of Canada.

We cannot go into the details of the war, which the Virginians called the French and Indian War; but we will view
Braddock's ill-fated campaign of 1755, for it so well reveals the support the French received from the Indians.

General Edward Braddock, a British general, moved
west from the Virginia-Maryland frontier across the mountains and down the Monongahela in the summer of 1755 to

attack Fort Duquesne. He cut a road as he advanced to provide a passageway for cannon and for a wagon train. On this advance he adhered to correct European military tactics. Washington and other colonial officers described to him the American way of fighting with swift-moving troops, who could subsist by hunting. But Braddock could not move his army in that fashion. His men, many of them London boys, did not even know how to roast a deer, let alone follow his track and kill him. Had Braddock ordered his men to feed themselves in the wilderness as Washington did in the subsequent Indian campaigns, they would have starved to death without even coming up to an enemy. The only way that Braddock could move his army was by taking along a wagon-train of food, and that meant that the army could advance only a few miles a day.

While Braddock was cutting the road, Pierre de Contrecœur, commandant at Fort Duquesne, had abundant time to dispatch runners to Niagara to bring on the Indians and woods rangers mobilized there. They moved down to Duquesne, and soon 700 warriors were pitching their tee-pees about the fort or were living in half-faced camps. Never again will America see such an assemblage. And what a tribute their presence paid to the brotherhood between the Indians and the French!

There came Algonquins from the St. Lawrence, Abenakis from the forests of Maine; Miamis, Kickapoos and Mascoutins led by Francis Lignery; Chippewas, Ojibwas, Pottawatomies, Hurons and Ottawas from Green Bay and Mackinac headed by Charles Langlande, a half-breed Ottawa; more Ottawas and Hurons from Detroit following their own chief, Pontiac; Illinois and Kaskaskias from the

Mississippi; and mounted tribesmen from beyond the Missouri—Otoes, Kansas and Osages—commanded by the youthful Pawhuska, in whose honor Pawhuska, Oklahoma, is named and whose fame rests largely on the fact that his daughter married a Kaw Indian chief and became the great-grandmother of Charles Curtis, who became vice-president of the United States. The forest Indians, who had never owned a horse, gazed in amazement and envy as their prairie allies performed daredevil feats of horsemanship.

Besides the Indians Contrecœur had a handful of regular soldiers and some woods rangers. He sent out scouts, both Indian and white. They crept through the forest, watched the movement of Braddock's army from the concealment of thickets, captured a few British soldiers for torture and brought back one captive alive. This man, James Smith, after running the gauntlet, was kept a prisoner at Fort Duquesne, and he has left us a description of what happened there. The scouts were worse than useless. As they observed the British army, they were moved to fear and admiration.

The British were in bright scarlet uniforms, while the Virginians were in drab blue. The Virginia uniforms were more suitable for concealment in the forest, but as the Indians and woods rangers saw the brilliant uniforms of the British, heard the blare of their bands and viewed the floating flags and guidons, they slunk back to their camps to report that the British were invincible.

Nearer and nearer to Fort Duquesne the British advanced as they cut a roadway twelve feet wide. After many weeks they were only seven miles from the fort, and on July 7 they went into camp beside the Monongahela River, planning to cross it in the morning. Contrecœur was so certain of defeat that he was deliberating on whether to destroy Fort Duquesne or to surrender it. One man and one alone, Captain Lienard de Beaujeu, believed the British could be beaten. On that July seventh, he begged for permission to attack the British on the following day as they would be hampered at the crossing of the Monongahela. Contrecœur had little hope of success, but he consented to the plan as worth trying. He ordered the woods rangers and the regular soldiers to be ready to march in battle array at eight o'clock the next morning.

The Indians, however, obeyed no commands except those agreed upon after debate. Beaujeu therefore called them into council. Although he was a native of Montreal and had had much experience with the Indians, he could not stir them that night to a willingness to risk a battle. Late at night the council broke up and the Indians slept. Beaujeu spent a restless night. Before breakfast he called the warriors to another council. Time, he knew, was precious. Already the English were crossing the river, and unless the French and Indians marched promptly the opportunity of fighting them at the ford would be lost.

Beaujeu told his hearers that battles are not won by brilliancy of scarlet, gilt of epaulets, blare of trumpets, roll of drums, shine of bayonets and rumble of wagons. He appealed to their greed by declaring that the advancing army offered great opportunity for plunder. He asked if they would not like to wear those brilliant scarlet coats with braided gilt. He insisted that all they needed to do to become horsemen like Pawhuska's Osages was to kill the British and take their horses. The prospect of plunder had its effect. A few of the boldest of the warriors offered to go if Beaujeu would provide them with powder and lead. But one cautious forest orator quenched their ardor. Because of the sultry heat of the July morning he came stark naked to the council. Rising in his place he shouted to Beaujeu:

"Do you want to die, father, and sacrifice us besides?"*

Grunts of accordance greeted the words, and the warriors who had responded to the lure of plunder laid down their weapons again. At this juncture Beaujeu flung back:

"I am determined to meet the English. What, will you let your father go alone?"*

It proved to be the right appeal given at the right time. According to James Smith, watching from the fort, the camp was converted into a frenzy of activity. Contrecœur ordered his men to roll barrels of ammunition from the fort, and as the heads of the barrels were knocked in, the Indians crowded around to fill their powder horns and bullet pouches.

Beaujeu, seeing that he had succeeded, hurried to the priest in the fort's chapel, quickly confessed his sins and took the sacrament. Then he sped back to take command.

What a strange army he led that day to fight the disciplined ranks of the splendid Braddock! He stalked at the head, clad in fringed buckskins and with nothing to indicate his rank except his officer's hat and a silver gorget at his throat. Down the forest aisle moved 36 French officers, 72 uniformed regulars, 146 woods rangers and 637 Indians —891 in all. They straggled like a rabble, the Indians fol-

*Reprinted from Francis Parkman's *Montcalm and Wolfe* by permission of the publishers, Little, Brown & Company.

lowing their chiefs and the white men about their officers.
Just two leagues away were more than 1500 scarlet- and
blue-clad men in gorgeous array. In the van rode Captain
Thomas Gage, later to command a British army in the
American Revolution. Guiding Gage were six blue-clad
Virginia horsemen. Some authors have called the battle an
ambuscade. It was nothing of the kind. Braddock had organized his army correctly according to European usage.
He had an advance guard and flankers on both sides of the
army in the woods. The six alert Virginians saw the enemy
the moment that Beaujeu sighted them.

Since the Virginians were expecting an attack, they were
not in the least surprised. The one surprised was Beaujeu.
He had hoped to fight the British at the crossing of the
Monongahela, but the delay in persuading the Indians had
cost him much time, and Braddock had accomplished the
crossing more quickly than had been thought possible. By
the time of Beaujeu's arrival, the entire army had crossed
the river. Beaujeu had to form a new plan of battle on the
instant. Only his complete knowledge of the lay of the
ground enabled him to proceed at all.

Turning about, he took off his hat, the agreed signal for
his men to spread out on either side of the enemy behind
the cover of the trees and lash him with a cross fire. Those
unfamiliar with Beaujeu's plan may wonder why he divided
his force in the presence of a more numerous enemy. He
did so to prevent the British from seeking protection of the
trees, for while a man could protect himself by a tree from
fire in one direction, he would yet be exposed to the cross
fire from the rear. As the narrative of the battle unfolds,
we shall learn that Beaujeu did not need to avail himself of

a fire from the rear, but he could not foresee that Braddock abhorred the idea of fighting under cover.

The battle began simultaneously on both sides, the French and Indians firing at will, the British firing under command. Gage wheeled his advance column into perfect alignment and shouted orders. A sharp volley barked from the British muskets. Bullets screamed through the forest glades and thudded against the trees.

"Reload!" cried Gage. "Ready! Aim! Fire!"

A second burst of flame flashed from the muskets and again bullets whistled through the leaves. Beaujeu darted from one group of men to another, urging them all to keep cover and telling them to note that the British were making a wonderful noise but doing no real damage. Beaujeu alone exposed himself. Success required that he continue darting from group to group to hearten his men. Unfortunately the third British volley found him exposed as he was crossing the enemy's front. He tripped to the ground and lay still. Faithful Indians recovered his body and found that he was dead.

Panic spread through the ranks. A majority of the woods rangers and Indians, except those near the officers, fled toward Fort Duquesne, howling to each other that Beaujeu was a fool and that all was lost. Not more than 200 remained to oppose the splendid Braddock.

Victory was in the hands of the British. The 300 Virginia bluecoats knew the art of Indian warfare, and despite their exposure to cross fire could have disposed of the 200 men remaining. As the fight opened, the Virginians scurried to the shelter of the trees to fight frontier fashion. This act of mere common sense shocked Braddock and his offi-

cers, who had been schooled in Europe to regard a soldier
as a coward unless he let himself be a fair mark. Consequently he dashed among the colonial troops and beat them
away from the trees by striking them with the flat of his
sword. Other British officers followed his example. The
bewildered Virginians were completely at a loss to know
what to do.

Dumas, Langlande and Lignery, who were now left in
command of the French and Indians, watched the British
officers in amazement. Langlande led his Green Bay and
Mackinac followers along the British line until he came to
a twisting ravine, the banks of which formed a breastwork
for his men. By following the ravine he was able to come
within a short distance of the enemy, where his men poured
in a raking fire at close range. Braddock ordered up cannon
to clear the ravine, but the cannon balls harmed only the
branches of the trees.

Gradually the Indians and woods rangers gained a contempt for the volleys and the cannonade. Slowly they
loaded, carefully they aimed, grimly they noted that almost
every shot brought down a redcoat. The British performed
with the discipline and coolness of men on parade. They
shouted "God save the king," and fell with the shout on
their lips.

For an hour the British stood fast. Two hours later found
the scarlet and blue column torn and bleeding. The Indians
and woods rangers who had scattered at the opening volley
now began to return and to steal among the trees on either
side of the British lines, fighting in independent units without command and picking off the enemy at will. The poor
British complained that they could not even see the enemy.

BEAUJEU AT THE BATTLE OF THE MONONGAHELA

He is lifting his hat as the signal for his French and Indian followers to spread
out on both sides of Braddock's army and rake the British with a cross fire.

Zolnay's statue on the St. Louis City Hall Square.
Photo by courtesy of Frank W. Taylor.

PIERRE LACLEDE

He founded St. Louis, the last of the cities built by the
French fur traders.

At the end of three hours Braddock realized that defeat was inevitable and ordered a retrograde movement. The retreat had just begun when Braddock fell from his horse wounded. He begged to be left to die on the field, but Washington ordered that he be carried away in a wagon. He lived for three days. Washington took command of the Virginians in person and protected the retreat of the demoralized army. The British officers, who had cursed the cowardly Virginians at the outset of the battle, were too busy in their retreat to molest Washington as he and his men took to the trees as they fell back before the allies in the forest.

Had the Indians rushed in, there is not the slightest doubt that they could have destroyed the remnant of Braddock's army as effectively as the Pawnees had annihilated Villazur's Spaniards on the plains thirty-five years before. They could have closed Washington's career on the Monongahela had they only chosen to do so. But their minds were filled with what Beaujeu had told them of plunder. They wanted their share of scarlet coats and blond scalps. They made no effort to follow and kill the British to the last man. Dumas and Langlande urged their followers to continue the battle, but their urging was in vain. And so Washington did not die with Braddock and so he was allowed to escape and live to become the father of his country.

Of Braddock's total force of 1460 men and 86 officers, 980 enlisted men and 43 officers lay dead. French losses were 5 Canadians, 4 French regulars, 27 Indians and 7 officers.

We have evidence that the Indians prized the plunder

they took that afternoon. Eight years later, a Captain Morris of the British army met a Maumee chief in a village in the present Ohio, mounted on a horse taken from the Braddock field. He also met an Indian carrying a copy of Shakespeare taken that day from the kit of one of the officers.

Fifty-one years after Braddock's disaster, Zebulon Montgomery Pike, on his exploration of the Great Plains, stopped at an Osage village to visit Pawhuska, then an old man. In Pawhuska's lodge Pike found a scarlet coat and a blond scalp, which the old chief said he had taken that sultry July afternoon in 1755 on the Monongahela.

We will not go into the succeeding campaigns of the Beaver War. We will mention that Washington and his men were forced to fight for years to defend the frontier from the raids of Indians. But in the end William Pitt, the British prime minister, reorganized the British army. He sent Wolfe and Forbes and Bouquet and Amherst and others to take the place of Braddock. His armies drove the French out of India. In America they captured Quebec and Montreal. An army finally marched back to Fort Duquesne and took it. To Washington was given the pleasure of raising the British standard over that thrice-contested forest citadel, the name of which was changed to Fort Pitt in honor of the prime minister, and it is from Fort Pitt that we have derived the name of Pittsburgh.

The French were overwhelmed in the end on every front. When peace was concluded in 1763, England acquired Canada and all of Louisiana east of the Mississippi with the exception of New Orleans. Spain had been an ally of France in the war, and she demanded pay for her losses.

To reimburse her, France transferred to her New Orleans and that part of Louisiana west of the Mississippi. New France was no more.

Among those to mourn at the death of New France was Bienville. To him fell the sad lot of seeing his native Canada fall a prey to the British and his beloved Louisiana pass from under the French flag to that of the nation against whose aggression he had successfully defended the colony through forty-three years. Bienville died in Paris in 1768, a lonely, childless man of eighty-seven years.

CHAPTER XV

THE FRENCH AT ST. LOUIS

THE defeat of France in the Beaver War ended her authority in the new world, but her spirit flamed from St. Louis, a trading post founded by Pierre Laclede, a native of France, who came to America in the year that saw Beaujeu and Braddock meet on the Monongahela. At first Laclede engaged in the fur trade at New Orleans. Seven years later he and a partner obtained the monopoly of the trade of the Missouri River, the partner agreeing to take charge of the business of shipping furs to Europe from New Orleans and Laclede to trade with the Indians and forward the furs from the Missouri to New Orleans.

Laclede's family, which he took with him to the Indian country, included his wife, Marie Chouteau; a stepson, Auguste Chouteau, age fourteen; a son, Pierre, age five, and three daughters. Although four of the children were Laclede's own, they never were known by his name but were called Chouteau, the name of their mother's first husband, from whom she had separated. Since the old Louisiana law did not provide for marriage of separated couples, children born of a union such as that of Pierre Laclede and Marie Chouteau went by their mother's and not their father's name.

Laclede sailed with his family and a crew of thirty *voy-*

ageurs for the north in August, 1763, six months after France had lost Louisiana as a result of the Beaver War.

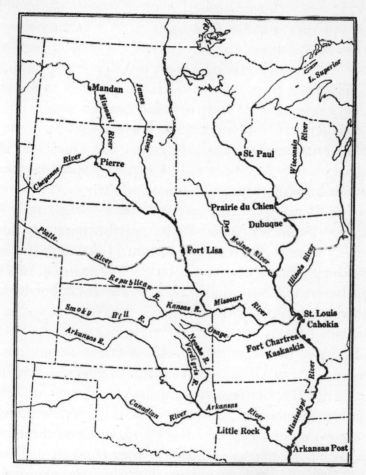

The St. Louis Trade Territory in the Days of Laclede and His Sons

No ship, however, had come to New Orleans with the bad news so that Laclede knew nothing of his country's loss. As his barge cast off from the levee on this epoch-making voyage, it is probable that his heart was gay as he stood at the stern steering with a long oar and singing the verses of a nonsensical song. Of course he sang, for the *voyageurs* believed that singing lightened labor. A master who could sing well always had willing boatmen. It was the custom for the master to sing the verses while the crew responded with the refrain. So general was the practice of singing that the hills beside every important inland waterway of America have resounded at some time to French *chansons*.

If singing really lightens labor, it certainly was needed for the back-breaking task of breasting the Mississippi. A tedious journey faced not only Laclede's toiling oarsmen but also his four younger children and their mother, confined as they were to the cramped space of the barge. It was less irksome for Auguste. His stepfather permitted him at times to steer the boat and to lead in the singing. For three long months the crew contended against the Mississippi before they brought the barge to rest at last beside the old walls of Fort Chartres.

It was November. Leaves were rattling from the trees, and the breath of winter was in the air. It must have seemed severely cold to Marie Chouteau and her children, none of whom had ever been north of the magnolia groves of New Orleans. The chill of the north wind, however, could not compare to the bleakness of heart they felt as the commandant at Chartres told them of word from Detroit that King Louis XV had given away all of Louisiana east of the Mississippi to England as a prize of war and all west to Spain for aid in the war. Laclede was stunned. What good now was his monopoly of trade on the Missouri? What good had been the thousand-mile river voyage to which he had exposed his wife and children?

A less courageous man would have returned to New Orleans. Laclede left his wife and small children at the fort and voyaged with Auguste and the crew to seek a location for the building of a trading post. Auguste was delighted that his stepfather, whom he always called father, should take him along. Although Auguste had been born in New Orleans and had grown up in that warm climate, he faced the north winds of December with a warm heart. Travelling northward, Laclede and his crew examined various places on the west bank of the Mississippi. He chose the west side because it was in Spanish territory, while the east side of the river was now a possession of England. Since Spain had been an ally of France in the Beaver War, the French naturally felt more kindly toward her than toward England.

Eighteen miles below the mouth of the Missouri, they found the site that suited them best. The men blazed trees to mark the location of the trading fort and of houses. They blazed another tree at the water's edge to serve as a landmark. This place Laclede named St. Louis, not for the profligate Louis XV, who had just divided Louisiana and given it away, but for a nobler king, Louis IX, the crusader. Their work done, the men boarded the barge and floated with the current back to Fort Chartres, where all celebrated Christmas as merrily as though nobody had ever heard that the English and Spanish were coming to rule Louisiana.

The Christmas season passed. January proved too cold for work and so the colonists remained to bask in the warmth of the fireplaces of Chartres. February brought a thaw. As the ice melted and the ravines ran full of snow water, Laclede directed Auguste to proceed with the barge and thirty men to the site of St. Louis and commence the building of log houses. Laclede had every confidence that his stepson, who lacked a few weeks of being fifteen, could manage the building as well as a grown man. The workmen too had confidence in the boy and obeyed his orders as readily as though their master had commanded in person.

After the barge had gone, Laclede visited the settlement at Kaskaskia, where he found the people saddened at the prospect of being placed under British rule. To cheer them, he suggested that all move to St. Louis, where they could be under the rule of the friendly king of Spain. A few of the settlers accepted the invitation, but since removal to St. Louis meant the abandonment of their homes and farms, the majority decided to remain and try out English rule before abandoning the country.

Returning to Chartres, Laclede rented a two-wheeled cart in which he transported his family to Cahokia. There he also invited the French settlers to move to St. Louis, which was just across the river. Leaving his family at Cahokia, he crossed to St. Louis to complete the building operations, after which he brought his wife and children to their log home.

There they were soon joined by about one hundred families from Vincennes, Fort Chartres, Kaskaskia and Cahokia. Some of those who came from Kaskaskia abandoned farms on which their grandparents had settled sixty-four years before. Rather than live under English rule, they gave up the comfort of well-built homes and cleared farms to start life in a wilderness.

St. Louis in that first year was a village of a few log

houses in the midst of a lovely forest of hickory, oak, walnut and elm trees. The children could gather pawpaws, persimmons, wild grapes, hickory nuts and walnuts in abundance. But while the wild fruit and nuts were a delight to children and birds and squirrels, the trees had to be chopped down and burned before the farmers could grow crops. It required a year of hard work to clear only a few acres of forest. Nothing but a deep distrust of the English could have induced men to abandon the cleared farms of the Illinois country to become pioneers at St. Louis.

Firm in their belief that song lightens labor, the new settlers sang as they cleared the land. They planted corn and sowed wheat among the tree stumps. They built a water-power flour mill. They erected a church upon the hill facing the Mississippi. In less than a year St. Louis grew into a settlement of 500 people. Not even Detroit or New Orleans began so well. As was the custom of the French settlers, they built their homes in a village beside the river, then laid out farms and cleared the forest adjoining the village to the west. Each farm was a long, narrow strip of land extending farther westward each year as each farmer cleared more land.

One thing the colony lacked. There was no government of any sort. Had St. Louis been settled by Englishmen, they would have elected town officers and governed themselves. The French, however, had never taken any part in their own government and had not the slightest idea how to proceed. They had always looked to the king to appoint their governors, who in turn appointed the commandants of the towns, who told the people what to do. Laclede had no authority to govern the people; but when they asked him for deeds to their lands, he granted the necessary papers, although he was not sure he had a right to do so. When boundary disputes arose between neighbors, they came to him, asking that he be their judge. In that manner, without any appointment or any election, he became judge and ruler of the village. When the Spanish governor arrived at New Orleans, he was so busy with affairs there that he had no time to think of sending a ruler to command St. Louis and gave no consideration to the question of the monopoly of the Missouri River trade for a long time.

A ruler for St. Louis at last came from an unexpected source. When the British soldiers arrived from Canada to take charge at Vincennes, the French commandant who had the sorrowful duty of surrendering the town was Louis St. Ange, who will be remembered as an officer under Bourgmont at Fort Orleans in 1724. St. Ange had grown old in the service of his country in the Mississippi Valley. He had fought in the wars against the Fox Indians and in the campaigns against the English. Since the death of Vincennes he had been serving as commandant at Fort Vincennes, a position he held for twenty-eight years. Having surrendered Vincennes, he took command at Fort Chartres. For eighteen months he was left in command there. Other French forts in America had long been surrendered before an English captain finally came to Chartres late in 1765. For the last time St. Ange hauled down the flag of his king. Not wishing to become British subjects, he and his soldiers departed with their families for St. Louis. Let it be said in passing that the English did not long remain at Fort Chartres. The Mississippi channel undermined the foundations. Today only a flood of water marks the site of the last fort in America to fly the lilies of France, but on the adjoining river bank the State of Illinois has dedicated a state park.

Laclede was pleased to welcome St. Ange to St. Louis and so were the people of the young town. Those who had come from east of the river had been accustomed for many years to recognize him as their ruler. Now they turned to him once more, and Laclede gladly resigned the management of public affairs to St. Ange's experienced hands. Although neither Laclede nor St. Ange had been elected or appointed to office, their rule in St. Louis was so just that everybody accepted their decisions. Eventually the Spanish governor learned that St. Ange was giving satisfaction. He therefore appointed him to be the first governor of a region to be known as Upper Louisiana and which included all the Spanish possessions in the Mississippi Valley above Arkansas Post. St. Louis became the capital of the region. St. Ange served as governor until 1770, when a Spaniard replaced him. After that he continued to live in St. Louis as a private citizen. Let it be said of the new Spanish governor, that he did not interfere with the lives of the people. St. Louis continued to be French in language, in customs and in the love of her people for adventure.

Laclede, being relieved of the government of his colony, devoted his entire time to business. He invited the Indians to trade their furs for manufactured articles, and each spring large numbers pitched their teepees at the river front to engage in trade with Laclede and his stepson.

Business, however, did not thrive. Laclede trusted everybody, and some of those he trusted cheated him. Debts piled up for a dozen years. Eventually his partner summoned him to New Orleans to help straighten out affairs. He was gone almost two years. At last he was permitted to return home. He fell ill on the voyage, and his crew took him to Arkansas Post in the hope that rest from the voyage would benefit him. Instead of improving, he grew rapidly worse and died at the post in 1778.

Upon Laclede's departure for New Orleans, he left his stepson in charge as manager. Auguste Chouteau refused credit to those who made no attempt to pay their debts. He managed affairs so well that he soon turned loss into profit. He sent his eighteen-year-old half-brother, Pierre, to the Osage River to trade with the Osages. He discharged employees who had been cheating Laclede. When news came of Laclede's death, Auguste remained in charge as manager. He was then twenty-nine years old. He and his brother won the confidence of the Indians by fair dealing and their business grew. It is due to the Chouteau brothers that St. Louis expanded from a village into a city.

Through the next seventy years the trade increased, until St. Louis became the chief market for the Missouri and Upper Mississippi Rivers, for the Rocky Mountain region, for Santa Fe, El Paso and Chihuahua, for the Great Salt Lake Basin, for Oregon and for California. It became the chief trading place for two thirds of the land area of the present United States.

Nor did the fur empire at St. Louis end with the Chouteaus. Even today raw furs come to St. Louis on the backs of men, by parcels post, by express and by freight. St. Louis buys furs not only from the United States, but from Canada, from Alaska, from the Pribilof Islands and from Siberia. The city is today a greater fur market than ever, and the

St. Louis fur auctions are attended by buyers from all over the world.

The first extension of the St. Louis fur trade was to the Indian tribes on the lower Missouri River. The Spanish governors granted to the Chouteau brothers the right to the trade of the Osages. Licenses to trade with tribes beyond the Osages were given to other merchants. Traders pushed their *pirogues* up the river to the villages of the Kansas, the Otoes and the Pawnees. They not only traversed the Missouri but explored the various tributaries of that stream. It was they who named the Missouri, the Osage and the Kansas for the tribes dwelling upon their banks. They gave the French names by which the Gasconade, the Chariton, the Grande, the Platte, the Loup, the Marias des Cygnes, the Verdigris and the Marmaton are today known. They also named the Solomon, the Saline, the Blue, the Stranger, the Republican and many other rivers which today bear English names that are merely translations from the original French names.

The naming of the Republican is of peculiar interest, because it reveals that the French trappers who named it were so ignorant of the different forms of government, they did not even know the difference between a republic and a monarchy. They first heard the name Republican in 1776. At that time the English colonies were in revolt against the British king and had established the republic of the United States. While George Washington was leading the American armies against the British in the east, George Rogers Clark was driving the British from the French villages of the west. In 1778 he took Kaskaskia and Cahokia and the following spring took Vincennes. The thing that impressed the trappers was that the United States had rebelled against the British king. The form of government meant nothing to them. Likewise when the French people beheaded King Louis XVI and set up a republic patterned after that of the United States, the trappers once more were impressed with the revolution and not with the form of the government.

Accordingly, when part of the Pawnee tribe revolted against their chiefs and followed new chiefs away from the Grand Pawnee villages on the Platte to live farther south, the trappers named the rebellious tribe the Pawnee Republic, although the form of government was exactly the same as that of the Grand Pawnees. They named the river, on which the Pawnee Republic established itself, the Republican River.

While the French of St. Louis traded on the lower Missouri, the French of Canada continued to carry on trade with the tribes of the Upper Missouri and Upper Mississippi as they had done since the days of Duluth and the Verendryes. While the Canadian traders were Frenchmen, they no longer represented the old French monopolies. Following the British victory in the Beaver War, two British monopolies divided the beaver trade of Canada. The Hudson Bay Company, organized at the suggestion of Radisson and Chouart, continued to operate from Hudson Bay. A new association, the Northwest Company, operated at Montreal instead of the French. The Northwest Company sent Scotch and English traders to take command at the most important forts in the fur country and employed French *voyageurs* and *engagées* to fill the lesser positions.

Some of the new British officers were men of great en-

terprise. Alexander Mackenzie is especially worthy of
mention. He came to Canada as a clerk for the Northwest
Company. Eventually he was promoted to the command
at Fort Chippewyan on Lake Athabaska. While there he
conceived the idea of finding the Arctic Ocean by an overland expedition. At the head of a party of five he discovered the Mackenzie River, so named in his honor, and descended it to the Arctic in 1789. To illustrate how completely the French *engagées* filled the lesser positions, let
it be said that not one of Mackenzie's companions on this
exploration was of British birth. One was a German and
the others were Canadian French. Next, Mackenzie, with
one Scotch companion and six French Canadians, crossed
the Canadian Rockies and discovered the long-sought route
to the Pacific in 1793.

Under the leadership of such men as Mackenzie, the
British controlled the Indian trade far south of the present
Canadian border. After the American Revolution, the
boundary between Canada and the United States was fixed
at the middle of the Great Lakes where it is today. In spite
of that boundary, French employes of the Northwest Company and their English leaders traded with the Indians
south of the Lakes. In the present Wisconsin they carried
furs from the Mississippi River up the Wisconsin and
down the Fox to Lake Michigan and to Canada. Their
merchants occupied the town of Prairie du Chien on the
Mississippi at the mouth of the Wisconsin and there traded
with the Sioux, the Sacs and the Foxes.

The Fox tribe, alone of western Indians, had always
been hostile to the French. Prior to the Beaver War they
had fought the French in several campaigns. They were

willing to come to Prairie du Chien and trade, but did not allow the French to invade their territory.

It remained for a St. Louis schoolmaster, Jean Baptiste Trudeau, to find a river passage around the Fox Indians. Trudeau arrived in St. Louis from his Canadian birthplace in 1774. For more than a quarter of a century he was schoolmaster for the children of such families as could afford to pay the tuition. School in those days lasted only two or three months in the year. For the rest of the year Trudeau engaged in the fur trade. He ascended the Mississippi, probably in 1775, to the mouth of the Des Moines River, and there, instead of going up the Mississippi past the villages of the unfriendly Foxes, he sailed up the Des Moines all the way across the present Iowa to the headwaters of the Des Moines in the present southern Minnesota. There he traded with the Sioux and brought their furs to St. Louis. Since the Des Moines watered a region west of the Fox villages, travel by that route was safe. For twenty-six years Trudeau continued in charge of the trade of the Des Moines. It is due to the French explorers that the river today bears its French name of Des Moines (the monks), and it is from the river that the capital of Iowa takes its name.

While Trudeau was avoiding the Foxes, another Canadian, Julien Dubuque, who arrived in Prairie du Chien in 1785 from Canada, began making their acquaintance. In order to gain influence over them, he pretended to be a great mystery man. The Fox Indians at first laughed at him and called him the Little Cloud. They called him *little* because he was only five feet six inches in height. They called him *cloud* because his hair was black and his features were fierce and threatening like a storm cloud. As an illustration of his methods in gaining influence over the Foxes, this story is related:

Dubuque once invited the Fox warriors to a council beside a pool of water into which he had previously poured a keg of turpentine. When the Indians had assembled, he threatened to burn up all the creeks, river and ponds around their villages. At this threat the Indians smiled, for they did not believe it possible for any man to burn water. To convince them of his power, Dubuque threw a firebrand into the pool. Instantly the turpentine burst into flames and the Indians believed the water was afire. Fearing that all of their drinking water would be consumed, the warriors begged him to quench the blaze. He therefore ordered the fire to cease burning and in a short time it burned itself out.

The amazed Indians were grateful when he promised them that out of his great friendship for them he would never set fire to water as long as they returned his friendship. They were pleased to have the friendship of so wonderful a man and were delighted when he married Potosa, the chief's daughter, and came to live with them.

It may be that Dubuque's friendship for the Foxes came from the fact that he had learned of lead deposits in their country. For a long time it had been known that lead existed in the Mississippi Valley. Tonty, while yet at Starved Rock, wrote of finding lead. Cadillac, it will be recalled, visited the Galena lead deposits. After his return to France, Cadillac evidently reported the existence of lead; for Phillippe Francis Renault came from France in 1721, imported Negro slaves from the West Indies and operated the Galena mines for twenty-three years.

Dubuque, having gained the fear and friendship of the Foxes, obtained permission to mine lead in the present Iowa just across the Mississippi from Galena. Employing several Canadian friends, he opened a mine and built a smelter and village on the site of the present Dubuque, Iowa, in 1788. Since the Mississippi offered a ready means of transportation to St. Louis, he formed a partnership with Auguste Chouteau, shipped the lead to Chouteau and sold it in St. Louis. The production of the Dubuque mines increased until it amounted to 40,000 pounds of pure lead a year. Part of this was manufactured into bullets at St. Louis, part into colored ornaments for the Indian trade and part was shipped to New Orleans for use there or for export.

Through the influence of Dubuque much of the fur trade of the Foxes also was carried to St. Louis instead of to Canada. Dubuque continued to operate the lead mines until his death in 1810. The Foxes regarded him so highly that upon his death they buried him in the same grave with their chief.

While Trudeau and Dubuque extended the trade of St. Louis to the Sioux and the Foxes, Jean Monier ventured up the Missouri River beyond the mouth of the Platte in 1789 and won the trade of the Ponca tribe.

Word of Monier's success came to Jacques D'Eglise, who, although he could neither read nor write, was a man of courage and enterprise. Being a Canadian by birth, D'Eglise formed a partnership with a St. Louis merchant, Joseph Robidoux, who also was a Canadian by birth. Both had migrated to St. Louis after the British conquest of their native land. Robidoux provided trade goods for a venture on the Missouri and also obtained a license from the Span-

ish governor for D'Eglise to discover the tribes beyond
the Poncas and to trade with them.

Although we use the word discover in connection with
the voyage of D'Eglise, it is likely that others had previously voyaged up the Missouri before him. But these voyages had been made by woods rangers in the days of Bienville. No authentic record had been kept of them and in
St. Louis there was no knowledge of what lay to the
north of the villages of the Poncas. D'Eglise therefore regarded himself as a true discoverer and in reality he was one.

With only two companions D'Eglise ascended the Missouri in a little *pirogue* in the summer of 1790. At times he
and his men drove the boat with oars. At times they pro-
pelled it by pushing with poles set against the bed of the
river. At other times when the *pirogue* could not be forced
against the powerful Missouri current in any other way,
they drew their boat with a tow line. All summer they
toiled and it was autumn before they arrived in the land
of the Sioux in the present South Dakota. Farther north
they came to the Arickarees. Continuing their voyage,
they came in late autumn to the Mandan village discovered
fifty-one years before by the Verendryes. Here they were
hailed in French by employes of the Northwest Company.
One of these traders, named Menard, had been trading with
the Indians of the Upper Missouri for forty years. He had
ascended the Yellowstone for 450 miles and was familiar
also with the Big Horn and other tributaries of the Yellowstone. He had visited the Black Hills. The names of all of
the important rivers of the Dakotas and of eastern Montana
and Wyoming are of French origin. Today we call these
streams by the English equivalent of their original French

names with a few exceptions, which, like the Belle Fourche and the Cheyenne, yet bear the original French and Indian names the early traders gave them.

The trade of the upper Missouri had not been greatly developed by the Canadians because of difficulties of transportation. Trade goods from Montreal had to be carried in boats up the St. Lawrence, across the Great Lakes, up Rainy River and across Lake of the Woods. After passing many portages, the goods finally had to be packed on horses to the Missouri. D'Eglise saw at once that the natural outlet of the trade of the Dakota country was down the Missouri to St. Louis. When he came home after a two-year absence, the tales he told of the abundance of fur on the upper Missouri caused other merchants to seek a share of that business.

The Chouteaus engaged Pierre Dorion, a former employe of the Northwest Company, to handle their trade with the Sioux. Trudeau engaged in the Missouri River trade for two years and then returned to the Des Moines. Solomon Petit, who had been trading with the Kansas tribe, Regis Loisel, a St. Louis merchant, Jean Monier of the Ponca village, and others went to the upper Missouri. D'Eglise continued his voyages to the upper Missouri for several years. He once formed a plan for crossing the Rockies to the Pacific, but nothing came of it.

With furs arriving from as far as the Yellowstone, the trade of St. Louis grew rapidly. In 1786 ten barges were required to transport the year's beaver trade from St. Louis to New Orleans. Ten years later the annual shipment was valued at $200,000. Among those to witness the arrival of the furs from St. Louis with covetous eyes was Manuel

Lisa, born in New Orleans of Spanish parents. As a youth he had sailed the seas and had served in the Spanish West Indian fleet. He had later engaged in fur trade at Vincennes and at New Madrid, a new town founded by Yankees and Spaniards on the Mississippi below St. Louis.

Lisa called on the governor and told him that since Spain owned Louisiana, it was not fair that Frenchmen should control the fur trade at St. Louis. He asked for and was granted the monopoly of the trade with the Osages on the Osage River. If he imagined that he could take over the trade of the Osages by merely gaining a monopoly from the governor, he underestimated the hold that Pierre Chouteau had on the hearts of the Osages. In 1802 Chouteau persuaded more than 3000 of these Indians to abandon their homes on the Osage and to migrate to the Neosho and Verdigris, streams which head in the same country as the Osage but flow south and empty into the Arkansas. This was outside of the limit of Lisa's monopoly.

From a new post on the Arkansas, Chouteau transported furs bought from the Osages directly down the Arkansas and Mississippi to New Orleans. We can imagine that Chouteau's *voyageurs* roused the echoes of the hills of the Arkansas with the notes of their songs. One of these hills is especially interesting. The French called it *La Petite Rochelle* (little rock). It is from this rock that the capital of Arkansas takes its name.

The quarrel between Chouteau and Lisa had but a short time to live, for an event in France soon put an end to Spanish monopolies. In France Napoleon was ruling the country in place of the Louis who had governed so badly. Napoleon thought to regain Louisiana for France.

He agreed with the king of Spain to help the king's son-in-law, the Duke of Parma, in a war for a kingdom in Italy in exchange for Louisiana. The treaty was signed in 1800, but was kept secret because Napoleon was unable to dispatch soldiers to take possession at New Orleans. Consequently the king of Spain agreed to continue his rule of the colony until such time as Napoleon gave the word.

Three years elapsed and the secret leaked out. At the same time Napoleon became embroiled in war with England. Fearing that the British navy might sail at any time to the conquest of Louisiana, Napoleon sold the colony to the United States for $15,000,000. New Orleans was actually under the French flag for only seventeen days. A French officer took over the governor's mansion on November 30, 1803, and hoisted the French tri-color. This was not the old French flag of the lilies, such as had floated over Fort Chartres, but the flag of the French Republic. It was allowed to fly until December 17, when the Stars and Stripes were hoisted in its place. At St. Louis the Spanish governor of Upper Louisiana continued to rule until March 9, 1804.

On that day, as Captain Amos Stoddard of the United States Army was about to take over the city, he was accosted by citizens who begged that the French flag be allowed to fly over St. Louis if only for a few hours. Stoddard graciously complied with the request. As the Spanish colors were lowered, the French flag was run up. At Stoddard's command, the American soldiers fired a salute. The French residents shouted with joy and danced in the streets, even though to them the tri-color was a strange flag, for they had known the flag of the lilies.

After giving them time for rejoicing, Stoddard signalled for the lowering of the tri-color and for the hoisting of the Stars and Stripes. Thus by peaceful means did the American Republic extend her dominion to the west bank of the Mississippi.

CHAPTER XVI

UNCLE SAM MOVES WEST

PRIOR to the purchase of Louisiana by the United States, President Thomas Jefferson planned an expedition to discover the long-sought route across the Rockies to the Pacific. The purchase was concluded while the expedition was being organized under the joint command of Captain Meriwether Lewis, the President's private secretary, and Captain William Clark, younger brother of General George Rogers Clark, conqueror of Kaskaskia and Vincennes during the American Revolution. Lewis and Clark departed in May, 1804, at the head of twenty soldiers, nine Kentucky volunteers, eleven St. Louis *voyageurs* and George Drouillard, who deserves special mention.

He was of French and Indian ancestry, could speak both English and French, knew several Indian tongues and was a master of the Indian sign language of the Plains. As a hunter he surpassed any other man in the party, which means that he was one of the best in America; for the expedition was composed of picked men of rugged physique, inured to hardship, expert with rifle, skilled at trailing both men and animals and able to find their way through a forest, on plain and in mountains.

The expedition travelled in a barge and two *pirogues* in which they carried provisions for the journey and a supply of gifts for the Indians. The boats ascended the Missouri for twenty-nine miles, where they passed St. Charles, a French village of 400 people, whose chief business was hunting, trapping and trading with the Indians of the Missouri River region. A little beyond St. Charles they came to La Charette, last French village before entering the Indian country. This settlement was composed of seven families, including that of Daniel Boone, Kentucky pioneer, who had moved from the United States to the Missouri while it was yet a possession of Spain.

Since Drouillard was a superior hunter, he was relieved from the toil of helping to man the boats. Instead he ranged the woods for deer, bear, squirrels and game birds to provide meat. Each night as the boats came to camp, Drouillard was there ahead of them with a plentiful supply of food. The monotony of the voyage was broken from time to time as the adventurers encountered *pirogues* laden with furs on the downstream voyage to market. The Americans were surprised at the volume of the commerce on the Missouri. They met Frenchmen with beaver from the Missouris on the Grande, the Osages on the Osage, the Kansas on the Kansas, the Pawnees on the Platte, the Sioux on the James, the Arickarees on the Cannonball and the Cheyennes in the Black Hills. In a single day they met four *pirogues*.

The Frenchmen in turn were astonished when told that the United States had bought Louisiana and that Lewis and Clark were exploring their country's new possession after which they intended to find a way to the Pacific.

So difficult was the voyage that fifteen miles was a good day's journey. The months seemed unending to the Americans. They soon learned from the French *voyageurs*, however, to be cheerful and to sing as they rowed, poled and towed against the hostile river. Unfortunately neither

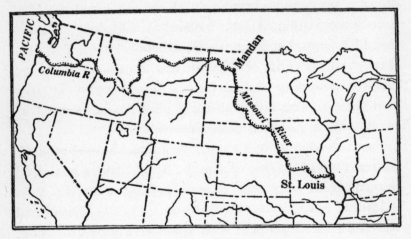

Route of the Lewis and Clark Expedition

Lewis nor Clark knew the knack of leading in the singing of the French songs. So slow was the progress that the Fourth of July, the first to be celebrated in Louisiana, arrived by the time the boats came to the site of the present Atchison, Kansas, where the explorers named a small stream Fourth of July Creek. They landed there and one of the men was bitten by a rattlesnake, but he recovered. Continuing their voyage, they camped that night on the site of Doniphan, Kansas, beside a stream which they named Independence Creek in honor of the day. By way of celebration Lewis and Clark issued a gill of whisky to each of the men.

Summer was more than half over before they saw the Platte, which was regarded by the *voyageurs* as the dividing point between the lower and the upper Missouri. In early autumn they visited with the Sioux, where Pierre Dorion, who had lived for twenty years with that tribe, served as interpreter. It was late autumn by the time they came to the Mandan village. Here they built log huts and went into winter quarters. They improved the winter by making friends with both the Indians and the French Canadian employes of the Northwest Company. They enlisted three of the Canadians to accompany them to the Pacific. One of the three was Toussaint Charboneau, who had been so long among the Indians that he had adopted their customs, even to marrying three Indian wives, the youngest being only seventeen or eighteen years old and the mother of a baby boy, Baptiste.

This wife, Sacajawea or Bird Woman, was of the Snake or Shoshonee tribe, which lived in the Rockies and was unfamiliar with white men. The Snakes were surrounded by enemies, the most ruthless being the Minnetarres, who, armed with French guns, invaded the Snake country, defeated the Snakes in battle and captured Bird Woman at the time she was twelve years old. They took her to their home on the Missouri below the mouth of the Yellowstone, where she was adopted by a Minnetarre family and remained several years. Charboneau, while on a trading expedition to the Minnetarres, met and married her. She could not speak French and he could not speak the Snake dialect. Consequently they conversed in Minnetarre.

Knowing how glad his wife would be to have a chance to visit her own people once more, Charboneau proposed to Lewis and Clark that she be taken with the expedition to serve as interpreter to the Snakes. Since her people owned horses, the captains hoped that she might help in buying animals on which they could transport their cargoes from the boats on the Missouri across the Rocky Mountains to whatever westward-flowing river they might discover. She, accordingly, was allowed to accompany her husband, while his other two wives remained at home.

With the coming of spring, the captains sent back a part of their force to St. Louis, thereby reducing the party to thirty-two men. Bird Woman and her baby increased the number to thirty-four.

Since Bird Woman tried to suppress any show of emotion in the presence of the white men, we can only guess that she must have been greatly excited with the hope of again seeing her own people. This excitement must have increased as the boats moved through the Minnetarre country, past the mouth of the Yellowstone and up the river toward the snow-capped Rockies of her childhood. At the Great Falls the expedition was delayed while the boats were moved on rolling logs for twelve miles around a series of falls and rapids. As this long portage was being accomplished, the Americans met their first grizzly bears. These huge beasts had been accustomed for generations to rule their country. Even the Indians, armed only with bows and arrows, fled before them. When they met the impudent Americans, who refused to get out of the way, the bears became infuriated and charged them. Among the first to be attacked unceremoniously was Drouillard. He whipped the butt of his rifle to his shoulder, took quick aim and sent a bullet through the animal's heart. But so furious was the on-

MERIWETHER LEWIS

KASKASKIA INDIAN

This is a striking example of the romantic conception of the American Indian generally held by European artists and writers. Indians taken to London and Paris never failed to excite the greatest curiosity.

slaught that the bear, even after receiving a fatal wound, was carried forward by its own momentum, and Drouillard had to leap aside to escape the dying monster. He skinned it, butchered the meat and that night served grizzly-bear steak.

Several hundred miles beyond Great Falls, the men came to a place which was to become a noted landmark known as Three Forks. Here the Missouri divides into three tributaries. Lewis and Clark named the largest the Jefferson in honor of the President; the next, the Madison, for the secretary of state, who later became President; and the third, the Gallatin for the secretary of the treasury. Selecting the Jefferson as the main fork of the Missouri, they ascended it. Not far from Three Forks, Bird Woman recognized the spot at which she had been captured by the Minnetarres.

At last they were in the Snake country, but they looked in vain for Snakes. Only abandoned camps showed where they had been. These Indians, hearing the firing of the rifles, feared that the Minnetarres were returning and fled into the mountains. In order to overtake them and gain their confidence, Lewis and Drouillard and two other men preceded the rest up the Jefferson River. The river narrowed to a creek and then to a rill. So narrow did it become that one of the men walked with a foot on either bank and exclaimed:

"I thank God that I have lived to walk astraddle of the Missouri!"

They continued along the rill until it became nothing but a trickle and at last disappeared altogether. There the men discovered a pass through which they crossed to the

Pacific side of the Continental Divide. The next day they came in sight of a mounted Indian, who viewed them from a distance but could not be coaxed to come nearer, even though Lewis held up tempting gifts and rolled up his sleeve to show that he was a white man and not a Minnetarre. At last the frightened Snake whipped his horse to ride away at breakneck speed.

Once more the scouts took up the hunt. When they did meet the Snakes it was in a sudden and unexpected manner. They were following a faint trail, which led to a thicket of service berries, where they saw three women picking berries. Lewis and Drouillard pounced forward and each seized a woman before she could get away, but the third eluded capture and ran like a frightened rabbit. The scouts were in a serious situation, for the running woman, if allowed to reach the Snake camp, would put everybody into flight. Since the Snakes had horses and the scouts were afoot, there was not a chance of running them down. The only possibility of averting the misfortune was to win the confidence of the two captives and have them call the running woman back.

Lewis opened his pack and presented each woman with a few trinkets. He then opened a paper of paints and began to paint their faces. This adornment delighted them. Seeing that they were pleased, Drouillard explained by the sign language that the four white scouts were friends, that they had boats on the Jefferson River in which were gifts for all and that instead of being Minnetarres, they were white people. To prove it, Lewis rolled up the sleeve of his shirt and showed his white arm. At Drouillard's request the captive women called to the third one and convinced her that she ought to return to receive her share of gifts and to have her face painted. Curiosity and a desire to share good fortune overcame her fears and brought her back to hold up her face for Lewis to paint. He did so and also presented her with trinkets. Drouillard next persuaded the three women to lead the way into the Snake camp.

Their unexpected arrival startled the village. The women and children began a retreat, while the men seized their weapons to defend their families. The three women, however, calmed the panic by shouting that the men were a new kind of friendly people and not Minnetarres. Drouillard by signs and Lewis by gifts won their confidence and Cameahwait, the chief, extended a cordial reception. After much palaver, Lewis persuaded the Indians to recross the mountains and meet the boats on the Jefferson River. As the Indians moved eastward, Drouillard supplied food for them, killing three deer at the outset of the march. These were quickly consumed by the 200 men, women and children.

When almost in sight of Clark's boat, the Indians became alarmed for fear that Clark's men would fire upon them. Lewis calmed their fears by donning Cameahwait's headdress and giving the chief his own hat. The other white men also exchanged headdresses to show they had confidence that Clark's men would not shoot at Indians.

It was Bird Woman who first saw her approaching kinspeople. As they came into sight down the river bank toward where Clark and his men were toiling with the boats, Bird Woman was walking ahead with Baptiste upon her back. With cries of gladness, she ran forward to hug the women she recognized.

Captain Lewis led Cameahwait directly to Captain Clark. Blankets were spread and the three sat down for council. After passing the peace pipe, Clark called to Bird Woman to assist as interpreter. As she drew near and was about to speak, she looked at Cameahwait and he at her. In that instant they recognized each other as brother and sister. She ran to him and threw her arms about him, while he also embraced her. So overcome was she at the meeting that she burst into uncontrollable tears. Embarrassed at the show of emotion in the presence of the white men, she unfolded her blanket and flung it wide so that it fell over herself, her baby and her brother, thus permitting them to visit under the blanket unobserved.

Later Captain Clark once more attempted to use Bird Woman as an interpreter. This proved to be a cumbersome process. Clark first spoke in English to Drouillard, who translated the words into French for Charboneau, who then spoke in Minnetarre to Bird Woman, who translated to Cameahwait in Snake. Then the chief replied in Snake, his sister in Minnetarre, Charboneau in French and Drouillard in English. With so many translations the meaning of the words became confused. It was found to be more accurate to talk by signs, and it was by the sign language that Drouillard effected the purchase of the horses. Although Bird Woman did not help in the buying of the horses, she later proved of utmost worth to the expedition. Some of the Snake warriors plotted to steal back the horses they had sold. Since they spoke to each other by words and not by signs, Drouillard knew nothing of the plan, but Bird Woman overheard them talking and reported to her husband, who in turn told Drouillard, who notified Lewis and

Clark. They summoned Cameahwait before them and sternly accused him of treachery. He confessed that some of the warriors had planned to stampede the horses in the night, but denied having had a part in the plot himself. The captains warned him that they would defend their property with their rifles and that loss of life would result to the Indians who attempted to steal the horses. The warning had the desired effect and no attempt was made at a stampede.

One of the warriors, however, did snatch up Drouillard's gun and ride off with it on a fleet horse. Drouillard mounted another animal and, after a chase of ten miles across mountain trails, overtook the thief, tussled with him as the two rode side by side and wrested the gun away. In justice to the Snakes, let it be explained that for generations they had been surrounded by enemies. From childhood they had been taught that all strangers were foes and that it was a praiseworthy act to steal from them.

Lewis and Clark were glad to transfer their cargo to the horses and to move across the Continental Divide westward out of the Snake country and down the Pacific slope where no white man had ever been. In what is now central Idaho they discovered a river, which they named the Salmon, because it was squirming with salmon swimming up from the Pacific to deposit their eggs. Here they built canoes and, after making presents to the Nez Perce (pierced nose) Indians, left their horses with them for safe keeping until their return. Launching their canoes upon the Salmon, they sped with the current and were carried to a larger river, which they named Lewis for Captain Lewis, but which is more commonly called the Snake for the Snake Indians.

The Snake carried them to still a larger river, which proved to be the Columbia, discovered at its mouth by Captain Robert Gray, American navigator, who in 1792 had entered it from the Pacific Ocean and explored its lower course.

As Lewis and Clark neared the ocean, they noted that the Columbia broadened until at its mouth it expanded into an estuary seven miles wide. It was November, 1805, when they completed their journey and stood on the shores of the Pacific to watch the waves roll eastward from China to break and foam against the rocks of the Oregon coast.

Mackenzie had been first to cross the American continent from Canada, but the Lewis and Clark Expedition had been first to come to the Pacific from the United States. They had completed the quest of Champlain, Nicolet, La Salle, Jolliet, Marquette, the Verendryes and D'Eglise.

Some miles back from the sea on ground above tide water, they built winter quarters. They expected a cold winter, for the Columbia is in the same latitude as northern Maine, but due to the warming effects of the Japanese Current, the temperature rarely fell below freezing. Instead of heavy snow, there came fogs and a deluge of rain. The air was damp and chilly. The skies were overcast. Added to the gloom of clouds was the shadow of hundreds of miles of deep forest—a forest of trees much taller than any in eastern America. Captain Clark measured a fir tree 12 feet in diameter and 210 feet tall, and there were thousands of others just as tall and taller. Masses of moss hung from the limbs of the trees, and the floor of the forest was a tangle of thorny brambles and brakes of ferns as high as the men. As they floundered through the brambles and waded in the mud, the ferns slapped their shoulders, beating water through the seams of their clothing to chill their bodies.

The noise they made as they moved through the brakes frightened away the game. Food supplies ran low. The captains reduced the rations, yet the supplies ran still lower. Hunger was ever present until Drouillard restored the spirits of the men by killing seven elk in a single day. His skill at hunting and his expert marksmanship caused Captain Clark to write in his journal:

"We would scarcely be able to subsist were it not for the exertions of this most excellent hunter. The game is scarce, and nothing is now to be seen except elk, which to almost all the men are very difficult to be procured; but Drewyer (Clark's way of spelling Drouillard), who is the offspring of a Canadian Frenchman and an Indian woman, has passed his life in the woods and unites in a wonderful degree the dexterous aim of the frontier huntsman with the intuitive sagacity of the Indian in pursuing the faintest track in the forest."*

The new year, 1806, arrived and the wet weather continued. Late in winter the explorers abandoned the camp to escape from the continuous rains. Slowly they toiled up the Columbia and the Snake rivers and came once more upon the Nez Perce, from whom they recovered their horses. In order to explore more territory, the expedition divided into three sections, after agreeing to reunite at the mouth of the Yellowstone. One returned to the Jefferson, found the boats abandoned the year before and floated downstream to the appointed *rendezvous*. The second party, headed by

*Quotations in this chapter are all from *The Original Journals of Lewis and Clark.*

Lewis, explored the Marias River, which enters the Missouri from the north side.

Clark took a third party, including Charboneau and Bird Woman, to explore the Yellowstone. As they moved southeast across the country from the Jefferson, Bird Woman pointed out at long distance a pass through which they could travel by easy grades to the Yellowstone. Since Bird Woman was but twelve years old at the time of her capture, her recollection of this pass, by which the Snakes were accustomed to travel from the Missouri to the Yellowstone, shows how well her wilderness life had schooled her in observation. Her remarkable feat of memory on this occasion has given rise to many fiction stories in which she is characterized as the guide of the Lewis and Clark Expedition on the march to the Pacific. Even some history writers have followed the lead of the fiction writers and have called her the guide of the expedition. A study of the Lewis and Clark journals, in which she often is praised for her assistance, fails to support the tale that she was a guide except on this one occasion and also at the time on the Jefferson when she remembered the scene of her capture by the Minnetarres. This is written not to belittle the services of Bird Woman, but to correct a prevalent error. Upon arrival at the Yellowstone, Clark's men built boats and descended to the river's mouth and there awaited the coming of Lewis.

When Lewis joined Clark, he reported an unfortunate encounter with a band of Blackfeet, two of whom he and his men shot and killed to prevent horse stealing. This was the beginning of seventy years of hostility between the Americans and the Blackfeet.

The three sections of the expedition having been reunited, they turned loose their horses on the prairie and rode by boat to the Mandan village. Here they were greeted by several American trappers bound for the Rockies, who requested that John Colter, a soldier of the expedition, be granted his discharge by Lewis and Clark so that he might guide them to the headwaters of the Missouri and share in the profits of their trapping venture. Colter was eager to go back. In the mountain streams he had noted many beaver dams and believed that a fortune could be harvested there by trapping. He was given his discharge from the army and once more turned his face toward the west.

At the Mandan village Charboneau and his wife and son also left the expedition. Little Baptiste, who began his career as an explorer at the age of ten weeks, was now a year and a half old. He had grown into a husky lad and was a favorite of Captain Clark, who had taught him to speak English. He also was learning French from his father and Snake from his mother. He later went to St. Louis to be educated at Captain Clark's expense. Some writers say that he also attended school in Germany. Eventually he returned to the Rockies to serve as guide and to find employment as a trapper and hunter. Upon parting from the Charboneaus, Clark wrote in his journal:

"This man has been very serviceable to us and his wife particularly useful among the Shoshonees (Snakes). Indeed she has borne with patience truly admirable the fatigues of so long a route encumbered with the charge of an infant."

The Missouri, which had retarded the expedition on its upstream voyage, sped the boats swiftly downstream with the current. Riding at ease, the men glided past the Platte, the Kansas, the Osage and the Gasconade. They passed La Charette and St. Charles in a hurry and arrived at the St. Louis levee in September, 1806, two years and four months after their departure. One man died early on the journey. Another remained on the upper Missouri. The remainder completed the hazardous expedition, in which they had suffered hunger, cold, rain and arduous toil, all in robust health.

While Lewis and Clark were journeying to the Pacific, another army officer, Lieutenant Zebulon Montgomery Pike, was sent to seek the sources of the Mississippi. With a party of soldiers and *voyageurs* and with Pierre Rosseau of St. Louis as French interpreter and guide, Pike visited Julien Dubuque at his lead mines, paused at Prairie du Chien and proceeded northward to the site of the present St. Paul, near where he met Jean Baptiste Faribault, an employe of the Northwest Company, who was carrying furs from the upper Mississippi to Canada. Pike won the friendship of Faribault, who later became a useful citizen of the United States. In 1841 Faribault assisted Lucien Gaultier, a French priest, who founded the mission of St. Paul, from which the capital city of Minnesota takes its name. His sons founded the city of Faribault, Minnesota. Pike continued his exploration and mapping of the Mississippi almost to its sources and then returned to St. Louis in 1806.

He was then ordered on a second tour of exploration, this time across the western plains to the Rockies. With a party of twenty soldiers and two French interpreters, he moved up the Missouri River to the Osage where he visited the Osage Indians. Here he met Pawhuska, Osage chief who had fought in the Battle of Monongahela. Pawhuska proudly displayed the British uniform and the British scalp he had taken on that occasion. Marching west from the Osage village with a train of pack horses bought from the Indians, Pike came to the Pawnee Republic where a Spanish flag was floating. The Spaniards, learning of Pike's expedition, had come out from Santa Fe to notify the Indians that they were living under Spanish protection and should turn all American trespassers back. Pike disregarded the warning and persuaded the Pawnees to replace the Spanish flag with the Stars and Stripes. Here he dismissed Belle Oseau, a half-breed interpreter, but retaining A. F. V. Baronet, who could speak Spanish as well as French, marched westward along the Arkansas River to the Rockies. At both the Osage and Pawnee villages Pike found French traders. After leaving the Pawnees, he met no more people, not even Indians, until he finally came to the Rio Grande River.

Across the Plains he travelled through the rich game country where Bourgmont had been so charmed more than eighty years before. Sighting a great mountain to the north of the Arkansas, he marched north to stand at its base and to admire it. Although the Spaniards and French had seen this mountain long before, Pike was the first to give a written description of it. From this fact it is known as Pike's Peak. Advancing up the Arkansas canyon into the defiles of the Rockies, until winter came with its bitter cold, Pike turned south in an effort to cross the mountains to the Red River. After severe suffering from cold and hunger and after losing some of his men from freezing, he finally led his party to a river which proved to be the Rio Grande and not the Red. Here Spanish soldiers arrested him for trespass and took him to Santa Fe.

He was well treated by the Spanish officers and allowed

the freedom of the city. In that way he met two men who
had preceded him across the Plains to Santa Fe only a short
time before. One was Baptiste La Lande, a rascally Frenchman from St. Louis, who had formed a partnership with
William Morrison of Kaskaskia, by which Morrison provided trade goods for fur trade with the Indians. La Lande
ascended the Missouri to the Platte, bought horses from the
Pawnees and proceeded over the route followed by the
Mallet Brothers to Santa Fe, where he arrived in 1804 and
sold his goods at prices ten times their worth in St. Louis.
Instead of returning to share his profits with Morrison, La
Lande remained at Santa Fe and became a Spanish subject.

Next Pike met James Purcell, a native of Kentucky, who
had gone to St. Louis before the Louisiana Purchase, had
travelled to the Pawnee country with French traders, had
wandered with the Indians in the Rockies and had come to
Taos and to Santa Fe in 1805. There he was employed as a
carpenter. Purcell took Pike to one side and emptying his
bullet pouch poured out several bits of shining, yellow
metal. It was gold. Purcell had found the nuggets near
Pike's Peak and kept them hidden in his pouch from the
eyes of the Spaniards.

After a stay in Santa Fe, Pike was taken to Chihuahua,
where the Spanish authorities released him and conducted
him back to the United States by way of Texas.

While Pike cannot be classed as a discoverer of the lands
he visited, he was the first to give the world maps of the
upper Mississippi and of the Southwest Plains and Rockies.
The expeditions of Lewis and Clark and of Pike added
much to man's knowledge of American geography.

CHAPTER XVII

LISA MANS THE LONG–OAR

GEORGE DROUILLARD, upon coming home from the Lewis and Clark Expedition, found employment awaiting him with the Missouri Fur Company, a new organization, headed by Manuel Lisa. After the Louisiana Purchase put an end to Lisa's monopoly of trade with the Indians on the Osage River, he began the formation of a new fur company to include all in St. Louis interested in the trade. Although Lisa was a Spaniard who spoke French badly and English hardly at all, he overcame his handicaps so well that he was able to persuade the members of the old French families and also the newly arrived Americans that they should invest their money in his enterprise and make him the president.

He even made peace with his former rivals, the Chouteau brothers, and induced them to become his partners. When Clark came back from the Lewis and Clark Expedition and made his home in St. Louis, Lisa persuaded him also to become a partner. The Missouri Fur Company was composed of twelve associates, six being English-speaking Americans, five being of the old French families and the twelfth being Lisa, the New Orleans-born Spaniard.

While we speak of the English-speaking inhabitants of St. Louis as Americans, all were now Americans since the

United States had extended her domain to the west bank of the Mississippi. As for Lisa, he became as true a patriot of the United States as Captain Clark himself.

To transport the cargoes of the Missouri Fur Company, Lisa discarded the *pirogue*, which had been the commerce carrier of the Missouri from the time of Bourgmont, and bought a keel boat. This new American-made craft was built on a keel like a sea-going ship, was well streamlined, and could carry a burden of twenty tons. It was decked over to protect the freight from rain and had a small cabin on deck for the comfort of the master and other officers. It was equipped with a rudder, but since a rudder might become enmeshed in submerged tree branches, Lisa removed it and steered with a long-oar. Since he had been a sailor in his youth and knew how to employ the power of the wind, he rigged a mast and sail. Of course the Missouri, lined as it was with high bluffs and fringed with forest, could seldom be navigated by sail. Generally the crew drew the boat by a towline or drove it with oars or poles.

Although Lisa spoke French badly, he realized that the *voyageurs* expected him to lead them in the singing. He therefore mastered all the favorite river *chansons*. The bluffs of the Missouri have echoed the notes of his lusty voice twenty-six times, for he voyaged thirteen times up river and thirteen times down, sometimes going as far as the Platte and sometimes to the Rockies. It has been estimated that on those thirteen round-trip journeys he spent what would equal three full years and that he travelled more than 26,000 miles on that stream. His crews responded to his leadership so wholeheartedly that they outvoyaged all rivals.

Accompanied by the dauntless Drouillard, he embarked on his first voyage as the head of the Missouri Fur Com-

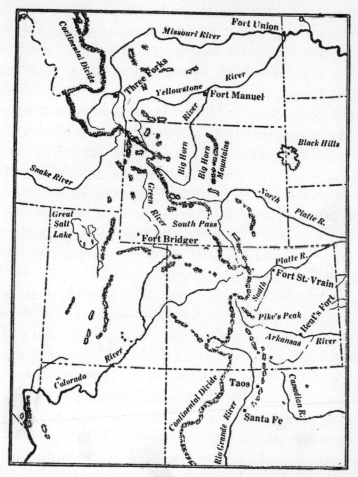

The Trapping Ground of the Mountain Men

pany in the spring of 1807 with a fur brigade of picked men. A tragic incident occurred on this voyage, which shows that even picked men do not always measure up to expectations. Antoine Bisonette, one of the greenhorns of the party, became homesick soon after the boat's departure. The farther the boat travelled, the greater his homesickness became. One evening after the boat had tied up for the night and the men were making camp, he slipped away quietly into the woods, intending to hide from Lisa and catch a ride back to St. Louis on the next downstream *pirogue*.

In those days desertion from a fur brigade was as much of a crime as desertion from a ship at sea. Lisa accordingly ordered Drouillard to find Bisonette and bring him back. It is not at all likely that Lisa meant for Drouillard to shoot Bisonette; but when the hunter received his orders, he picked up his rifle, trailed the fugitive as he might have trailed a wild beast, found him and ordered him to return to his master. At this Bisonette resisted capture, broke loose and ran. Drouillard, unwilling to lose his quarry, fired. Shouldering his wounded victim as he might have carried a deer, he brought him back to the boat. Lisa, distressed at what had happened, put Bisonette to bed in his own cabin and nursed him, but it was a fatal wound. Bisonette died. The next year Bisonette's relatives had Drouillard arrested and tried in St. Louis for murder, but the jury found the shooting justified.

Some days after Bisonette's death and burial, the keelboat crew sighted a *pirogue* coming down the river. As the vessels drew alongside to exchange news, Drouillard recognized Colter and his two companions who had gone on a trapping expedition to the Yellowstone. They had been very successful and the *pirogue* was heavily laden. Lisa, upon learning from Drouillard that Colter was one of the best men of the Lewis and Clark Expedition, invited him to return up river with the keel boat. It had been three years since Colter had seen a white man's town, but he already was homesick for the mountains. He quickly arranged for his two partners to sell his share of furs for his account. Then picking up his long rifle and elk-skin bag, he sprang aboard the keel boat. For the third time he set his face toward the shining Rockies where stirring adventure awaited him.

Up the river moved the keel boat. In the Sioux country Lisa paused long enough to establish a trading post and left a few of his men in charge. He opened a second station with the Arickaree Indians and a third with the Mandans, after which he ascended to the Yellowstone and up the Yellowstone to the mouth of the Big Horn where he directed the building of Fort Manuel in the heart of the Crow country, this being the first white settlement in the present Montana.

The Crows were indeed glad to welcome Lisa, for his coming meant that they could trade for guns with which to defend themselves from the Blackfeet, who, armed with muskets bought from the British of the Northwest Company, often attacked the Crows to rob and to slay. Fort Manuel was to be more than a mere Indian trading post. In Lisa's brigade were several expert trappers equipped with the latest American-made traps. He expected these men would catch more beaver than could be hoped for from many times their number of Indians, who trapped only when they wanted beaver skins to trade for manufactured goods.

Leaving most of his men at Fort Manuel, Lisa returned to St. Louis, arriving before winter. No other trader had ever before gone to the upper Missouri and back the same season. His voyage proved the superiority of the keel boat, which now replaced the *pirogue* as the commerce carrier of the Missouri.

As Lisa departed down river, Colter, with a string of traps on his back, followed the Yellowstone farther into the mountains than any white man had been before. He came one day to a spring beside which he paused for a cooling drink. As his lips touched the water and he was about to take a gulp, he suddenly leaped to his feet and spat out the water. It was scalding hot. He had heard of hot springs before, but none so hot as this. Advancing farther, he found more hot springs. One day he came upon a jet of roaring water and hissing steam spouting out of the earth and into the air in a fountain as high as the flagpole in St. Louis. He began to wonder if he had come to the gates of hell where Satan was boiling water in a mammoth underground kettle. Some of the geysers he discovered flowed steadily, but most of them spouted in periods of activity with alternate periods of quiet.

Upon his return to Fort Manuel from the region now included in Yellowstone National Park, he told of his discoveries, but the trappers burst into shrieks of incredulous laughter. They voted him the best and biggest liar in the brigade. Not until they saw the "devil's teapots" with their own eyes could they believe him.

Colter had one other hair-raising adventure. With a companion named Potts, he crossed the mountains by way of the pass through which Bird Woman had guided Captain Clark in 1806. Arriving at the three forks of the Missouri, he and Potts found abundant beaver and expected to reap

MANUEL LISA

From a painting. By courtesy of the Missouri Historical Society, St. Louis.

MARY HEMPSTEAD LISA

First white woman of the Upper Missouri.

a harvest of fur. But a band of Blackfeet arrived and sur-rounded them. Colter saw that resistance to the Indians was useless. He therefore surrendered and urged Potts to fol-low his example. Potts, however, fired upon the warriors and wounded one. Before he could reload, he was riddled with bullets and arrows. This unexpected action of Potts put Colter, who already had handed over his rifle, in a serious predicament. The Indians were infuriated with Potts, but, having killed him, they had to take their ven-geance out on Colter. After a conference among them-selves, they asked Colter in the sign language if he was a good foot racer. He replied that in his native state of Ken-tucky he was regarded as one of the poorest runners who ever engaged in a foot race.

That answer suited their purpose. They stripped Colter naked, even removing his moccasins. They told him that they would give him an opportunity to run for his life in competition with the best men of the Blackfeet tribe. Since he had modestly called himself a poor runner, they gave him a good head start to make the race more interesting. The signal was given and the race was on. The course of the race was over six miles of plain on which grew masses of prickly-pear cactus. The spines of cactus pierced his bare feet, inflicting cruel pain at every step; but his only hope lay in running as fast as he could to reach a river he could see on the other side of the six-mile plain. For three miles he kept ahead of his pursuers. Then, when he felt he could run no longer and would have to give up, he heard the footfalls of a runner behind him.

Glancing back, he saw that the approaching warrior was carrying a light lance and was poising it for a cast. At this Colter exerted himself until he burst a blood vessel in one of his lungs, and blood gushed forth to spread a crimson dye over the front of his body. He managed to remain in the lead of his opposing racer for two more miles, when once again he heard the sound of closely pursuing feet. Certain that the runner was again poising the lance for a cast, Colter stopped suddenly, wheeled about and spread his hands wide. The sudden pause, the gesture of the spreading arms and the sight of the white man's body smeared with blood must have astonished the lancer so much that it spoiled his aim. The lance fell short, striking the ground at Colter's feet and breaking the handle. In a flash the Kentuckian grasped what was left of the broken handle, jerked the lance from the ground, rushed upon his enemy and thrust him through, pinning him to the ground.

The other warriors raised an angry yell, but they were too far in the rear to do anything. At the end of the sixth mile Colter came to the river and there saw a jam of logs and trees entangled on a sand bar. Diving into the river, he came up under the log jam and hid there under a log. When the Indians arrived, they swarmed over the logs looking for him. At times they came so near to him that he feared they could hear the chattering of his teeth. The dive into the cold water after the exhausting race left him weak and suffering from cold. The log jam had been caused by a spring freshet, which had washed the trees down from the mountains. Since the logs were spread over the sand bar and over the water to form an island an acre in extent, the Indians failed to find him.

Colter waited until night, when he dived once more into the water, swam beneath the surface until he was below the

Indian camp and came to the river bank. The night was cold and he had to walk to keep up circulation. The next day he found roots to eat and in that way satisfied his hunger. Eluding the Indians, he crossed the mountains, and after seven days and nights, staggered into Fort Manuel.

To understand the hostility of the Blackfeet toward the Americans, it must be recalled that they traded with the British of the Northwest Company and therefore regarded the British as their friends. On the other hand Lisa had built Fort Manuel in the heart of the Crow country. Since the Crows and Blackfeet were enemies, Lisa's act was regarded as unfriendly to the Blackfeet. The fact that Captain Lewis's men had killed two Blackfeet horse thieves on the Marias River was not sufficient cause of hostility. The Blackfeet recognized the right of a man to protect his own property and might have forgiven Lewis had not Lisa traded with the Crows.

The Americans also believed that the British traders encouraged the Blackfeet in their hostility toward the Missouri fur brigades, for the British regarded the upper Missouri as a part of Canada and regarded the Americans as trespassers.

Disregarding the hostility of the Blackfeet, Lisa sent a brigade of trappers to the Three Forks in 1808 and there they built a fort known as Three Forks. Andrew Henry, one of Lisa's associates, and Pierre Chouteau, another associate, were in command at Three Forks at various times and Drouillard was second in command. For two seasons the fort successfully resisted the attacks of the Blackfeet, but in 1810 they began a continuous siege. In April they waylaid and killed five men from the fort at one time. It became so dangerous to leave the palisade that only the bravest could be persuaded to go out to examine the beaver traps.

In May Drouillard was leading a small party of mounted men to follow the trap line and bring in the fur, when a large band of Blackfeet charged the party and killed ten of the trappers at the outset. Drouillard might have escaped by riding to the fort, which was only two miles away. Instead he dismounted and stood beside his horse resolved to teach the Blackfeet a lesson. Maneuvering his animal to serve as a shield, he warded off the attack first from one side and then from the other.

While warding off the enemy, he kept up a steady fire, loading rapidly and taking careful aim across the back of his horse. The Blackfeet howled in rage and chagrin as their best men fell, one at each crack of Drouillard's rifle. Unable to get a fair shot at him, the Indians killed his horse. As the faithful animal fell, it exposed him to a fusillade from all sides at once. In a moment the battle was over and Drouillard died beside the Jefferson River he had helped to discover.

No doubt the Blackfeet carried away his scalp to dry it on a loop in the smoke of their wigwams and to dance the scalp dance around it. But that scalp was a dearly won trophy, for Drouillard had taken with him many Blackfeet warriors to the Land of the Hereafter. More white scalps were needed to even up the score. They therefore pushed their war so ruthlessly that Fort Three Forks had to be abandoned. Chouteau departed before the decision was made to retreat, and Henry led the remnant of the brigade across the Rockies to the headwaters of the Snake River.

From there he sent a messenger by a roundabout way to ask for re-enforcements from Fort Manuel. Unfortunately the trappers at Fort Manuel became panic stricken and fled down the river to St. Louis, arriving in the autumn.

The cowardly abandonment of Fort Manuel roused the contempt of the Sioux and Arickarees. They too joined in the hostility toward the Missouri Fur Company. Lisa was disgusted when his men arrived in St. Louis from Fort Manuel. Nothing could be done, however, until the following spring when he once more arranged to return to the Yellowstone.

That same spring a fur brigade of the American Fur Company, with headquarters in New York, planned to ascend the Missouri with a view of crossing the continent and founding a fur-trading city at the mouth of the Columbia. Head of the American Fur Company was John Jacob Astor, a German by birth, who began his business career in London as a penniless clerk, and who came to America to engage in the fur trade on the Great Lakes where he amassed a fortune. He became an American citizen, but he had no strong loyalty for his adopted country and failed to see danger in employing British subjects for his colony on the Columbia. Most of his employes were experienced fur men formerly in the employ of the Northwest Fur Company. They included Scotch, English and French residents of Canada. Only a few of the members of his expedition were native Americans, one being Wilson P. Hunt.

Hunt was placed in command of the brigade, which was to proceed from St. Louis. A second crew was sent by sea around Cape Horn. Astor's plans included not only the control of the fur trade of the Columbia Valley, but also trade up and down the Pacific Coast, with the Hawaiian Islands and with China. He planned to build a fleet of ships and control the commerce of the entire North Pacific. From the fact that his name was Astor, the men of his brigade were known as Astorians.

Hunt was ready to depart from St. Louis in March, 1811. Lisa was unable to get ready for three more weeks, and he asked Hunt to delay his departure so that they might go up the Missouri in company for mutual protection from the Indians. To this proposal Hunt gave an evasive answer. Among the Astorians were two men who formerly had been rivals of Lisa on the Upper Missouri. They told Hunt that Lisa was a treacherous man who would be apt to turn the Sioux against the Astorians if he had a chance. Hunt, fearing to have any dealing with such a person, rode to St. Charles where his boat was awaiting him and departed upstream on March 12. The main bulk of the Astorians had wintered in camp at the mouth of the Nodaway River, about halfway between the mouth of the Kansas and that of the Platte. Hunt voyaged to the Nodaway as fast as his crew could navigate, ordered his brigade to break camp immediately and continued his flight. It was a grand sight as the keel boats moved away from Nodaway, the master of each vessel singing and the *voyageurs* responding as they plied their oars.

Lisa, upon discovering that Hunt had gone, hastened to complete his arrangements; yet despite his haste, it was April 2, or just twenty-one days after Hunt's departure from St. Charles, before Lisa left the same place.

There followed the most memorable keel-boat race in

history. It has been described by three distinguished writers. Henry Brackenridge, traveller and author, was a passenger on Lisa's boat. John Bradbury, noted botanist of his time, rode with Hunt. They both have left a day-by-day account of the voyages of each party, while Washington Irving, historian of the Astorians, also has written an account. Two distinguished frontiersmen, Daniel Boone and John Colter, witnessed Lisa's brigade as it passed their cabins. Colter regretted that he could not go to the mountains for more adventure, but he was married and was living on a Missouri farm, which claimed his time. Two other noted persons were on Lisa's boat. These were Charboneau and Bird Woman, who had come to St. Louis a year or two before at the invitation of Captain Clark; but tiring of town life, they were returning to their home at the Mandan village.

Hunt had eighty-five men in his brigade and several keel boats. Lisa had twenty-five *voyageurs* in addition to his three passengers. It was because of his superiority of men that Hunt saw no need of the company of Lisa in passing through the Sioux country. The men of both brigades were well armed and each keel boat carried a small cannon, mounted on a swivel, in the bow.

Bad luck dogged the Missouri brigade for the first three or four days of the race. Again and again the boat ran afoul of submerged sawyers. The Missouri is infested with perils of this kind. The swift and powerful current is forever undermining the bluffs of the stream. Cliffs crowned with forest trees are continuously being caved into the river. A tree is washed into the main channel of the stream and its roots become embedded in the mud and sand of the river's bed. The rest of the tree rises and falls with the current somewhat like a saw, from which comes the word sawyer. The passing boatman becomes so practised that he can usually tell by the swirling of the current where a sawyer is hidden beneath the murky water. But even the best pilot will be deceived. Even Lisa, who knew the Missouri as well as any man, ran repeatedly above these submerged trees, which sawed upward just in time to entangle the boat. On such occasions Lisa would rush to the bow, grappling hook in hand, to take the lead in freeing the boat. When all was clear, he would bound back to the long-oar to steer the boat and to take up the song where he had left off.

The life of the keel-boat men was a continuous round of toil. They were often soaked to the skin from dawn to dark, for they worked through rainstorm as well as through fair weather. Often they had to wade in the water as they towed their craft. After a day of gruelling work—towing, rowing and poling—they came to camp at night where their food was hominy and pork. After passing the settlements and coming to the region where there was abundant game, the menu was changed to hominy and wild meat. A day of such back-breaking work generally resulted in only fifteen miles of progress. Under the circumstances wages were pitifully small. Men today could hardly be found to do such work at any wage, yet Lisa's *voyageurs* were generally good-humored and willing to sing or joke.

For several days Lisa travelled less than fifteen miles a day. He knew he was losing time on Hunt. Yet when he came upon an ox mired in the quicksand at the river's edge, he gave orders for all hands to cut poles and bring the towline. Hastily constructing a crude winch and crane, they hoisted the animal from the mire and set it free on solid ground. This delay cost several hours of valuable time. The men, smeared with mud from their labor, were discouraged as they returned to the boat. They were grumbling to each other about their master, who seemed to think more about an ox than about getting them through the Sioux country in safety. They were still grumbling when a stiff breeze sprang up from down stream. This enabled them to spread sail and travel with the wind while they had a chance to rest. The wind carried them along at a fast rate so that by night they had made more mileage in a few hours than they had ordinarily been making in a whole day. At this the men praised their master. They declared that the freeing of the ox had brought them luck. As they wrapped themselves in their blankets and lay down with their feet to the camp fire that night, their hearts were full of hope that under Lisa's leadership they would overtake Hunt before they met with the Sioux.

When they came to Cote Sans Dessein, a new settlement near the mouth of the Osage River, which had replaced La Charette as the westernmost white man's town, they eagerly inquired of Baptiste Louis Roi, leading citizen of the town, concerning Hunt. Roi replied that Hunt had passed nineteen days before, which meant that they had gained two days. At the mouth of the Nodaway they examined Hunt's winter camp. Here, by signs unknown today except to expert woodsmen, they learned that they had gained several days more. Whenever they noted one of the Astorian camps on shore, they paused to examine it and read signs telling how long it had been since the passage of Hunt. At each place they were encouraged to note that they were gaining.

But when they came to the southern hunting ground of the Sioux, they were still four days in the rear. Here Lisa dispatched two runners to overtake Hunt and request that he await their arrival. Since men on foot could avoid following the detours of the river and since a man on foot could easily outwalk a keel boat, they overtook Hunt quickly and delivered the request. It had an effect opposite from that intended. The Astorians, amazed that Lisa was so near, redoubled their efforts. A day or two later they came to a band of Sioux in war regalia, who demanded that Hunt give them presents. At this, two of Hunt's men resorted to a despicable trick to get rid of the Sioux. They told the Indians that the gifts were on a boat which was following only four days in the rear. They also reported that the boat in the rear had but twenty-five men aboard. The Indians, unwilling to take the gifts forcibly from Hunt's eighty-five armed men, decided to waylay the twenty-five who were following.

Lisa, upon learning that the Astorians were redoubling their efforts, urged his Missourians to catch up as a matter of pride. They ate their breakfasts before day so as to be ready to sail at the first light of dawn. They even travelled at night. This proved to be a fortunate thing, for one night they passed the Sioux camp without rousing the Indians and thus eluded them.

On the morning of June 2, just two months after they had left St. Charles, Brackenridge left the boat to climb a hill. This gave him a long view ahead, and just around the bend he saw the Astorian fleet. Hastening back, he roused the *voyageurs* to new exertions. Their oars rose and fell in perfect cadence. So fast did they go that they overtook the Astorians at 11 o'clock that day. They had voyaged from St. Charles to the Grand Detour of the Missouri, a distance of 1100 miles in sixty-one days, at an average of eighteen miles a day.

Since Hunt could not escape from Lisa, the two parties travelled together until they came to the Arickarees, where the Astorians bought horses and marched overland, crossing the Continental Divide far south of the Blackfoot country. Hunt led his brigade to the mouth of the Columbia, where he met the crew travelling by sea. They together built the fort and log-hut village of Astoria, the first American settlement on the Pacific. Lisa, after separating from Hunt, continued up the Missouri, rescued Henry, and once more engaged in the fur trade.

A new difficulty now arose. The United States, although utterly unprepared, declared war against Great Britain. The cause for declaration was the insistence by Great Britain on the right to search American ships for British seamen who had deserted their navy for the higher pay offered by American captains. It is not our purpose to review the War of 1812 except as it affected the West.

The declaration of war gave the British fur merchants opportunity to do openly what they doubtless had been doing secretly for a long time. They bribed the Indians to wage war upon the American fur brigades and upon exposed frontier settlements. In a very short time Lisa was compelled to withdraw down the Missouri to a point a short distance above the Platte where he built Fort Lisa. This was the beginning of an important trading center of which Omaha, Nebraska, and Council Bluffs, Iowa, are now a part.

Captain Clark, having been appointed governor of Upper Louisiana, the name of which had been changed to Missouri Territory, asked Lisa to help him by serving as subagent for the Indians. Lisa was prompt to act in counteracting the influence of the British agents working with the Indians. He had in his employ men who had spent most of their lives among the Osages, Kansas, Otoes, Poncas and Pawnees and had their friendship. He sent these men to call upon the Indians and urge them to kick back the gifts offered by the British.

Nothing, however, could be done to influence the Blackfeet, Arickarees, Sioux, Sacs and Foxes. The Foxes, who had traded with the St. Louis merchants during the life of Dubuque, eagerly turned back to British influence. A band of Sacs and Foxes swooped upon Cote Sans Dessein and probably would have massacred the inhabitants had they not been discovered by Osage hunters, who sounded the warning. Baptiste Louis Roi led the men of the settlement out to meet the enemy, routed them in battle and saved the town. The Indians, turning eastward, attacked Boone's settlement where they killed several settlers, including Captain James Calloway, grandson of Boone. Farther east they approached St. Charles and even St. Louis.

Lisa replied to the Sac and Fox raids by arming war parties of friendly Indians and sending them overland from the Missouri to the Mississippi to attack the Sacs and Foxes in their villages. This proved to be good strategy. It forced the roving warriors to hurry home for the protection of their own country.

While Lisa was successful on the Missouri, the Americans suffered elsewhere. At Fort Dearborn, on the site of Chicago, the American troops surrendered to the British on promise of safe conduct. No sooner had they given up their arms and marched out of the safety of the fort than they were set upon by Indian allies of the British, who killed men, women and children without distinction. Disaster also befell Astoria. The British arrived at the mouth of the Columbia during the absence of Hunt. Thereupon, Astor's British employes eagerly surrendered, and the Northwest Company took possession of the Columbia Valley.

By the terms of the treaty of peace signed at the close of the war, the British agreed to surrender all captured posts. They did not, however, surrender the Columbia Valley. We can only conjecture what would have been the fate of the West had Lisa and his associates not held the lower Missouri. In all probability the British would have remained on the Missouri had they taken it. But with the lower Missouri as a base, Lisa returned to the upper Missouri immediately after the war. He quickly regained the fur trade he had lost. He could do this because he was able to ship his cargoes on the Missouri, while the British had a long overland haul as well as a difficult water passage to bring cargoes from Montreal. In a few years the British yielded to the Americans and agreed to fix the boundary between Canada and the United States at the Forty-ninth Parallel as far west as the Rockies. No agreement could be reached concerning the ownership of the Columbia basin. The Hudson Bay Company succeeded the Northwest Company there and remained in possession.

Lisa was at the height of his prosperity when he was married for the third time in 1818. His first wife, a French woman, had died. His second was an Indian, whose marriage he annulled. His third was Mary Hempstead Keeny, a widow who spoke only English. Lisa's success in courting her, when he could scarce speak her language, again calls attention to his facility in overcoming handicaps. Despite differences of language, they were fond of each other and Mrs. Lisa accompanied him to Fort Lisa where they spent the winter of 1819–20. As far as the records show, she was the first white woman to live on the Missouri beyond the Platte.

The following spring they returned to St. Louis. There Lisa fell suddenly ill. He grew rapidly worse and in a few days the founder of the Missouri Fur Company was dead.

CHAPTER XVIII

THE CHOUTEAU BROTHERS

As LONG as Lisa lived, he held the leading merchants of St. Louis united in the Missouri Fur Company so that they worked together like the fingers of a hand. His death was the signal for several rival companies to spring into existence. The associates remaining in the Missouri Fur Company looked for a leader strong enough to take Lisa's place. Auguste and Pierre Chouteau were both yet living, but neither wished to return to active management.

Next they turned to two sons of Pierre Chouteau, both of whom had been with Lisa on the Upper Missouri and were familiar with the fur trade. Both of these boys were named Pierre. The elder was Auguste Pierre and the second Pierre. To distinguish them, the elder was called A. P., and the second Pierre "Cadet." Both had gone to the French school of the fur-trading schoolmaster Jean Baptiste Trudeau. Both had travelled as boys with their father to the Osage country and to the upper Missouri. It was as natural for them to take to the fur trade as it is for a bird to take to the air.

A. P. Chouteau at one time determined to be a soldier and attended West Point where he was graduated with an officer's commission. He remained in the army, however, only a short time. During the War of 1812 he served in the Missouri militia. As soon as the war was over, he led an expedition to the Pike's Peak region, where for two years his brigade trapped for beaver with great success on the headwaters of the Arkansas. This was in disputed territory. The United States claimed it as a part of the Louisiana Purchase, while Spain claimed it by right of discovery and exploration. The Spaniards arrested the men of Chouteau's brigade in 1817 and locked them in a dark, damp, filthy prison at Santa Fe. For forty-eight days they were left to worry about their fate. Their prospect was bad indeed, for in 1811 several Americans had been arrested, and sentenced to nine years imprisonment, and forced to work in the silver mines of Chihuahua.

Chouteau was wondering if he would be sentenced to suffer a like fate when he was brought out into the daylight. He shaded his face from the glare of the sun, which hurt his eyes after seven weeks of confinement in the dark. Into the adobe Palace of the Governors he was led and commanded to kneel before the judge. Although a citizen of a free republic, Chouteau obeyed and knelt as ordered. Then the judge read his decision. All of Chouteau's furs, merchandise, traps, horses, and other equipment, of a value of $30,000, was confiscated. Each man was allowed to keep one horse and his rifle on condition that all would return to St. Louis again and never more return to the upper Arkansas. Since he could do nothing else, Chouteau promised. The judge handed him the paper on which the decision was written and a bailiff ordered him to kiss it. Since he could not help himself, he pressed it to his lips and kissed it as reverently as though it were a holy thing. The judge, satisfied, gave him and his men their freedom. They were glad to escape.

Rather than risk a second arrest, Chouteau assisted Lisa on the upper Missouri. Then he returned to the Arkansas in the present Oklahoma and built a trading post and residence on the Verdigris River north of its junction with the Arkansas. His trading post became a well-known place. There he entertained many noted men. Samuel Houston was often his guest. Washington Irving, while on his tour of the prairies, was entertained there and has left us a description of the residence and surrounding farm. Trade on the Arkansas proved profitable, and A. P. Chouteau had no desire to succeed Lisa on the Missouri.

This left his younger brother, Pierre "Cadet" Chouteau, as the next best man. He was thirty-one years old and had been active in the fur trade since the age of fifteen. Upon becoming the leader of the Missouri River trade, his first problem was that of coming to terms with John Jacob Astor, president of the American Fur Company. After the Canadian boundary was set at the Forty-ninth Parallel, the British had to withdraw. The Northwest Company therefore sold its forts on the upper Missouri to the American Fur Company. Astor did not care to engage in a rivalry with Chouteau. The two men therefore agreed to merge their companies into one. Since Astor lived in New York and often voyaged to Europe where he was in close touch with the fur markets of London, Paris and Berlin, he agreed to handle the sale of furs on the markets of the world. On the other hand, Chouteau agreed to take active management of the trapping brigades and Indian trade of the Missouri. Under the terms of the merger, the Missouri Fur

Company became the Western Division of the American Fur Company.

Chouteau's men took over the old trading forts of both the Missouri Fur Company and the Northwest Company. He also built several new forts. At the junction of the Yellowstone and Missouri he built Fort Union. He rebuilt Fort Manuel at the mouth of the Big Horn. Advancing into the Blackfoot country, he built a fort at the mouth of the Marias. When Fort Tecumpseh on the Missouri fell into decay, he directed the building of a new fort there. When it was completed, the engineer in charge named it Fort Pierre in honor of Chouteau. Since it was a log fort, it has long since disappeared, but the city of Pierre, capital of South Dakota, perpetuates its memory. This city is only a short distance from the site of the old fort. Fort Lisa continued to be occupied until it was replaced by a new fort.

That Chouteau had a good eye for the location of future cities is shown by the fact that so many of the forts he built are now the sites of cities. He realized as early as 1822 that the mouth of the Kansas River was a strategic trading center. There he built Chouteau's Landing. Since this was one of his most important trading centers, he placed his younger brothers, Francis and Cyprian, in command. Later their still younger brother, Frederick, joined them. When Congress set aside the present Kansas, Oklahoma and Nebraska to be an Indian Territory and removed the Delawares, Shawnees, Pottawatomies, Sacs and Foxes, Kickapoos and other tribes from east of the Mississippi to settle in the present Kansas, Chouteau's Landing became an important trading center. Today two cities, Kansas City in Missouri and

m a contemporary portrait. By courtesy of the Missouri Historical Society, St. Louis.

PIERRE "Cadet" CHOUTEAU

Painting by C. H. Bodmer. From Maximilian Wied-Neuwied. "Voyage in the Interior of North America." By courtesy of the New York Public Library.

ENCAMPMENT ON THE MISSOURI

Kansas City in Kansas, with a combined population of half a million, mark the site of old Chouteau's Landing.

In connection with the forts on the Missouri, mention needs be made of Joseph Robidoux's trading post at the Blacksnake Hills. Robidoux was a son of the Joseph Robidoux who financed the ventures of Jacques D'Eglise. To-day the city of St. Joseph, Missouri, founded by Robidoux and named for his patron saint, stands upon the site of the trading post.

Not only was Pierre "Cadet" Chouteau a founder of trading posts that grew into cities, he designed a steamboat for navigation of the Upper Missouri. The first steamboat to come to St. Louis arrived from Pittsburgh in 1817. Two years later four steamboats, the *Jefferson*, the *Johnson*, the *Expedition* and the *Western Engineer*, left St. Louis for the Yellowstone. The *Jefferson* was snagged by a slivered log at the mouth of the Osage and sank. The *Johnson* and the *Expedition* turned back at Cow Island, near the present Atchison. The *Western Engineer* managed to reach Fort Lisa, where she remained frozen in the ice during the winter of 1819–20. She gave up the voyage and doubled back to St. Louis the following spring.

The back-breaking labors of the keel-boat *voyageurs* induced Chouteau to study the river and its problems until he devised the steamboat *Yellowstone*. She was 130 feet long, 19 feet beam, with paddle wheels on either side and so designed that when loaded with a 75-ton cargo, she drew only 6 feet of water. A boat of such shallow draft could sail to the mouth of the Yellowstone in early summer, at which season melting mountain snow raised the river level. Astor supplied Chouteau with the $7000 necessary to construct the boat. She made her first voyage in 1831, ascending beyond the Grand Detour. The following year she ascended to the Yellowstone. The Indians regarded her as a living creature. Fascinated by her revolving paddle wheels, they called her "the boat that walks upon the water."

The success of the *Yellowstone* resulted in the construction of more steamboats on the same pattern for use on the Missouri. Soon the song of the keel-boat *voyageur* was forever stilled. In its place the bass whistle of the steamboat woke the echoes of the bluffs of the Missouri.

Chouteau, of course, knew that his success in steamboating was only partly due to the design of his boat. Part was due to his skilful pilots, who understood the varying moods of the treacherous, shifting Missouri and who could tell by the tint of the water or the swirl of the current where to steer the boat to avoid submerged snags and sawyers or hidden sand bars. Chouteau's pilots were recruited from the best of his keel-boat *voyageurs*. Other steamboat owners followed his example and also employed *voyageurs* as pilots. These French-speaking pilots introduced into our language of steamboating many French words. It is because of them that even today we speak of the steamboat landings at New Orleans, St. Louis, St. Joseph and at other river cities as *levees*. From them we learned the French word *detour*, a bend in the river. Even though today we drive motor cars instead of steamboats, we still use the word *detour* to signify the place where we are turned from our course.

CHAPTER XIX

MOUNTAIN MEN

Oｎｅ of Lisa's associates, who was driven from Three Forks by the Blackfeet to seek refuge west of the Rockies in 1810, was Andrew Henry. While west of the Rockies, he learned that the region was exceedingly rich in beaver. After Lisa's death Henry discussed with William Henry Ashley, a new arrival at St. Louis, the possibilities of a beaver harvest across the Continental Divide. The two men formed a partnership in 1822, and while Henry became discouraged at reverses and withdrew from the company, Ashley persisted in the business which resulted in the formation of the Rocky Mountain Fur Company.

Ashley's first employes were largely French *engagées* of St. Louis, but he also employed Delaware and Shawnee Indians and young Americans of English origin, who were flocking to the west bank of the Mississippi eager for adventure. In 1823 he engaged three greenhorns from the east, who soon became his most able associates. They were: Tom Fitzpatrick, known to the Indians as Broken Hand after one hand had been shattered by the explosion of a gun; Jim Bridger, a Virginian, who discovered hundreds of mountains and valleys in the Rockies, and Jedediah Smith, a New Yorker, known as the praying trapper from his practice of carrying a Bible with him and of reading from it every night.

Through the winter of 1823–24 Ashley's brigade was housed in a log fort at the south of the Big Horn River. Early in 1824 Fitzpatrick learned from a Crow Indian of a pass across the Continental Divide where the slope to the summit was so gentle that a man could not even know he had crossed it until he came to a westward-flowing stream. The trappers called it South Pass, because the Indians said it lay to the south of other known passes of the Rockies. While it was yet winter, Fitzpatrick, with fourteen mounted men, set out to find the pass. They moved southward up the valley of the Big Horn until they came to the headwaters of the Platte in the present southern Wyoming.

Turning westward, they followed a creek until it headed as a tiny rill in a bank of snow. Higher and higher up the slope advanced the men, but since the rise was so gradual, they had no idea that they were crossing the backbone of America until they noted that the melting snow was flowing west. It was exactly as the Crows had said it would be. They had crossed the Continental Divide at an elevation of 8000 feet without knowing it. All the way they had been travelling over a gently undulating plain.

Fitzpatrick's men are entitled to credit for discovery of South Pass, although they were not the first white men to use it. Several Americans of the Astorian Expedition returned to St. Louis. They came eastward from the Snake River to the Platte and no doubt traversed South Pass late in 1812. Leaders of this group of eastward-bound Astorians were Robert Stuart, Ramsay Crooks and Robert McLellan. Their discovery of the pass was of no lasting value because no further use was made of it. When the men of the Missouri fur brigade arrived in the West, they had no knowledge of the existence of the pass until told of it by the Indians.

In the Green River Valley beyond the Divide, in what is now southwestern Wyoming, they found a region where the beaver were so ignorant of traps they seemed anxious to be snared. It was early spring. The weather was yet cold and furs were at their best. So rich was the daily catch, the trappers feared that they had not enough horses to pack home their harvest. Then came something that was worth worrying about.

The Snake Indians, discovering the white men without being seen themselves, came one morning at a mad gallop, howling like wolves and flapping blankets. Fitzpatrick's twenty-five horses took fright and stampeded far away to the hills where the Indians ran them into a dead-end canyon and lassoed them. The men were for following the Indians afoot and fighting them. Fitzpatrick, however, directed them to continue their trapping.

"The weather is cool now," said Fitzpatrick. "The fur is prime. Trap beaver while you can. After the weather warms up and fur is no good, we will find time to get back our horses."

The trappers delayed pursuit so long that the Indians concluded they had lost hope of recovering their horses. Accordingly they became careless. No longer did they think it necessary to put out horse guards. That was just the time for Broken Hand and his men to act. They followed the Indians to their camp almost a hundred miles away.

One night, during the dark of the moon, a Snake was

roused by the barking of a dog. Other dogs took up the howl. The warriors, seizing their weapons, rolled from their blankets and rushed out of their teepees. By that time the dogs were barking furiously, and looking up the valley toward the grazing horses. The war chief urged his men to save the herd. At the same time Fitzpatrick gave a signal. His men sprang forward. Each seized the mane of a horse and leaped to the animal's bare back. Yelling like demons and firing rifles, the mountain men put the entire Snake herd into a stampede. Right through the Indian village galloped the horses and out upon the plain beyond. All night the men rode and all day. They kept up the race until they were back to their old camp.

With as many horses as they needed they packed the furs upon forty animals and hurried through South Pass to deliver the harvest to Ashley. The discovery of South Pass changed Ashley's plan of operation. Thereafter he transported furs and trade goods by river only between St. Louis and the mouth of the Kansas. At most he used the river only as far north as the mouth of the Platte. From one landing or the other he transported goods by pack train across the plains to the gateway of the Rockies at South Pass.

He arranged with the mountain men that each year he would bring out supplies from St. Louis, while they would catch beaver and prepare the furs for his coming. Each summer he would appoint the place where he would meet them the following summer for exchange of furs and provisions. Since so many of his men were French in speech, they called the annual meeting place the *rendezvous*. This is another word which has been adopted from the French into our language. That the mountain men had an eye for beauty is shown from the lovely spots they chose for the annual *rendezvous*. Today Americans tour the Rockies and enjoy to the full such spots as Jackson's Hole, Pierre's Hole, Cache Valley, Green River and other mountain parks where rugged peaks look down on forests of poplar, pine and aspen. Without exception these parks were all at one time or another the *rendezvous* of mountain men.

Under the leadership of Fitzpatrick, Bridger and Smith, the exploration of the Rockies was carried on. Bridger, upon being told by an Indian of a body of salt water, marched to find what he supposed was the Pacific. Instead of coming to the ocean, he discovered Great Salt Lake in 1825.

Jedediah Smith, turning south from Salt Lake, discovered the Virgin River. He followed it to its union with the Colorado, descended the Colorado to the Yuma Desert, crossed the desert and then passed over the mountains to arrive at the Spanish seaport town of San Diego. Late in the winter of 1827 he led his men northward along the western front of the Sierra Nevada Mountains, whose saw-edged peaks rake the sky above snow line. At the headwaters of the Merced River, he discovered a pass across the mountains through which he came eastward back to the north side of Salt Lake in time for the summer *rendezvous*, in Cache Valley. For the first time a man had travelled by a practical wagon road from the Atlantic to the Pacific.

Unlike the rugged Rocky Mountain pass discovered by Lewis and Clark, South Pass could be crossed by wagons. Smith had completed the route to the Pacific by discovering two wagon roads over the mountains to California.

After the *rendezvous* Smith embarked on a second journey of exploration in an effort to tap the beaver country which supplied the British of the Columbia. He was to be gone two years on this hazardous journey in which more than half of his brigade was to suffer death. Instead of striking out directly toward the Oregon country, Smith turned southward once more toward southern California. This he did because he knew that snows would block his entrance to Oregon when he came to the mountains. By entering through southern California, he could march northward up the California valleys to arrive in the Oregon fur territory by early spring when fur would be at its best.

His first brush with the Indians came before his arrival in California. Several of his men were killed, and the survivors came to San Gabriel Mission, near the Spanish village of Los Angeles, where they remained until time to march north late in the winter of 1828. On this journey Smith and his men passed up the Sacramento Valley past the foot of Mount Shasta, whose slopes are cloaked in an evergreen forest and whose head is eternally hooded under ten thousand winters of snow.

In the Oregon mountains Smith's men gloated over the abundance of beaver. It kept them busy taking the animals from the traps, skinning them and baling the skins in hundred-pound packs. All went well until July when the Indians, resenting the presence of the strange white men, launched an attack. They beat the Americans, killed several of them and robbed them of the beaver skins. The robbery of the beaver packs, however, proved to be a mistake. Smith had marked each pack and his marks resulted in the undoing of the robbers. Mourning over the loss of his friends, Smith and the survivors of his brigade sought refuge with John McLoughlin, commandant at Fort Vancouver, which the Hudson Bay Company had built on the Columbia to replace Astoria. McLoughlin welcomed the Americans, invited them to spend the winter at his fort and listened attentively as Smith told the tale of his explorations and adventures. One day several Indians came to the fort to trade beaver packs for merchandise. McLoughlin turned the packs over and quickly noted the marks placed by Smith, which the Indians had failed to see.

Leading the Indians into Smith's presence, McLoughlin sternly accused them of murdering the Americans and stealing their beaver. The Indians, not knowing how McLoughlin had discovered their misdeeds, broke down and confessed. Not knowing any better way to punish them, the commandant ordered them to bring in all the other stolen packs and deliver them to Smith. This the Indians did, for they feared to rouse McLoughlin's displeasure. Then McLoughlin paid Smith for the beaver at the prevailing market price. No one could have treated the Americans better. Smith remained at Fort Vancouver through the winter and returned for the *rendezvous* of 1829 by way of the Columbia Valley. He had mapped three routes to the Pacific and had explored more miles of undiscovered territory than any other American in history. And yet this praying trapper, who brought to the United States the knowledge of the road from South Pass to California, whose discoveries were of greatest importance to the United States, has been almost forgotten.

Because of McLoughlin's kindness, Smith persuaded his

associates of the Rocky Mountain Fur Company to leave
the British in undisturbed possession of the Columbia Valley. The mountain men respected his wishes in this matter
as long as Smith remained with them. Ashley, having made
a fortune in the beaver trade, sold his interest to his associates in the mountains and returned to St. Louis, where he
was elected to Congress. Smith remained for a time, but he
also left the mountains to engage in the Santa Fe trade. He
was killed by Comanche Indians on the Santa Fe Trail and
his body was left unburied upon the sands of the Cimarron
River.

Fitzpatrick and Bridger, however, could not be persuaded to leave the mountains. They loved the Rockies and
loved the free life of the trapper and hunter. After Smith
had gone, the remaining mountain men competed with the
British for the fur of the Columbia. They invaded the
Blackfoot country and fought those Indians. They marched
far south and discovered the petrified forest of Arizona.
They explored practically every river, valley, creek, plain
and mountain between the Rockies and the Sierras and also
discovered several new passes through the Sierras with better grades for wagons than the pass found by Smith.

Bridger married an Indian woman and lived with her on
the Green River where he built a log structure, known as
Fort Bridger. It became the gathering place for mountain
men and here they assembled every winter to sit before the
fire and spin tall tales of their exploits. Some of their tales
have come down to us and will bear repeating. One tale
concerned the Little People, who lived in the mountains
and could pull the doors of the mountains shut after them
when they wished to hide. These Little People had double-

hinged knees and swivelled necks. When they were walking in one direction and wished to turn to go the other way, they did not turn their bodies as do other men. They simply turned their heads on their swivelled necks, and since their knees were hinged for walking either way, they could walk backwards as well as forwards.

Bridger himself became one of the most gifted of tall-story tellers. In telling of his first visit to the petrified forest, he said that he found not only petrified trees but also petrified deer. Since all the animals were petrified, he became hungry and shot a bird, which, perched on the limb of a petrified tree, was singing. Although shot, the bird continued to sing. Bridger, puzzled, picked up the bird and discovered that it was petrified and that the song also was petrified.

Bridger's favorite story, which he told often for the benefit of strangers, ran something like this:

"Ever hear anybody tell about the time the Injuns chased me up a canyon? Wul, when I saw them coming, I rode my hawrse like lightning and the Injuns lit out after me like lightning. I kept going as tight as my hawrse could travel right up that canyon, until I come plunk to the head of a dead-end. 'I'm sure a gone beaver,' I said. There I was, walls straight up to the right of me, walls straight up to the left of me, and walls straight up at the dead end of the canyon in front of me, while the Injuns were a-coming up behind me. Waugh!"

At this point Bridger always paused in his story while his listeners waited in suspense. When he failed to continue, one of his listeners would urge:

"Go on, Jim. What happened next?"

"Whut happened!" he ejaculated. "Whut do you think happened? Why the Injuns killed and sculped me."

The best known of the mountain men were of English-American origin. This is due to the fact that when they returned to St. Louis to visit, they were sought by newspaper writers, who published the stories of their adventures in *The St. Louis Republic* and other papers of that day. Since the reporters did not speak French, they did not interview the French-speaking trappers. Yet those Frenchmen have left us innumerable French place names in the western mountain states.

For example: In Wyoming are the Three *Tetons*, which is French for the three breasts. In Idaho are the *Cœur d'Aline* (awl-hearted) Mountains. In Oregon is *Des Chutes* (the shoots) River. In Colorado is *Cache a la Poudre* (hidden powder) River. The capital of Idaho is *Boise*, named for *Boise* (woods) Creek, so called because of the timber lining its bank.

Names of numerous streams mark the spots where trappers of old St. Louis French families were slain by Indians. In Idaho is *Portneuf* River, where a St. Louis man named Portneuf was "rubbed out." In Wyoming is the town of *Laramie* on *Laramie* River, where Jacques Laramie was killed by the Arapahoes. In western Nebraska is *Gonneville* Creek, where Louis Gonneville died in a battle with the Sioux. One of the partners of Bridger and Fitzpatrick was Etienne Provot, the discoverer of Utah Lake and the Jordan River. The town of *Provo*, Utah, is named in his honor.

CHAPTER XX

THE BENTS AND THE ST. VRAINS

S T. LOUIS was a glamorous town for romantically minded youngsters in the days of the fur brigades. Instead of reading adventure tales in books, children of old St. Louis heard true, wild-west thrillers, straight from the lips of buckskin-clad actors upon a living stage. Among these with ears atune for the latest exploit of the river men and mountain men were the eleven boys and girls of Judge Silas Bent. Born in Boston, Judge Bent came to make his home in St. Louis shortly after the Louisiana Purchase.

Adventure coursed through the blood of the Bents. Judge Bent's father had helped start the American Revolution by participating in the Boston Tea Party. All of the Judge's children were ambitious to do stirring things like their grandfather. But of all the family none was more desirous for adventure than twelve-year-old William. He could hardly wait to grow up so that he could leave home and be a trapper.

Once for a few days he was diverted from his purpose late in the autumn of 1821 when a shaggy-headed backwoodsman came to St. Louis from Arrow Rock, a village of central Missouri, and bought a bill of printed cloth, tools and other merchandise in quantities ten times larger than a man of his class could afford to buy. But when this man,

William Becknell, got ready to pay, he banged one bulging, whang-hide bag of strange silver after another down on the merchant's barrel head and told him to weigh it up. That must have startled the merchant. Silver was rare even in St. Louis, while backwoodsmen usually came to town with beaver, bear or coon skins or perhaps a few hams or sides of smoked bacon. The merchant, opening a bag, saw silver bracelets, silver combs, silver breeches buttons and Spanish silver coins.

"Where did you get this stuff?" he wanted to know.

"It's genuine stuff," was the reply. "Bite it and see."

The merchant put a coin in his teeth and bit. By biting hard enough he could dent it, for unalloyed Spanish silver was soft enough to bite.

"Ring it," challenged Becknell.

The merchant clinked a coin on the barrel head and it rang true.

The backwoodsman was not very talkative, but word of William Becknell already was spreading over Missouri like a fever. With four companions he had gone to Santa Fe with all the trade goods he could buy and borrow. This was the same Santa Fe that had denied the Mallet brothers the right to trade and which had forced A. P. Chouteau to kneel before the governor and promise never to come back. But Mexico had broken the Spanish yoke at last and Santa Fe was now a free city. Becknell had entered there in the summer of 1821 and had been wildly welcomed by a throng in the public square of the Palace of the Governors. They paid him ten times St. Louis prices, bought all he had and clamored for him to come back with more. And so Becknell was outfitting for a second journey to the land where they paid silver for cheap, cotton, printed goods.

What Becknell could do, others could do. Farmers, trappers and merchants packed horses and filled wagons for the Santa Fe trade. Nineteen-year-old Ceran St. Vrain, who had grown up in St. Louis with the Bents, caught the fever and joined a Santa Fe caravan either the next spring or the year after. William Bent was tempted to run away and go to Santa Fe, but finally he decided to stick to his original plan.

"Let others deal in silver and merchandise," he said to himself, "I'm going to be a trapper and do bigger things than even my grandfather."

In the spring of 1823 William's older brother Charles signed up with Pierre Chouteau's brigade to ascend to the fur country. William gained permission from his father to go with him. He was fourteen that summer and his brother nine years older. William picked up Indian tongues with the ease of a Jolliet or a Drouillard. He had not been on the Upper Missouri long before he could speak readily in both the Cheyenne and Sioux tongues and had mastered sign talk. The Indians liked him and called him Little White Man. In the fall when the Bent brothers came home, they exchanged stories of their adventures with St. Vrain who was back from Santa Fe.

St. Vrain, because he was a son of one of the old St. Louis French families, had seen things in the streams about Santa Fe which meant nothing to the Yankee traders who had gone with him. The mountain streams of the Southwest were swimming full of beaver. Nobody had ever tried to catch them with the exception of the men of A. P. Chouteau's brigade. Here then was opportunity.

St. Vrain and the two Bent brothers put all their savings together, borrowed more money from Judge Bent and formed a partnership, which later was to be known as Bent, St. Vrain and Company. The partners bought trade goods suitable for the New Mexican market, transported the goods by steamboat to Franklin, a river harbor near Arrow Rock, and there transferred to wagons for shipment to Santa Fe. Arriving at their destination, they traded for silver, wool and mules. Silver is small in bulk. Wool is light in weight. Mules can walk. That left their wagons only partially loaded for the return to Missouri.

Herein lay the advantage of combining Santa Fe trade with beaver trapping. While other Santa Fe merchants had the expense of paying wages to men for driving half-empty wagons 800 miles back from Santa Fe to Franklin, the Bent brothers and St. Vrain filled their wagons to the full with beaver skins so that the back haul was not wasted.

The partners divided their work. St. Vrain took charge of the wagon trains as they shuttled back and forth between Franklin and Santa Fe. Charles Bent opened headquarters at Taos whence he sent brigades to trap on the headwaters of the Rio Grande and westward as far as the Gila of Arizona. He also bought the fur catch of Antoine Robidoux. This brother of the founder of St. Joseph, Missouri, built two forts west of the Continental Divide, one on the Gunnison River in what is now western Colorado and another in the present Utah. There he traded with the Indians and managed fur brigades to collect peltry to ship by pack train to Taos.

Charles had not lived in Taos long before he was captivated by the flashing smiles and dark Spanish eyes of

CERAN ST. VRAIN

ROBERTA ANN BURNS

This Cheyenne girl resides at Weatherford, Oklahoma, and is proud to claim descent from William Bent and Owl Woman.

Senorita Marie Ignacia Jaramillo, whom he married. St. Vrain too fell in love in New Mexico and married Senorita Luisa Branch. Each spring Charles Bent collected peltry for shipment to Missouri.

William Bent remained with his brother at Taos the first year; but when he was seventeen, he headed his own brigade to venture to the headwaters of the Arkansas, where A. P. Chouteau had found beaver so abundant. He built a stockade on the Arkansas west of the present Pueblo, Colorado, and led his brigade to the mountain streams of that region. He trapped in the Pike's Peak region and to the west of Pike's Peak. He found that he could trap in the lower streams early in the season, but by going higher and higher up the mountains he could trap at an elevation of 11,000 feet in midsummer amid melting snow banks and find beaver in prime condition even at that season. Each winter he retreated down through Royal Gorge to his stockade.

In 1832 the partners completed Bent's Fort on the Arkansas River at the point where the Santa Fe Trail left the river to turn south toward Raton Pass on the way to Santa Fe. After that William Bent made his headquarters at the fort. This structure was situated about fifteen miles west of the present La Junta, Colorado. It was of adobe construction and became the best known of all fur-brigade forts in the West. Charles Bent, from his residence in Taos where adobe was generally used for house building, directed the erection of Bent's fort, employing Mexican laborers. He used adobe, for a building of that material is cool in summer and warm in winter. It cannot be set afire from the outside by hostile Indians and it will last longer than a log fort. For defense against attack two bastions were placed at diagonal corners. These were thirty feet high and armed with cannon and loopholed for rifles. Over the main gate a high watch tower commanded a view of the Arkansas Valley for many miles. In order to assist the watchman in seeing long distances, the partners bought a spyglass. This was mounted on a swivel so that it might be turned in any direction. So strong was the fort and so carefully was it managed, the Indians respected it; and its cannon never were fired in its defense.

Adjoining the watch tower was an aerie in which Bent housed two tame, bald eagles. These birds became so attached to the fort and its master that when allowed to fly free, they always came back to the aerie for the night. A feature of the fort was a game room at the rear where men might play billiards. The game room was built at the wish of Robert and George Bent, two younger brothers, who came out from St. Louis to serve as clerks for the company.

William Bent was a friend and a brother to the Indians. When he came to the Southwest he found the Cheyennes and Arapahoes, who roamed the Plains from the Black Hills to the Arkansas, in a deadly feud against the Comanches and the Kiowas. Through Bent's influence these warring tribesmen met in the Big Timber below the fort where they concluded a peace which has never been broken.

Bent also was a friend to travellers. Since the Santa Fe wagon trains passed the fort, travellers were constantly coming and going during the summer. Bent welcomed them as his guests and feasted them at his hospitable table on meat of the buffalo, elk, deer, antelope and mountain sheep.

Living far from his native St. Louis, Bent was deprived of the society of white women. He did not care for the girls of Taos, whose lips were all smiles and whose eyes were all twinkles. He chose for his wife a Cheyenne girl, Owl Woman. She was the daughter of White Thunder, a famous Cheyenne and keeper of the medicine arrows. That this was a true love match and not a passing whim is evident from the fact that Bent was a devoted husband. When Owl Woman died twenty-two years after their marriage, he felt his loss keenly. Although he later married his wife's younger sister, he never ceased to mourn for his first wife.

Five children were born from the two marriages, four of them being the offspring of Owl Woman. The children were well educated in St. Louis, but since they were half-breed Indians they could not fit well into the life of the white city. All returned to the Plains and today their descendants may be found among the Cheyennes of Oklahoma where they are proud to claim William Bent and Owl Woman as their forebears.

Bent's Fort was so successful as a trade center that the partners built a second fort on the South Platte under the direction of St. Vrain, from which fact it was known as Fort St. Vrain. In command of this fort the partners placed Marcelline St. Vrain, a younger brother of Ceran. He directed fur brigades from this center to trap the headwaters of the South Platte and hunters to bring in buffalo robes from the surrounding plains. St. Vrain River, which rises in Rocky Mountain National Park, flows down St. Vrain Canyon to join the Platte opposite the site of the old fort. Today a fine highway extends from Denver up St. Vrain Canyon to Rocky Mountain National Park. Tourists by the thousands use that highway every summer. In the park they have opportunity to see wild beaver, descendants of those which escaped the traps of St. Vrain's fur brigades.

In this account of Bent, St. Vrain and Company, mention should be made of Kit Carson, most famous of the company's employes. He came as an ignorant lad who did not even know how to keep himself clean and became one of the most famous of mountain men. Reared as he was on the frontier, he had no schooling and could neither read nor write. His father died and his mother bound him out to a tanner at Franklin. Not liking the confinement of the tannery, he ran away in 1826 at the age of sixteen and joined St. Vrain's wagon train as it was rolling out of Franklin for Santa Fe. St. Vrain, upon discovering that the boy was infested with vermin, had him take a thorough bath. Before he began scrubbing himself to get rid of the lice on his body and in his hair, St. Vrain told him to place his clothing on a hill of big red ants. The ants rummaged through the garments and made short work of vermin concealed there.

From a partnership formed by three boys, Bent, St. Vrain and Company grew in a few years to become a formidable rival of the largest fur companies of the West. Under St. Vrain's direction, its wagon trains carried goods not only to Santa Fe but south to El Paso, Chihuahua and Durango.

CHAPTER XXI

BRIDES IN THE ROCKIES

THE year 1833 was one that every man in the beaver trade and every Indian on the plains remembered to his last day. Even now, although more than a century has elapsed, the older Cheyenne Indians of Oklahoma recall hearing their grandmothers speak of 1833 as *The Year the Stars Fell*. It must have been a dazzling spectacle as flowing fire streaked in every direction across the heavens. Begining with November 13, the meteoric shower flamed in the eastern sky after midnight for three successive nights. Stars fell in such numbers that the mountain men wondered how any could be left. They told each other that such a thing was bad medicine. From that time they kept looking for bad luck, and when bad luck befell the beaver trade, they blamed it on the falling stars.

John Jacob Astor was in London when the stars fell. But he was too busy thinking of silk hats to pay any attention to such a thing as meteors. He saw that men were buying silk hats and throwing away their beaver hats. Three centuries of slaughter had so reduced the supply of beaver that it cost eight dollars a pound to buy fur in the Rockies. By the time the skins had been shipped by pack train or wagon train and steamboat and sailing ship from the Rockies to Paris and had been handled in warehouses at St. Louis and New Orleans, the cost to the Paris hat makers was a dozen times that paid the trappers. The hat makers therefore cast about for a substitute for fur and learned to make hats of silk.

Silk hats came into style over night. The only market left for beaver fur was for use as wraps for women. Astor, foreseeing the collapse of the beaver market, sold his stock in the eastern division of the American Fur Company to his New York associates and in the western division to his St. Louis associates headed by Pierre Chouteau.

Chouteau, knowing full well that beaver prices would fall, called his fur brigades from the mountains and put them to hunting buffalo for robes. It happened that just as beaver hats went out of style, buffalo-hide lap-robes became fashionable. Stylish men and women therefore were demanding buffalo robes to spread on their laps when driving in chilly weather.

Bent, St. Vrain and Company also converted their fur trappers into buffalo hunters. Beaver were scarce, but millions of buffalo roamed the Plains to be had for the killing. Kit Carson and many other trappers readily became hunters.

There were a few mountain men, however, who refused to leave their beloved Rockies. Among them were Jim Bridger and Tom Fitzpatrick. They and their friends brought their fur to the *rendezvous* in 1834 and sold it for what it would bring. The *rendezvous* was held again in 1835 but fewer men came. In 1836 still fewer men came, less than 200 in all. They assembled on Green River on July 1, the day set for the *rendezvous;* but the merchants from St. Louis had not yet arrived with their wagons. Finally several scouts were sent to look for the missing merchants. The scouts rode to South Pass, crossed to the Sweetwater, and what they saw there caused them to wheel about and ride like crazy men. On the morning of July 4 they galloped into the Green River camp, shouting: "White women! Waugh!"

The mountain men were incredulous. No white woman had ever come to the mountains and no mountain man expected a white woman ever to come to the mountains. The scouts, however, insisted that they had seen one riding horseback and another riding in a wagon. The women, so the scouts reported, were travelling with the wagon train of the St. Louis merchants and were headed for the *rendezvous*. The woman who rode horseback was the wife of Doc. Whitman, they said.

Whitman! The mountain men knew Doctor Marcus Whitman, whom they called "Doc." He was a doctor-missionary for the American Board of Commissioners for Foreign Missions and had been in the mountains the year before selecting a site for a mission on the Columbia River. He was a capital fellow and had "butchered" an arrow out of Jim Bridger. Butchered is the correct word. Bridger had stretched himself on a blanket. Since anesthetics were unknown in those days, Bridger had to "grin and bear it," while the Doc. removed the arrow. Whitman had told the mountain men that he would return to the Columbia mission, but he also had told them that he was unmarried.

"Doc.'s a bachelor," declared the trappers.

"Wul," explained the scouts, "he's got him a woman now. She's a bride!"

"Bride! It doesn't make sense. Who would come to the Rockies for a honeymoon?"

"Both the women are brides," declared the scouts. "The other fellow is a preacher named Spalding—Henry Harmon Spalding. He has just been married too."

The two scouts were so serious that the mountain men were convinced that the impossible had happened. White women had come to the Rockies. Bridal parties were honeymooning in the Rockies.

The mountain men leaped to their saddles and were off. What a motley gang to welcome the first white women to cross the Continental Divide! They were the toughest lot of unshaven, sooty-faced half-humans in America. When Etienne Brule went at Champlain's command to be the first woods ranger, he set a style for woods rangers, which had been followed ever since by woods rangers, *voyageurs* and mountain men. Some who rode that morning to greet Narcissa Whitman and Eliza Spalding had fled to the Rockies to escape punishment for murder. Some had been river pirates and their chief boast was that they were half horse and half alligator. A few were from homes of refinement. But all were clad either in nondescript buckskins or in breechclout and leggings like Indians.

Joseph Meek led the charging horsemen; and everything he did, the others did. They howled like panthers. They fired rifles in the air. They pirouetted their horses. They rode round and round, acting half the time like savages capturing a wagon train and half the time like rowdies serenading a bridal party at a backwoods charivari. The women, taken by surprise, were alarmed at first. They had seen many rough frontiersmen since leaving St. Louis, but

From a painting by Mary C. Allen. Photo by courtesy of Dr. Stephen B. L. Penrose.

NARCISSA WHITMAN

She and her husband were killed in the Indian massacre of 1847.
No portrait from life of Mrs. Whitman exists. This portrait follows detailed descriptions of her and her dress with great fidelity.

JOSEPH JUNEAU

The capital of Alaska is named in Juneau's honor. It is one of the seven state and territorial capitals that bear French names.

none like these mountain men, whose long hair streamed in the wind as they rode. At length, tired of their antics, the mountain men rode up to the train, dismounted and stood staring in childlike admiration. They were especially pleased with Mrs. Whitman, who had ridden horseback all the way across the plains and whose plaits of hair reflected the sunlight. At her home in New York State she had sung in the church choir and she had a sweet voice. Jim Bridger drew near to greet Doctor Whitman, who introduced him to his wife and the Spaldings. Bridger shook hands all around. It had been thirteen years since he had shaken the hand of a white woman.

He later became well acquainted with Mrs. Whitman. After she had established a home on the Columbia, Bridger brought his half-breed daughter Ann to live with her where she might learn to live like a Christian, to sing hymns and to be a white woman.

The coming of the two women to the Columbia deserves to rank in importance in American history with the discovery of South Pass. After Mrs. Whitman and Mrs. Spalding led the way, more women came to the Columbia with their men. Each year saw more families from Illinois and Missouri crossing the mountains to settle on farms in the Columbia River valley. By 1843 the number going to Oregon in one year exceeded 1000, men, women and children. Some of the mountain men, Joseph Meek among them, joined the settlers there and married daughters of the farmers.

In 1845 the farmers set up their own government on the Columbia. They outnumbered the British ten to one and this induced them to send Meek to Washington to ask the President for admission into the Union. Great Britain, unable to cope with the American tide, agreed to share the Columbia Valley with the United States. That north of the Forty-ninth Parallel fell to Canada and all south to the United States.

The British had conquered Astoria through the disloyalty of Astor's own men. John McLoughlin had conquered Jedediah Smith through kindness. The American women who made homes and reared children were unconquerable.

The migration of Americans to Oregon was repeated in California. Antoine Robidoux, while on a visit to St. Louis, met a group of Illinois farmers with their covered wagons on the way to Oregon. He told them that California was a sunny country with a milder climate. These men with their families therefore resolved to go to California. After crossing South Pass, they engaged mountain men to pilot them across the Sierras to the Pacific slope where they settled on American River. More followed. In 1846 more than a thousand settlers streamed through the Sierras into California.

Once in the Mexican province, they joined with the Spanish residents of California in a revolt against Mexican rule. First they set up the Bear Flag Republic, which later was taken as a part of the United States during war between the United States and Mexico.

In the same war the Spanish residents of New Mexico willingly surrendered to an approaching army. The United States troops were welcomed into Santa Fe, and the people accepted Charles Bent as the first American territorial governor of New Mexico.

At last one flag floated from the Atlantic to the Pacific.

There remained but one more task for the fur trapper. Alaska was purchased by the United States from Russia in 1867. While the Russians had explored the seacoast and the Yukon River, most of the interior of the territory was unknown. Alexander "Buck" Chouquette came to the territory six years before the American purchase and found a mine of gold on the Stickine River.

Next arrived Joseph Juneau, member of a well known family of fur traders and trappers. His uncle, Solomon Juneau, had trapped and traded in the present Wisconsin until the invention of the silk hat. He then founded the city of Milwaukee and taught himself to read English so that he might serve as his city's first postmaster.

Joseph Juneau, after his arrival in 1878, founded a partnership with Dick Harris and they trapped beaver and prospected for gold on streams flowing into Gastineau Channel in southeast Alaska. One afternoon while setting a trap in a creek, in 1881, Juneau saw a glint of yellow in the gravel. He scooped up a quantity of sand in his frying pan and washed out a teaspoonful of yellow grains as fine as sand but much heavier. Heating the grains over his camp fire, he fused them together into a solid lump. Then he hammered the lump. Fool's gold will crumble under the hammer, but this lump flattened out like a pancake until it was thin as tissue paper. Juneau lifted the sheet by a corner and punched it with the point of his knife. The point did not break the sheet of metal. It merely dented it. It was gold!

The fabulous Treadwell mine, for thirty years the world's greatest producer, had been struck. Juneau and Harris sold the mine and founded a town, which is today the capital of Alaska and bears the French name of Juneau, being the seventh capital of our states and territories to bear a French name.

The Treadwell strike brought more men to Alaska. Most of them were both trappers and prospectors. Fifteen years after the discovery by Juneau, George Carmack and Joe Ladue hit pay dirt on the Klondike in the Alaskan interior. Fur, coupled with gold, led the way to the exploration of the last corner of the North American continent.

MEMORIALS

No longer does the explorer follow the tracks of the beaver, for today this animal thrives only in places where the government provides protection.

Gone too are the woods rangers, the *voyageur* and the mountain man. But from one end of America to the other we may yet enjoy the picturesque place-names he has bequeathed us, such as, for instance, *Terre Haute* (high land), *Lac Que Parle* (lake which speaks) and *Cote Sans Dessein* (hill without a plan). These names remain as memorials in the language of a half-forgotten era when a half-forgotten people blazed the way west.

GUIDE TO PRONUNCIATION

In the case of French words which have become American place names, the English pronunciation is first given, followed by the French.

Accau (ă-kō'), Michael

Algonquin (ăl-gŏng'kĭ-ăn)

Anayas (ă-nĕ'jàs), Gaspardo (gàs-pär'dō) de (dĕ)

Annahotaha (ă-nă-hō-tä'hä)

Antoine (ân-twàn')

Archévêque (àrsh-vĕk'), Jean

Baptiste (bà-tēst')

Baronet (bàr-ŏ-nĕ') A. F. Vasquez (văs'kĕs)

Barré (bär'ê), Fr. (bàr-ā'), Le Fèbre de la

Baton Rouge (bā'tôn rōōzh')

Beaujeu, Lienard de (bō-jū', lē-när' dĕ)

Belle Fourche (bĕl fōōrsh')

Belle Oiseau (bĕl wà-zō')

Bienville (bē-yăn-vēl'), Jean Baptist Le Moyne de

Biloxi (bĭ-lŏk'sĭ)

Boisbriant (bwä-brē-yân'), Pierre

Boise (boi'ză), Fr. (bwà-zā')

Bois Brulé (bois bru'lĕ), Fr. (bwà brü-lā')

Bouquet (bōō-kĕ'), Henry

Bourgmont (bōōrg-môn'), Étienne (Ā-ty-ĕn') Venyard (vĕn-yár') de

Brulé (Brü-lā'), Étienne (Ā-ty-ĕn')

Bruyère (brü-yĕr'), Andre Fabry de

Cache la Poudre (kàsh là pōō'dr)

Cadillac (kà'dĭ-làk), Antoine de la Mothe

Cahokia (kà-hōk'ĭ-à)

Calabozo (kă-là-bō'zō)

Cap Rouge (kàp rōōzh)

Carillon (kà-rē-yôn')

Cartier (kàr-tē-ā'), Jacques (Jàk)

Céleron (sā-l'rôn')

Champlain (shăm-plān'), Fr. (shâm-plân'), Samuel de

Charboneau (shàr-bŏn-ō'), Toussaint (Tōō-săn')

Chartres (shártr)

Chihuahua (shē-wä'wä)

Chouart (shōō-ăr'). (See Groseillers)

Chouquette (shōō-kĕt')

Chouteau (shō'tō), Fr. (shōō-tō'), Pierre

Cimarron (sĭm'à-rôn)

Coahuila (kō-ă-wē'là)

Cœur d'Alène (kûr-dà-lān'), Fr. (kūr-dà-lĕn')

Contre Cœur (kôn-tr kūr), Claude Pierre Pécaudy de

Cordell (kŏr-dĕl')

Côte sans Dessein (kōt sân dā-sân')

Crève Cœur (krĕv kūr)

Crozat (krō-zà'), Antoine

Cyprian (syp'rĭ-yân)

D'Argenson (dàr-zhân-sôn')

D'Artaguette (dàr-tă-gĕt')

D'Eglise (dā-glēz'), Jacques

Des Chutes (dà shōōt), Fr. (dā shüt')

Dollard des Ormeaux (dŏ-làr' dā ŏr-mō')

Drouillard (drōō-yàr'), George

Dubuque (dŏō-būk'), Fr. (dü-bük'), Julien

Duluth (dŏŏ-lōōth'), Fr. (dü-lüt'), Daniel Greysolon

Dumas (dü-mă')

Duquesne (dū-kĕn')

Du Tisne (dü tēn), Claude Charles

El Camino Real (ĕl kăm-ē'nō re'al)

El Quartelejo (ĕl kôrt-ĕl-ā'hō)

265

Engagée (ân-gă-zhā')
Étienne (ā-ty-ĕn')

Faribault (far-e-bō'), Fr. (fĕr-bō'),
   Jean Baptiste
Fèbre (fĕbr)
Frontenac (frôn-tē-nák'), Fr. (frônt-
   nák'), Louis de Buade, Compte

Gastineau (gàs-tē-nō')
Gaultier (gō-tē-yā'), Lucien
Glorieta (glŏ-rē-ĕ'tä)
Gonneville (gŏn-vēl'), Louis
Gravier (grăv-yā'), Jacques
Griffon (grĭ-fôn')
Grollet (grŏ-lĕ')
Groseillers, Médard Chouart Sieur de
   (grō-zĕ-yā', mā-dàr' shoo-ăr' sē-yēr'
   dē)
Gros Ventre (grō vântr')
Guyon, Marie Thérèse (gyôn, mà-rē'
   tā-rĕz')

Hélène (ā-lĕn')
Hennepin (hĕn'ē-pĭn), Fr. (ĕn-păn'),
   Louis

Iberville (ē-bĕr-vēl'), Pierre le Moyne
Iroquois (ĭ'rō-kwoi)

Jacques (jàk)
Jean (jân)
Jolliet (jō'lĭ-ĕt), Fr. (jŏ-lyĕ'), Louis
Joutel (joo-tĕl'), Henri
Juan (hwän)
Julien (jü-ly-ăn')
Juneau (joo'nō), Fr. (jü-no'), Joseph

Kaskaskia (kăs-kăs'kĭ-ä)

La Bête (là-bĕt')
La Chine (là-shēn')
Laclède (là-klēd'), Fr. (là-klĕd'),
   Pierre
Lac qui Parle (làc kē pàrl')
Ladue (là-dü'), Joe
La Harpe (là-àrp'), Bernard de

La Lande (là-lând'), Baptiste
La Mothe (là-mŏt')
Langlande (lân-glând'), Charles de
La Salle (là-sàl'), Robert Cavalier
   (kà-và-lyā') Sieur (sē-yēr') de
La Violette (là-vyŏ-lĕt')
Le Bœuf (lē-bĕf')
Le Moyne (lē-mwàn')
Levée (lĕ'vĕ), Fr. (lē-vā')
Lignéry (lē-nā-rē'), Francis Marchand
   (màr-shân') de
Lisa (lē'sä), Manuel
Loisel (lwà-zĕl'), Regis

Mackinac (măck'ĭ-nä)
Mallet (mà-lĕ'), Pierre and Paul
Manuela (män-wē'lä)
Marais des Cygnes (mà-rĕ' dā sēn-
   yà')
Marest (mà-rĕst'), Gabriel
Maricourt (mà-rē-koōr')
Marquette (màr-kĕt'), Jacques
Ménard (mā-nàr')
Monier (mŏ-nyā'), Jean
Monongahela (mō-nŏn-gą-hē'la)
Montagnes Rocheuses (môn-tăn-ya'
   rŏ-chûz')

Nacogdoches (năk-ō-dō'chĭs)
Natchitoches (năk'ē-tōsh)
Nicolet (nĭk-ŏ-lĕ'), Jean

Onondaga (ŏn-ŏn-dàg'à)
Ouachita (wàsh'ē-tä)

Perigord (pā-rē-gŏr')
Petit (pĕ-tē')
Pierre (pĕyr), Fr. (Pyĕr)
Pontchartrain (pŏn-shàr-trān'), Fr.
   (pôn-shàr-trăn')
Portneuf (pŏrt-núf'), Fr. (pŏr-nĕf')
Presle (prĕl)
Prèsque Isle (prĕs-kēl')
Provot (prō'vō), Fr. (prŏ-vō'), Étienne

Radisson, Pierre Esprit (rà-dē-sôn',
   pĕyr ĕs-prē')

Renault (rĕ-nō'), Philippe Francis
Richelieu (rē-shē-lyû')
Roberval (rŏ-bĕr-vál'), Jean Francis
de la Roque, sieur de
Robidoux (rŏ-hē-dōō'), Joseph
Roche Jaune (rŏsh-jōn')
Roi (rwá), Baptiste Louis

Sacajawea (să-ká-já-wē'á)
Saint Ange (săn ânzh). Louis St.
Ange de Bellerive ('bĕ-l'rĕv')
Saint Denis (săn dē-nē'), Louis
Juchereau de
Saint Vrain (sănt vrăn'), Fr. (săn
vrăn), Céran (sár-ân')
Sandoval (sân-dŏ-vál')
Saut (sō)
Sauvole (sō-vŏl')
Shoshone (shŏ-shō'nĕ)

Tadoussac (tá-dōō-sák')

Talon (tá-lôn'), Jean Baptiste
Terre Haute (tĕr-rĕ hōt'), Fr. (tĕr ōt')
Teton (tē'tŏn), Fr. (tĕ-tôn')
Ticonderoga (tī-kŏn-dĕr-ō'gá)
Tonty (tŏn'ty), Fr. (tôn-tē'), Henri
Toussaint (tōō-săn')
Trudeau (trü-dō') Jean Baptiste

Ursuline (ür-sü-lēn')

Venango (vē-nău'gō), Fr. (vē-nân-gō')
Verchères, Madeleine (vĕr-shĕr', má-
dĕ-lĕn')
Villazur (vēl-yá-sûr'), Pedro de
Vincennes (vĭn-sĕnz'), Fr. (văn-sĕn'),
Francis de
Voilà les Verts Monts (vwá-lá lā vĕr
môn)
Voyageur (vwá-yá-zhĕr')
Vérendrye (vĕ-rên-drē'), Pierre Gaul-
tier de la

REFERENCES FOR FURTHER STUDY

Alter, Cecil B., *James Bridger*, Salt Lake City, Shephard Book Co., 1925.

Andreas, A. T., publisher, *History of the State of Kansas*, Chicago, 1883.

Bancroft, Hubert Howe, *History of Alaska 1730–1885*, San Francisco, A. L. Bancroft and Co., 1886.

Billon, F. L., *Annals of St. Louis in Its Early Days Under the French and Spanish Domination*, St. Louis, 1886.

Bolton, Herbert E., *French Intrusions into New Mexico*, in Stephens H. Norse (Editor), *The Pacific Ocean in History*, pages 389–407, New York, Macmillan, 1917.

Bryant, William Cullen, *A Popular History of the United States*, Charles Scribner's Sons, New York, 1879, 4v.

Boucher, John Newton, *A Century and a Half of Pittsburg and Her People*, New York, Lewis Publishing Co., 1908, 4v.

Castle, Henry A., *Minnesota, Its Story and Biography*, Chicago, Lewis Publishing Co., 1915.

Catlin, George, *North American Indians, Letters etc., Amongst the Wildest Tribes of Indians in North America 1832–1839*, Edinburg, John Grant, 1926, 2v.

Chambers, Henry E., *A History of Louisiana*, Chicago, American Historical Society, 1925, 3v.

Champlain, Samuel de, C. P. Otis, translator, *The Voyages of Samuel de Champlain*, Boston, The Prince Society, 1878–82, 3v.

Chittenden, Hiram Martin, *The American Fur Trade of the Far West*, New York, The Press of the Pioneers, 1935, 2v.

Clark, Henry W., *History of Alaska*, New York, Macmillan, 1930.

Colby, Charles W., *Canadian Types of the Old Regime*, New York, Henry Holt, 1910.

Coman, Katharine, *How We Won the Land Beyond the Mississippi*, New York, Macmillan, 1921, 2v.

Crawford, Lewis J., *History of North Dakota*, Chicago, American Historical Society, 1931, 3v.

Du Pratz, Le Page, *Histoire de la Louisiane*, Paris, 1758, 3v.

Finley, John, *The French in the Heart of America*, New York, Charles Scribner's Sons, 1915.

Frémont, John C., *The Exploring Expedition to the Rocky Mountains, Oregon and California,* Auburn and Buffalo, Miller, Orton & Milligan, 1851.

Gayarre, Charles, *Histoire de la Louisiane,* New Orleans, Magne & Weisse, 1846–7, 2v.

Gregg, Josiah, *Commerce of the Prairies,* New York, Langley, 1845, 2 parts.

Harlan, Edgar Rubey, *A Narrative History of the People of Iowa,* Chicago, American Historical Society, 1931, 5v.

Hennepin, Father Louis, *A New Discovery of a Vast Country in America,* London, 1698. New edition edited by Reuben Gold Thwaites, Chicago, A. C. McClurg, 1913.

Herrman, Richard, *Julien Dubuque—His Life and Adventures,* Dubuque, Times-Journal Co., 1922.

Houck, Louis, *History of Missouri,* Naeter Bros., Cape Girardeau, 1908.

Howe, Henry, *The Great West,* Cincinnati, Henry Howe, 1852.

Irving, Washington, *Astoria,* New York, Peter Fenelon Collier, 1897.

Irving, Washington, *A Tour of the Prairies,* in his *A Crayon Miscellany,* pages 11–239, New York, G. P. Putnam & Sons, 1891.

Irving, Washington, *Adventures of Captain Bonneville,* New York, Putnam, n.d.

James, Thomas, *Three Years Among the Indians and Mexicans,* 1846, reprinted with notes by Walter B. Douglas, St. Louis, Missouri Historical Society, 1916.

Kellogg, Louise Phelps, *Early Narratives of the Northwest, 1634–1699,* New York, Charles Scribner's Sons, 1917.

Kellogg, Louise Phelps, *The French Regime in the Northwest,* Madison, State Historical Society of Wisconsin, 1925.

Laut, Agnes C., *Pathfinders of the West,* New York, Grosset & Dunlap, (c. 1904, Macmillan).

Laut, Agnes C., *The Conquest of the Great Northwest,* New York, George H. Doran Co. (c. 1918), 2v.

Laut, Agnes C., *Cadillac,* Indianapolis, Bobbs-Merrill (c. 1931).

Margry, Pierre, *Découvertes et Etablissements des Français dans l'Amérique, 1614–1754,* Paris, Maisonneuve et Cie, 1879–1888, 6v.

Moore, Albert Burton, *History of Alabama,* Chicago, American Historical Society, 1927, 3v.

Moore, Charles, *History of Michigan,* Chicago, Lewis Publishing Co., 1931, 4v.

Neihardt, John C., *Splendid Wayfaring*, New York, Macmillan, 1920.

Oudard, Georges, *Notre Louisiane*, translated by Bianco, Margery, as *Four Cents an Acre*, New York, Brewer & Warren, 1931.

Parkman, Francis, *California & Oregon Trail*, New York, A. L. Burt, n.d.

Parkman, Francis, *Conspiracy of Pontiac*, Boston, Little, Brown & Co., 1891, 2v.

Parkman, Francis, *Count Frontenac and New France Under Louis XIV*, Boston, Little, Brown & Co., 1892.

Parkman, Francis, *Half Century of Conflict*, Boston, Little, Brown & Co., 1892, 2v.

Parkman, Francis, *La Salle and the Discovery of the Great West*, Boston, Little, Brown & Co., 1892.

Parkman, Francis, *Montcalm and Wolf*, Boston, Little, Brown & Co., 1892, 2v.

Parkman, Francis, *Pioneers of France in the New World*, Boston, Little, Brown & Co., 1887.

Parkman, Francis, *The Jesuits in North America*, Boston, Little, Brown & Co., 1892.

Parkman, Francis, *The Old Regime in Canada*, Boston, Little, Brown & Co., 1892.

Pike, Zebulon Montgomery, *The Explorations of Zebulon Montgomery Pike*, edited by Elliott Coues, New York, Francis P. Harper, 1895, 3v.

Powell, Lyman P. (Editor), *Historic Towns of the Western States*, New York, G. P. Putnam's Sons, 1901.

Quaife, N. M., *Detroit Biographies; The Sieur de Bourgmont*, Burton Historical Collection, Leaflet VI, 4, Detroit, March, 1928.

Robertson, James Alexander (Editor), *Louisiana Under the Rule of Spain, France and the United States, 1785–1870*, Cleveland, Arthur H. Clark Co., 1911, 2v.

Robinson, Doane, *South Dakota*, Chicago, American Historical Society, 1930, 3v.

Roll, Charles, *Indiana*, Chicago, Lewis Publishing Co., 1931, 5v.

Ruxton, George Frederick, *In the Old West*, New York, Macmillan, 1922.

Sabin, Edwin L., *Kit Carson Days*, New York, The Press of the Pioneers, 1935.

Seton, Ernest Thompson, *Lives of Game Animals*, New York, Doubleday, Doran & Co., 1929, 4v.

Severance, Frank H., *An Old Frontier of France*, New York, Dodd, Mead & Co., 1917, 2v.

Sheldon, Addison Erwin, *Nebraska, Land & People*, Chicago, Lewis Publishing Co., 1931, 3v.

Smith, George W., *History of Illinois and Her People*, Chicago, American Historical Society, 1927, 6v.

Spears, John R., *A History of the Mississippi Valley*, New York, A. S. Clark, 1903.

Steck, Francis Borgia, *The Jolliet-Marquette Expedition, 1673*, Glendale, Arthur H. Clark Co., 1928.

Thwaites, Reuben Gold (Editor), *Early Western Travels, 1748–1846*, Cleveland, Arthur H. Clark Co., 1904–1907, 32v.

Thwaites, Reuben Gold, *France in America, 1497–1763*, Vol. 7 of series, *The American Nation*, New York, Harper & Bros., 1905.

Thwaites, Reuben Gold (Editor), *Jesuit Relations and Allied Documents, 1610–1791*, Cleveland, Burrowes Brothers, 1896–1901, 73v.

Thwaites, Reuben Gold (Editor), *The Original Journals of the Lewis and Clark Expedition, 1804–1806*, New York, Dodd, Mead & Co., 1904–1905, 8v.

Williams, Walter, and Shoemaker, Floyd Calvin, *Missouri, Mother of the West*, Chicago, American Historical Society, 5v.

Winsor, Justin, *The Mississippi Basin*, Boston and New York, Houghton, Mifflin & Co., 1895.

Wood, Edwin O., *Historic Mackinac*, New York, Macmillan, 1918, 2v.

ARTICLES IN HISTORICAL SOCIETY PUBLICATIONS

American Historical Review, New York, Macmillan: Trudeau, Jean Baptiste, *Journal of Jean Baptiste Truteau on the Upper Missouri, June 7, 1794–March 26, 1795* (in French), January, 1914, pages 299–333.

Illinois Historical Society Collections, Springfield: Rokker, H. W., *Henry de Tonty's Memoir of 1693*, 1903, 128–164.

Kansas Historical Collections, Topeka:

Chouteau, Frederick, from notes by Franklin G. Adams, *Reminiscences of Frederick Chouteau*, VIII, 423–428, 1904;

Dunbar, John Brown, *Massacre of the Villazur Expedition by the Pawnees on the Platte in 1720*, XI, 397–423, 1910;

Grinnell, George Bird, *Bent's Old Fort and Its Builders*, XV, 28–88, 1923.

Louisiana, Historical Collections of:
Joutel, Henri, *Journal of the Last Voyage Performed by La Salle to the Gulf of Mexico* (in French), I, 1875;
Tonty, Henri, *Memoirs of the Discovery of the Mississippi* (in French), I, 1875.

Mississippi Valley Historical Review, Lincoln:
Bolton, Herbert E., *The Location of La Salle's Colony on the Gulf of Mexico*, Sept., 1915, 165–182;
Hafen, L. R., *The Early Fur Trade Posts on the South Platte*, Dec., 1925, 334–341;
Lafarque, Andre, *The French Governors of Louisiana*, Sept., 1927, 156–167;
Libby, Orin G., *Some Verendrye Enigmas*, Sept., 1916, 143–160; Dec., 1916, 369–399;
Nasatir, Abraham P., *Jacques d'Eglise on the Upper Missouri, 1791–1795*, with original documents, June, 1927, 47–56;
Surrey, Mrs. N. M. Miller, *The Development of Industries in Louisiana During the French Regime*, Dec., 1922, 227–235;
Trudeau, Jean Baptiste, *Notes and Documents, Trudeau's Descriptions of the Upper Missouri*, with notes by Annie Heloise Abel, June–Sept., 1921, 149–179.

INDEX

Acadia, settled, 11

Accau, Michael, explores upper Mississippi, 90; captured by Sioux, 92; freed, 93

Alaska, gold strikes, 263-264

Albany, formerly Fort Orange, 26; merchants of buy furs from woods rangers, 64

Alberta explored, 158

Algonquin Indians trade with French, 11, 12; wars with Iroquois, 13; accompany Champlain in campaign against Iroquois, 14-17; at Long Saut, 41-44

Alton, site of, 79

American Fur Co., 223; operating on Missouri River, 235; Astor sells interest in, 258

Amherst, British general, 174

Anayas, Gaspardo de, governor of Coahuila, 126, 127

Annahotaha, Huron chief, 41; heroism of, 44

Anticosti Island awarded to Jolliet, 85

Arapahoes in peace treaty, 254

Arickaree Indians, visited by D'Eglise, 191; mentioned, 197, 217; contempt of for Americans, 223; sell horses to Astorian Expedition, 229; mentioned, 230

Arkansas Post, founded by Tonty, 104-105; visited by Tonty, 116; visited by La Harpe, 139; visited by Mallet Brothers, 153; travellers from reach Santa Fe, 155-156; Laclede dies at, 184

Arkansas River, noted by Jolliet, 81; by La Salle, 93; explored by Mallets, 152-153; Osages move to, 193; Chouteau's post on, 235.

Arrow Rock, Mo., 249

Ascontia River explored by Iberville, 113

Ashley, William Henry, fur trader, 239; uses South Pass, 242; withdraws from beaver trade, 246

Astor, John Jacob, fur trader, 223; in partnership with Pierre "Cadet" Chouteau, 235; sells fur business, 257-258

Astoria founded, 229; lost to British, 231

Astorian Expedition, 223-229

Astorians at South Pass, 240

Atchison, Kan., site of, 198

Bachelors, of Canada, 46; court maidens, 47

Baltimore, Lord, 21; buys Indian lands, 161

Baronet, A. F. V., interpreter for Pike Expedition, 211

Barr, English captain, on Mississippi, 116-118

Barre, Le Febre de la, governor of Canada, 96

Baton Rouge, origin of name, 113

Bear Flag Republic, 262

Bears, grizzly, 200, 201

Beaujeu, Capt. Lienard, opposes Braddock, 168-171

Beaver, 1; size and value, 2; trade at Quebec, 12; 250 canoe loads of, 34; trade at Detroit, 68-69, 71; limit of trade at Starved Rock, 106; furs brought to Mobile, 118; trade at Kaskaskia and Cahokia, 119; furs of sold by Bourgmont, 141; furs of on Ohio, 159; trade in at St. Louis, 183-185, on the Des Moines River,